MAASAI DAYS

Cheryl Bentsen

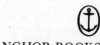

ANCHOR BOOKS
DOUBLEDAY

NEW YORK   LONDON   TORONTO   SYDNEY   AUCKLAND

An Anchor Book
PUBLISHED BY DOUBLEDAY
a division of Bantam Doubleday Dell Publishing Group, Inc.
666 Fifth Avenue, New York, New York 10103

Anchor Books, Doubleday, and the portrayal of an anchor
are trademarks of Doubleday, a division of Bantam Doubleday
Dell Publishing Group, Inc.

Maasai Days was originally published in hardcover by
Summit Books in 1989. The Anchor Books edition is published
by arrangement with Summit Books.

Library of Congress Cataloging-in-Publication Data
Bentsen, Cheryl.
  Maasai days / Cheryl Bentsen.
    p. cm.
    1. Masai (African people)   I. Title.
DT433.545.M33B45   1991   90-26186
967.62′004965—dc20   CIP
ISBN 0-385-41630-X

FOR CHUCK

▲ Contents

NOTE: *The spelling of "Maasai" varies as used by individual authors.*

They are dreaded as warriors, laying all waste with fire and sword, so that the weaker tribes do not venture to resist them.

—Dr. Ludwig Krapf,
*Travels, Researches,
and Missionary Labours* (1860)
(The first known written
description of the Maasai)

The word was passed round that the Masai had come. . . . Passing through the forest, we soon set our eyes upon the dreaded warriors that had been so long the subject of my waking dreams, and I could not but involuntarily exclaim, "What splendid fellows!"

—Joseph Thomson,
Through Masai Land (1885)

[The Maasai] had that attitude that makes brothers, that unexpressed but instant and complete acceptance that you must be Masai wherever it is you come from.

—Ernest Hemingway,
Green Hills of Africa (1935)

A Masai warrior is a fine sight. These young men have, to the utmost extent, that particular form of intelligence which we call chic; daring, and wildly fantastical as they seem, they are still unswervingly true to their own nature, and to an immanent ideal.

—ISAK DINESEN,
Out of Africa (1937)

What upstart race, sprung from some recent, callow century to arm itself with steel and boastfulness, can match in purity the blood of a single Masai Murani whose heritage may have stemmed not far from Eden?

—BERYL MARKHAM,
West with the Night (1942)

The Masai are not primitive in the way that pygmies and bushmen are. They are an intelligent people who have deliberately chosen to retain their own way of life.

—EVELYN WAUGH,
A Tourist in Africa (1960)

The Maasai, having no choice, altered his habits, but in a spiritual sense, he has ceased to exist as well.

—PETER MATTHIESSEN,
The Tree Where Man Was Born (1972)

1

THE VALLEY

I FIRST BEGAN to explore the land around Nairobi on a motorcycle. Looking back, it is hard to imagine seeing the country any other way. On a bike, with the air and landscape rushing around you, the views are immense, unobstructed by car roof or window frame. Up in the highlands, on a cool, misty morning, the curved terraces of the big tea plantations were rolling emerald seas. The motorcycles were my husband's idea, and most weekends Chuck and I took long trips, sometimes setting off across the grass-covered plains below the Ngong Hills, sometimes following a winding trail through a shaded forest, watching monkeys sail through the trees. The forest trail joined a road that encircled the hills, and around its last bend, the Great Rift Valley came into view—so sudden and startling it seemed to be the very edge of the world. The valley floor lay below, some two thousand feet deep and nearly forty miles wide, part of a tear in the earth that runs from the Jordan Valley to Mozambique. It was eerie and tremendous, studded with craters, like a landscape on the moon. The only trees were the scattered, flat-crowned acacia.

You could ride for hours—all the way to Kilimanjaro—without encountering a fence. The best days were overcast ones in early June, when the sky was flinty, and the air was scented by rain and moistened dust. The land took on a brooding look. As hawks circled above, we rode the rutted dirt trails with thunderclouds chasing behind us. Across the plains, a wall of rain descended like gray curtains slowly lowered to earth. After the shower, the valley was spanned by rainbows.

When the rain started, wildlife returned to the plains —ostrich, herds of zebra and wildebeest, eland, impala, and Thomson's gazelle, the latter's trim, twitching flanks marked by a dark racing stripe. In a single day, I once counted forty giraffes. Lions and leopards patrolled the valley, but I never saw them. There were birds—some with trailing iridescent plumage, others, including the hornbills, so strange or whimsical they might have been dreamed up by Walt Disney. Occasionally I would be startled when a gazelle—sometimes several—bounded across my path, hanging for a split second in midair, immune to gravity.

The long dry season transformed the valley into a hushed and barren place. The tall plumes of dust devils twirled across the plains. The animals vanished, and a gritty wind scoured the land. The sun bore down day after day until, by early March, the grass had turned the color of a lion's haunch, and the dust lay thick on the trails.

On a day like this, I rode alone along a deserted road to the soda lake at Magadi. The temperature was more than a hundred; the plains looked liquid in the shimmering air. I saw no signs of settlement. I stopped to get my bearings and check the map. Suddenly—out of the air, it seemed—a group of Maasai women appeared on the road, rushing toward me in red-and-white capes and beaded collars that bounced as they ran. Giggling and chattering away in Maasai, they surrounded me, holding out beaded ornaments they wanted me to buy. They had smooth copper skin, high cheekbones and small shaved heads that shone like polished mahogany. On them, baldness seemed a brilliant stroke of fashion. The holes cut in their earlobes were the size of half-dollars, the loops suspended with long wire earrings like mobiles, decorated with colorful beads and tin cutouts. The women fastened a large bib-style necklace around my neck and stood back to admire the effect, nodding in approval when I indicated that I would buy it. It was frustrating not to be able to speak their language, but when we had settled the business, I offered them a drink from my jug of water. Their faces became solemn as they each took a small sip, barely a swallow. I urged them to have more, but they declined. A drought was approaching; I suppose water must have seemed to them a great indulgence. This brief encounter—just thirty miles outside the city—heightened my curiosity. I found myself wondering about these women, where they lived, what their lives were like. Several times I went down that road again, hoping to see them, but I never did. Somehow I was convinced I would get to know more about them.

I had been living in Kenya for only a few months then. I arrived in 1980 when my husband was assigned there as a newspaper correspondent. Before that, I knew very little about Africa or its people, but I had heard of the Maasai whose legendary pride and physical courage seem to have impressed every foreigner who has ever seen them. I had read Karen Blixen's (Isak Dinesen's) tribute to Maasai warriors in *Out of Africa*, and I once watched an old Stewart Granger movie, *The Last Safari*, in which everyone but the white hunter was afraid of them. I pictured the Maasai as a carefree, independent people, roaming the plains with their cattle, unburdened by the problems of modern life.

I saw them for the first time the weekend Chuck and I arrived in Nairobi. We were taking a game drive through a national park, hoping to see lions; meanwhile, the Kikuyu driver was dutifully pointing out giraffes, kongoni, zebras and hippos, proposing that Chuck and I take pictures of them. I stood up through the open roof of the Land-Rover to get a better look when I noticed several tall figures dressed in red crossing the high grass of the plain. They were clearly Maasai. They carried spears and walked as if they owned the land.

"Isn't that dangerous, walking like that?" I asked, remembering the signs warning visitors not to get out of their cars. "What about lions?"

The guide laughed. "Madam, the poor lions are fear-ing the Maasai." He told us they lived on the plains and slept in dung huts. The young men hunted lions to prove their bravery. From the tone of his voice, I sensed that he did not approve of such primitive arrangements.

After that, I saw some Maasai in Nairobi. On city streets, in the midst of high-rise office buildings, boutiques and Western-dressed Africans, they seemed peculiarly anachronistic. The elders, wrapped in thick orange blankets, gave the impression of eccentric old aristocrats as they went about their brief business—buying snuff, tobacco, medicines for their cattle, blankets, glass beads and tea strainers—unfazed by traffic or crowds, oblivious to stares, seemingly incurious about the modern world around them.

The Maasai women were always more outgoing, selling their beaded ornaments outside the City Market and smiling at passersby with the insouciant air of professional partygoers. They wore their traditional *shukas* (togas), capes and beaded necklaces, but many of them had begun to wear vinyl-trimmed green canvas sneakers that I had seen displayed in store windows.

The warriors—tall, slim, angular young men with chiseled features—did not carry their spears to Nairobi; a city law prohibited it. On rare jaunts to town, they were still a sensation, appearing both daring and whimsical. I was downtown one day, shortly after I arrived, when a Maasai man entered a crowded elevator in an office building. Everyone automatically drew back to give him room. We all stared. The Africans seemed wary. The Maasai paid no attention and looked straight ahead. He wore a *shuka* checked like a tablecloth and sandals made from old rubber tires. His hairdo was an elaborate arrangement of plaits, a mop stained with what looked like greasy rust-colored clay. The loops of his ears were wrapped in beads; a sword was tied to his belt; and he carried a nasty-looking knobbed club. At the fourth floor, he stepped off the elevator and turned right. We all looked to see where he was going, but the doors slid shut. Nobody said anything, but a faint odor lingered, like the smoke of a cooking fire deep in a forest.

I was intrigued, but it was the Maasai I saw on my motorcycling in the valley who caught my imagination.

They always waved, as though delighted by any passing entertainment. I saw the edges of their strange, secluded world. Once, I stopped at Kisemes, a small trading center on the edge of the valley. Outside a rickety metal-roofed shack, a hand-lettered sign read: HILTON HOTEL. I went inside to buy a soda, and the owner, a Western-dressed Kikuyu, asked if I had brought a newspaper. "We don't hear much news out here," he sighed. Outside, a group of Maasai warriors in *shukas* and red-stained pigtails stood around the motorcycle and took turns studiously admiring their faces in the handlebar mirrors. I finished my soda and said goodbye to the shopkeeper, who seemed disappointed to see me go. The bike was balky when it was hot, and I had some trouble kick-starting it. This amused the Maasai men; but they jumped back respectfully when the engine caught and let out a roar. Some Maasai women, who had been watching, drew closer as I pulled on my helmet. One of them asked in Swahili, "Are you a man or a woman?" The younger children knew the Swahili word for motorcycle—*piki-piki*—and sang that funny word as I drove off.

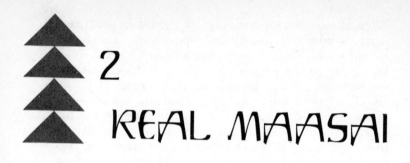

2
REAL MAASAI

In Nairobi, everyone seemed to have strong opinions about the Maasai. Foreigners, beguiled by their glamour, often perceived them as the model for the Hollywood noble savage. The stereotype was understandably offensive to progressive Africans, who derided the fame of the Maasai. The colonials were predictably disenchanted, but told some good stories.

I met a white game rancher, born in Kenya, who knew the Maasai well. "They were always circumspect and a bit superior," he said. "Their minds worked differently than the Kikuyu—they were more complicated, like the Somali." His grandfather had employed a few Maasai herders at his Lake Naivasha ranch. When gramophones were invented, he ordered one of the first and invited some elders up to the house to see the new things that were coming out of Europe. Wearing leather capes and earrings, the old Maasai stood around the contraption, listening to a scratchy recording, none of them saying a word. Finally, one elder turned to the others and observed, "It takes a small thing to amuse the mind of a white man."

Africans gave me amused or condescending glances when I mentioned my interest in the Maasai. Most of them resented the fact that a "backward" tribe featured so prominently in the national image. A history professor at the University of Nairobi dismissed them as drunkards, advising me that they were "best left alone." Others like him, who viewed the Maasai as degenerate, were baffled that foreigners, so long preoccupied with "civilizing the natives," were so fascinated by them.

Speaking before the Kenyan parliament, the country's former vice president Mwai Kibaki, a Kikuyu educated at the London School of Economics, summed up national sentiments by criticizing the tourist agencies that "depict Kenya on the brochures they dish out as a country of naked Maasai . . . jumping and exposing their gadgets." (Maasai warriors, called *ilmurran*—or moran, the shortened English version of their name—have a dance in which they jump straight-backed very high in the air.)

But the official pronouncements were only public posturing. Kenya's economy is dependent on tourism, and a profitable industry revolves around foreign fascination with the tribe. Kibaki's words had no effect. The travel brochures continued to play up the old stereotypes, breezily promoting the Maasai, along with the zebras, lions and elephants in the wildlife parks, exotic local attractions. Souvenir shops in Nairobi do a brisk business selling picture books, Maasai trinkets, carvings of warriors (made by another tribe) and six-foot lion spears that come apart and fit in a tourist's suitcase. Tea towels and pillows are printed with warrior images; postcard racks display pictures of moran in lions' mane headdresses; in one shop a Maasai—ostensibly a store detective—stands around in full regalia, lending atmosphere to the place and often startling shoppers.

Foreigners are, however, put off by recent changes in the Maasai. Browsing in a souvenir shop, I overheard two Americans complaining that when they visited a national park the moran had demanded twenty shillings to have their picture taken; more if they posed with spears. A few days before, at Kenya's National Museum, I too was disappointed; a display of traditional beaded Maasai ornaments included a plastic film canister, the type in which 35-mm film is stored. The Maasai now wear them as earplugs. They fit exactly the holes cut in their earlobes.

At a party some months later, I met an Indian pediatrician whose first job had been at a remote clinic in Maasailand. He was a great supporter of the Maasai, he said, though he had been very lonely that year, working by himself at a tin-roofed clinic—hardly more than a shack—several hours' drive from Nairobi. There were no towns or nearby villages, not even a real road. He sat for days by himself without any patients. From what he saw, the Maasai rarely got sick, and if they did they relied on home remedies: they cauterized wounds with hot ash, drank medicinal soups made from roots and bark, or, for difficult cases, visited the local herbalist or witch doctor.

To his surprise, he never saw evidence of complications following female circumcision, or clitoridectomy, a traditional practice among them. But once a warrior who'd been gored by a buffalo showed up at the clinic. It was the worst wound the doctor had ever seen. The moran's intestines had been ripped out, but he'd pushed them back into his belly, using a flap of skin to hold it all together. He had already lost a frightening amount of blood. Certain that the patient would not survive the drive over bad roads to a hospital in Nairobi, the doctor performed surgery with a textbook propped open in front of him. He had no experience, no anesthesia, and no blood for transfusion. The only painkiller in stock was aspirin. The Maasai remained stoical throughout the operation. In the morning, when the doctor went to check on him, he was gone. He returned months later in perfect health with the gift of a goat. The doctor said he missed the adventure of those days. He now had a downtown office, and his clients were mostly expatriate mothers who rushed their children to him for the slightest complaint.

I thought of his story, reading in the newspapers about a Maasai moran who had killed a lion with his spear in Amboseli National Park, after two lions had killed two of his father's cows and were attacking a third. He was badly mauled in the struggle with the lion and was arrested for killing a protected wild animal without a license. Kenya banned hunting in 1977, which put a strain on the Maasai, whose pastures are also home to dangerous predators. The case drew wide interest. Conservationists pointed out that a single lion—by some mysterious calculation of tourist dollars—had a value of $515,000 and suggested that some of the Maasai were poaching in the parks. Others defended the moran, questioning a policy that places the protection of wild animals above the safety of human beings.

When the moran's wounds had healed, he was brought before a Nairobi magistrate. He admitted his guilt, and spoke proudly about having killed the lion single-handedly. The Indian chief magistrate accepted the young man's guilty plea but discharged him and even commended his courage.

My curiosity about the tribe persisted. The old-timers had a name for it: "Maasai-itis," which they told me was common among newcomers. It was a pejorative term, coined by white settlers to describe a few Rift Valley farmers who had become fanatic admirers. Their leader, Hugh Cholmondeley (Lord Delamere), learned the Maasai language, struck up friendships, consulted the elders for advice about cattle and convinced a few Maasai men to work on his ranch. (The Maasai had cattle wealth, and few were interested in working for white farmers.) Otherwise known for his violent temper, Lord Delamere did not seem to mind when the Maasai repeatedly raided his stock but rather delighted in their skill and cunning. The majority of the settlers, on the other hand, feared Maasai raids, regarded Maasai customs as barbaric and saw their refusal to work—or to sell their cattle—as a liability to Kenya's development. They thought the land could be put to more productive use.

I heard the same kinds of criticism from modern Africans who described the Maasai as "stubborn" and "arrogant." Like the colonials, they also have their eyes on Maasai land. Kenya is smaller than Texas, with only 15 percent of the land suitable for agriculture. The country's 22 million population is the fastest-expanding in the world—something close to 4 percent annually—and will double by the year 2000. Shantytowns have already sprung up around Nairobi, farmland is becoming scarce and unemployment is rising. With growing pressures on the land, disputes between cattlemen and farmers are mounting. Kikuyu farmers, who make up Kenya's largest tribe and dominate national politics, have started buying up Maasai pastures to plant wheat. At some point, the land that now supports the pastoral life of the Maasai is likely to run out.

A friend who shared my interest took me to see the Keekonyokie Maasai in the Great Rift Valley. The Keekonyokie—"people of the red trees"—are a section of the tribe that lives on lands, including a part of the old Maasai reserve and the area around and beyond Lake Naivasha, once farmed by Lord Delamere and other white settlers. Nowadays, despite their proximity to Nairobi, the Keekonyokie are still counted among the "purest" Maasai in their resistance to change.

The Maasai dwellings we saw that day were low igloo-shaped huts, their frames made of woven branches and twigs, like upside-down baskets, plastered with cow dung to keep out the rain and wind. They blended so well with the landscape they seemed to be almost a natural feature, like boulders or termite hills. But many of them were cracked and looked abandoned. The Maasai were migrating; the rains had not yet started, and there was little grass here for their cattle. The only ones around were two young boys—their legs painted with red ocher, like patterned stockings—chasing each other with short metal swords. They were herdboys playing at being warriors. They had a few sheep and goats in their care, all of them scrawny. After a while they put away their swords, waved at us and headed home.

Since a bad drought in 1978–79, which killed large numbers of their cattle, some Maasai have taken up work as security guards in Nairobi. A man we knew, who traveled on business and worried about burglary during his frequent absences, had two Maasai night watchmen. Actually, he had hired only one, but the second showed up regularly to keep his friend company. Finally, he agreed to employ them both.

At first, he was pleased, though communicating with

them was a problem since they spoke only their tribal tongue. Still, in full costume with their capes and spears and sullen expressions, they were a sight to scare off any burglar. But after a while they began drinking, perhaps from boredom or homesickness, or sheer lack of supervision. Neighbors complained about the racket. Drunk, in the dark of night, one of them would roar like a lion. Much as our friend hated to do it—for he enjoyed their ornamental aspect—he fired them.

The old-timers in Kenya take a dim view of the present state of the Maasai. A former white hunter pointed out to me that the ones I saw in Nairobi were not "real Maasai." He'd known the real ones. He meant those untainted by the modern world and tourism. They were from the old days, he said, and they would not hang around city streets selling jewelry, work as watchmen, or wear film canisters stuck in their ears. "Real Maasai" looked down on all occupations except cattle herding. Soon, he said, the Maasai would become "like all the rest." It was hard to imagine Maasai moran exchanging their *shukas* and spears for flared pants and platform shoes, the outdated but current fashion in Nairobi. But there was pressure on them; I could see that. And I, like the old white hunter, felt dispirited by it, although I was not sure why.

3

SPLENDID
FELLOWS

FEW TRIBES in Africa have been as extensively studied as the Maasai. Anthropologists appear in Nairobi each year, carving out arcane areas of interest. I met one, an American woman, whose years of work focused solely on the philosophical implications in the designs of Maasai beadwork. Another was an expert on the Maasai "cattle complex." The bead specialist recommended to me a paper written by a colleague entitled "The Semiotics of Maasai Ritual."

But as I began my own haphazard research, visiting libraries and reading Maasai history, I noticed wide disagreement among the academics about the tribe's exact origins and its early history. Old romantic theories— now mostly debunked—suggested that the Maasai were a lost tribe of Israel or an offshoot of Mark Antony's army. And indeed the swords, shields, sandals, togas and helmet-styled hairdos of the warriors do give them a certain likeness to ancient Roman soldiers. A thorough history of the tribe has yet to be written, but current thinking suggests it is a mixture of the Nilotics, who lived in the Nile River basin, and the Cushites of North Africa, with whom they share Hamitic practices such as male age-grouping and ritual circumcision.

In a Nairobi thrift shop, I found a reprint of Joseph Thomson's *Through Masai Land* (the old-fashioned spelling), the Scottish explorer's account of the expedition he led in 1883. He was the first white man to cross Maasailand, then a dreaded region avoided by all but a small number of Arab slave traders. Little is known about the capture of Maasai slaves, but the reports on the tribe from the Arabs, intended to discourage European exploration and interference in their ivory and slave business, and from early European missionaries provided a fearsome picture of the Maasai.

A century ago, they were experts at war, favoring attack in a great phalanx, a terrifying advance in red paint, colobus-monkey anklets, and towering headdresses made from black ostrich feathers and lions' manes. With spears, swords and buffalo-hide shields, they drove rival tribes—especially despised agriculturalists like the Kikuyu—into the forests. They raided cattle as far south as Kilimanjaro and thought nothing of killing a man when a cow was at stake. It was an article of Maasai faith that Engai (God) had intended them to own all the earth's cattle; their raids were simply a means of collecting misplaced property.

At the peak of their power, in the mid-nineteenth century, the Maasai numbered about fifty thousand and controlled a territory slightly smaller than West Germany (some seventy-five thousand square miles), with boundaries that extended from the northern deserts beyond Mount Kenya to the Serengeti Plain south of Kilimanjaro, and from the eastern shores of Lake Victoria to the Indian Ocean.

Joseph Thomson, a twenty-four-year-old geologist, was already a veteran of two previous African expeditions when the British Royal Geographical Society hired him. There was great scientific curiosity about the region, and wide doubt about a missionary's report of a snowcapped mountain (Mount Kenya) straddling the equator. Thomson accepted the assignment with an ambition to equal the fame of Stanley, Speke and Burton—the giants of African exploration. Henry Morton Stanley, the journalist and explorer of the Congo, never met the Maasai but characterized them as "a tribe that specially delights in blood." His parting advice to Thomson was to take a thousand men or "write your will."

Backed up by 150 Zanzibari porters—"a flood of vagabondage," as he described them—80 of them armed with handguns, Thomson entered Maasailand near Kilimanjaro in April 1883. Advised by Swahili traders that the Maasai were particular about the gifts they accepted, he ordered his badly frightened men to string 60,000 beaded necklaces of regulation length and 300 approved war dresses. After joining up with a passing slaver's caravan en route to Maasai country, Thomson pressed on, buoyed by news that a rival German expedition, which had survived an earlier skirmish with the Maasai, had given up at Lake Naivasha and turned back because of illness among the porters.

Over a period of fifteen months, Thomson walked from the coast to the shores of Lake Victoria, a three-thousand-mile march across desert, marsh, plain, forest and mountains. He was ill with dysentery, barely survived a buffalo goring and had to be carried at times on a stretcher. Not all of his men survived: some died from illness, exhaustion or attacks by wild animals; one missing porter was later found on a trail, mutilated by hyenas.

Thomson met little hostility from the Maasai, describing the first warriors that he met as "splendid fellows"—an enchantment that flavors much of his book. But the Maasai were already in decline. Smallpox, cholera, drought, famine, a cattle plague called rinderpest and civil war had sapped their strength; old rivals were fighting back. An elderly, almost blind Maasai spiritual leader named Mbatien had predicted the disasters, as well as the arrival of hairy pink beings. The Maasai were not surprised to see the explorer, who posed as a friendly white magician. His feats included the removal of false teeth—a trick that backfired only once, when a cynical warrior tried to remove his nose—and the Maasai may have believed that his wizardry could help solve their problems.

Back in London, Thomson received the gold Founder's Medal of the Geographical Society. *Through Masai*

Land was published in 1885 and sold well in London, Paris, Leipzig and Boston. His descriptions of tribal customs were laced with Victorian titillation, but he also admired the tribe's dignity: "I gradually became accustomed to their arrogant ways; for, troublesome and overbearing as they were, they displayed an aristocratic manner and a consciousness of power, which seemed to raise them infinitely among the negro [*sic*]—as I had seen him."

He died in 1895, at age thirty-seven, his health giving out after three subsequent trips to Africa. The fame he coveted was not to last. An East Africa gazelle and a waterfall he discovered were named for him, but few visitors to Kenya nowadays know of the connection.

Within a decade of Thomson's exploration, the British and Germans had divided up East Africa and advertised for white settlers. The British started constructing a railroad in 1895 and hoped the enterprise of white pioneers who were offered cheap land would defray the building costs. Agreements with the Maasai in 1904 and 1911–12 appropriated tribal lands for the scheme. In exchange for the Laikipia Plateau and large areas of the Rift Valley, the Maasai were guaranteed tenure in two reserves. The native population in Kenya was small in comparison with the size of the land, but a final resettlement of the Maasai into a single large reserve cost them the alternative pastures they depended on during droughts.

The northern Maasai at first resisted but soon realized their spears were no match for British guns. The migration to the reserve—involving 10,000 Maasai, 175,000 cattle and more than 1,000,000 sheep—was a fiasco. Taking various routes south, they encountered drought and floods. Numbers of them died; some turned back; others lost their cattle to an outbreak of rinderpest. Stories about the tragedy were reported in London newspapers. At one point, some elders hired an English lawyer and obtained a temporary injunction, which halted the move. A year went by before the court heard their case and dismissed it. In 1913 the elders appealed, but lost again on a contrived technicality. Their lawyer was deported.

For the duration of British rule, the tribe was restricted to the reserve, and the Maasai kept mostly to themselves. Until 1952 there was only one secondary school in Maasailand. Maasai confrontations with government tax collectors were sometimes violent, and they resisted the draft of Africans to fight in World War I. In the postcolonial era, they were no longer so warlike, but they still maintained the mystique and preferred their traditional life and ancestral customs to those of the modern world. The young men today—at the risk of jail—still raid cattle and hunt lions to prove their bravery. In many ways, they are not much different from the time when Thomson first saw them.

At the library of a local newspaper, I found additional information about the Maasai. Around the time of Kenya's independence, the Kenyan Maasai, not happy at the prospect of Kikuyu-dominated rule, began to talk of secession and joining up with their Tanzanian counterparts. But the idea collapsed. Among the tribe's twelve major geographical sections (called *il-oshon*) and five blood clans, customs, dialects and opinions have always varied. The Maasai have never had a single leader or any central authority. The tribe's spiritual leaders—*iloibonik*—have declined in influence since Mbatien's son, Lenana, signed away their land to the British. Local matters are reviewed by councils of elders, with wider conferences called only on ceremonial matters, such as the initiation and naming of a new male age-set or the settling of intertribal border disputes. Each *ol-osho* has its traditional grazing territories, though exceptions are allowed during droughts. But sometimes the old system breaks down. When I arrived in Kenya, seven Maasai had recently died of spear and poison-arrow wounds inflicted in a border clash over grazing rights.

When Kenya conducted its first national census in 1979, university students were hired to do the counting, but the Maasai, superstitious about revealing personal information, chased most of them away. They live on both sides of the Kenya–Tanzania border, and their total population is estimated at around 300,000. They rank eleventh in size among some forty Kenyan tribes.

Many of the towns and geographical features scattered over Kenya and Tanzania, much of which once comprised Maasailand, have Maasai names. Nairobi is the Maasai word for "cold." The name Kenya may have been derived from a Maasai word, *e-rukenya*, which means "mist," their description of the country's tallest peak. Serengeti, Olduvai, Naivasha, Magadi and Ngong are names with roots in the Maasai language as well as landmarks set deep in the tribal memory.

In some ways, the Maasai act as if all the familiar land is still theirs. Blind to national boundaries, oblivious to political differences between capitalistic Kenya and socialist Tanzania, they continue to move with their herds wherever there is rain and pasture. They are often arrested, but are undeterred. Much of their rangeland, some sixteen thousand square miles, is semiarid, and recurrent droughts have reduced the tribe's once huge herds. Still, they are said to own three million cattle—more than any other single tribe in Africa—but rarely sell any, regarding cows as currency.

In some Kenyan national parks where Maasai pastures overlap with public lands, the tribe shares in a percentage of the profits earned from tourist lodges, an arrangement devised by a white game warden who admired them. The money is supposed to be used for development projects, but government efforts to redirect Maasai interests to modern practices have made little headway. In many parts of Maasailand where police have tried to force Maasai children into schools, harassed families have packed up and moved to more remote areas. The Kenyan president's reiterated warnings against female circumcision go unheeded.

Years ago, the former president of Tanzania, Julius Nyerere, said his country could not afford to maintain the Maasai as a "human zoo" for tourists. A law was passed in Tanzania that required male bus passengers to wear trousers, a measure obviously aimed at the Maasai, but they rarely travel by bus and are able to walk incredibly long distances without fatigue. The law sailed past them, like a spear thrown wide of the mark.

After Kenya's independence in 1963, a small number of Maasai who had been "kidnapped" by the British as children, put in boarding schools, and trained as tax collectors, court translators and clerks—or as soldiers sent to fight in Burma—returned to the bush, relieved to take up their old ways. Only about three hundred Maasai work at jobs in Nairobi. Very few have ventured outside the tribal circle for long. There are some notable exceptions, among them the heads of the dental school and the animal physiology department at the University of Nairobi. Kenya's first president, Jomo Kenyatta, was a Kikuyu who proudly claimed a trace of Maasai blood in his veins. The first vice president was a full-blooded Maasai, but a distaste for modern politics led him to resign. Tanzania had a Maasai prime minister who might have ascended to the presidency, but he was killed in a car accident. A young Maasai runner, Billy Konchellah, who attended an American college on an athletic scholarship, once won a medal at the World Track Championships in Rome. At Diani Beach, a resort on the Kenyan coast, a cheerful Maasai teaches wind surfing to tourists and once participated in an international competition in the Seychelles. But it is not easy to say what impact, if any, those who left had on those who stayed behind.

4

A HITCHHIKER

A FEW MONTHS after I arrived in Kenya, my friend
Stephanie Liss came on a visit from Los Angeles. I'd
written to her about the Maasai, and she wanted to see
them for herself. We drove from Nairobi on blacktop
through a suburb named for Karen Blixen to the Ngong
Hills. Passing the Kiserian market on the way, I saw a
young Maasai standing at the edge of the road, waving
his hand up and down. I hadn't seen many Maasai flag-
ging rides. I stopped—I wasn't sure why; I never picked
up hitchhikers, believing the warnings I had heard all
my life.

As I pulled over, he looked at me with surprise, but
quickly folded himself into the backseat. He spoke some
Swahili, a little of which I could understand, and said
his name was Ndika. He seemed the exception to tribal
beauty. He wore a *shuka* but no beads, not even a bracelet; the loops of his ears were comically hooked over the
top rims, as if their flapping were a mere annoyance.
He carried a wooden club, a cattle stick, and four big
pellets wrapped in newspaper, which he opened to show
us. *"Dawa,"* he said, medicine for sick cows. He looked
concerned. On an impulse, I said we would take him
home. He smiled and pointed the way.

We turned off the paved road at Kisemes, by the

"Hilton," and drove into the Rift Valley. Heavy rains had reduced some stretches of the muddy track to a dark goo, the consistency of axle grease. It was called "black cotton" in Kenya, and on a motorcycle you could always navigate around it. It was another matter in a car with only one spare tire and two-wheel drive. The low brush growing alongside the track had spikes the size of darning needles. I stopped and got out to look down the track. A pair of giraffes stood motionless a few yards away. Ndika was right behind me, using his sword to hack at the brush and uproot bushes. He rolled away the rocks that stood in our path and urged us on. When I started the car, the giraffes turned and galloped off.

After three hours of intermittent driving, brush clearing and getting stuck in the mud, Ndika assured us it was not much farther. I was starting to have doubts. It occurred to me that Ndika's conception of time might be different from ours; we might be hours or days away from his home. Fifty miles would seem a reasonable hike for a Maasai. I was covered with mud. We had slid into a ditch and spent forty minutes pushing the car out, using the rubber floor mats for traction under the back tires. Stephanie was tired, still jet-lagged and adjusting to the elevation. Even on the floor of the valley we were nearly a mile above sea level. She took some pictures of baboons. Ndika ripped off some leleshwa leaves from a clump of bushes scented like camphor and used them to wipe the mud off his legs. He handed us some, encouraging us to try them. The headphones from my cassette player were stuck over his big ears; he was listening to Vivaldi. Five young moran with red-stained mop hairdos approached us and stood at a distance leaning against their spears. "*Rafiki* [friends]," Ndika said, noticing them, but the moran were noncommittal and soon sauntered off. We got going, deciding to see where adventure would lead us.

"Just over there!" Ndika said, pointing to a steep hill. We tried to drive up it, but boulders blocked the way. He got out and ran up the hill. We locked the car and followed. The sun was sliding to the horizon. A hundred miles below the equator, it gets dark at six-thirty, and the sunsets are dramatic, but abrupt. All around us, the Rift Valley was turning a deep copper. The four peaks of Ngong, like a giant's knuckles, stood darkly outlined in the distance. Ndika strode ahead of us, trampling the tall grass and providing a trail. He became a dash of red against a backdrop of slate-colored hills, a figure like the first Maasai I had seen in the game park. We ran to catch up and were startled when a Maasai man in a blanket appeared from out of the shadows. He looked us over with glassy eyes and spoke harshly to Ndika. He was speaking Maasai; I couldn't understand a word. Ndika stared at his muddy toes; then, as if ordered, he handed me the cassette player and slunk off without a word. The older man came closer, and I smelled liquor. He motioned for us to come with him. I tried to talk with him, but my Swahili did not seem to get through. When I mentioned *simba* (lions), he smiled and waved his arms in all directions. We speeded up.

Not far from where we had left Ndika, we came to a *boma*, a dozen or so huts arranged in a circle and enclosed by a thick thornbush fence. A young boy, startled to see us, lifted the spiky branches to let us in. We were led to a hut, where we stooped down and felt our way through a tunneled entrance. Inside, it was dark and smoky and smelled of dung and burning wood. A small fire glowed on a bed of rocks. A hand reached out and guided us to a couple of tin-can stools. My eyes burned and watered from the smoke. I brushed against something woolly, which let out a tiny bleat. By the time our eyes adjusted to the dim light, the hut had filled up with curious Maasai. Across from us a woman sat at the edge of a sleeping platform nursing her baby. The firelight caught the sheen of the infant's skin and the bright colors of the woman's beaded necklaces. With her free hand, she offered us a gourd filled with sour milk.

In the darkness, a voice said carefully, in English, "Hello, my friends, how are you?" At first, I couldn't make out the face. Then a boy, who looked about fourteen or fifteen, came closer and said his name was Joseph. He introduced another boy, crouched beside him, as his friend Noah. The man who had brought us was

Noah's uncle, Musanka. An elderly man next to him was Noah's grandfather. Joseph's mother crawled out from the back of the sleeping berth, filled a teakettle with water from a plastic jug and set it on the fire.

Joseph said that he and Noah went to a primary school a few miles away. "It is built by missionaries," he said. "But now it is a government school."

Noah remained mute but looked at us intently, as did the others.

"Why are you here?" Joseph finally asked. I explained the situation and asked him why Musanka had sent Ndika away.

"Ndika is bad, a criminal," he said. "He steals cameras from tourists on the Ngong Hills." He spoke in Maasai to the others, who nodded gravely.

"Even I have seen the cameras myself," Noah suddenly boasted, also in English, and added that we were lucky to have met his uncle. "That man could kill you in the forest."

"But he seemed very nice," I said. "He said his cows were sick, and he was bringing *dawa* for them."

"The moran get sick when they see him," Joseph said, scrunching up his face.

The old man spat in the fire and said a few words to Joseph, who told us, "Noah's grandfather says he can curse Ndika, and then you will have no trouble from him." The old man spat again, closed his eyes and mumbled some words.

"Is he making the curse?" Stephanie asked.

"Not now," Joseph said. "First he can discuss with the *wazee* [old men]." He then asked where we were from and if we owned cows or sheep. I said my only animals were a dog and a cat, which did not impress them.

"We are interested to learn about the Maasai," I said, immediately realizing how absurd that sounded. I imagined the situation in reverse—a pair of curious Maasai, or Eskimos, showing up at my doorstep and asking for a look around.

But Joseph did not seem to think that my curiosity was unreasonable, and when he told the old man, he also nodded with approval and said something to Joseph.

"Noah's grandfather says he can tell you every story about the Maasai—he knows them all," Joseph translated. "He wants to give you a he-goat to take to your husband so he will not beat you for getting lost." The women giggled. Joseph asked if we would like to spend the night in his mother's hut. "No problem," he said, "my father is away with cattle." His mother smiled shyly. We thanked them but explained we couldn't stay. I said I would like to visit another time, to hear the old man's stories.

"What about the goat?" Noah asked.

"Next time," I said. The women looked worried. I described the hill where we had left the car. I wasn't sure I could find it in the dark.

"No problem," Joseph said. "We can go now." His mother gave us each a bracelet, and after a round of good-byes, Joseph and Noah led the way. A tall boy with a spear followed. It was pitch-black.

"Are there lions around here?" Stephanie asked Joseph.

"*Mingi*—many," he said. "But a big problem is leopards. They can jump on your head." The week before, leopards had come twice to eat his father's sheep. But Joseph said he and Noah knew how to kill a leopard.

"I can kill him with a rock," Noah said.

The boys scrambled barefoot down the hill and found the car. We followed clumsily, slipping on the loose rock. Joseph asked if he could sit in the driver's seat. "I have never done this thing before," he said, sliding behind the wheel. He examined the dashboard, and asked how to turn on the lights. Noah got in with him and startled himself by leaning on the horn. The boy with the spear watched with fascination, but dignity seemed to prevent him from getting in with them.

"You can teach me to drive another day," Joseph said, as he and Noah got out. Waving good-bye, Joseph suddenly remembered something he had forgotten to tell us and ran after the car. I rolled down the window. "Next time, bring *Newsweek*!" he shouted.

5

FIRST VISITS

A COUPLE of weeks after my chance meeting, I rented a Land-Rover and went back to visit the Maasai. I had the *Newsweek*s for Joseph, some ballpoint pens and candy for Noah and the other children, and a vague sense of the right direction. I had driven a few miles into the valley when I saw Joseph and another boy tending some goats and sheep. "You came back!" Joseph shouted when he recognized me in the truck. He told his friend to look after the animals, and we drove to his *boma*, taking a shortcut that he knew.

In the daylight, the *boma* looked grimier and more run-down than it had in the dark. The younger children ran around me yelling, *"Mzungu! Mzungu!"*—the Swahili term for a white person. A very small boy wearing only a strand of beads took one look at me and began bawling, refusing my offer of candy.

Noah was visiting their teacher, Joseph told me. But Musanka, the man who'd first brought me to the *boma*, was sitting on a rock outside the circle of huts whittling a staff, and an old woman was shaving a man's stubbled head with a razor. Most of the women were at a fertility ceremony at another *boma*, and the men were grazing the cattle.

Noah's grandfather and two elders were talking under an acacia tree outside the *boma*. Joseph said they were discussing an upcoming conference of witch doctors scheduled for the night of the next full moon. "We always watch the sky and the moon," he explained. "The Maasai can only have a big meeting when there is a moon, and the witch doctors only meet at night because they don't want anyone to see their medicines. But now they are complaining because no young men want to become medicine men. They don't believe in witchcraft anymore, so the old men are discussing about that."

"Do the witch doctors' medicines work?" I asked, thinking perhaps that was the problem.

"Their *dawas* work, but they taste terrible, very bitter, and people these days get medicines from the clinic because it is free," he said. "The witch doctors can charge a lot for a cure."

Joseph said if I had come the day before, I would have met his two older brothers, William and Kureko, moran who were staying in the forest at Mount Suswa. He pointed out the old volcano rising in the distance high above the plains. "The moran don't live at home," he explained. "They sleep in the bush and hunt lions, but sometimes they come home to sing and dance, and everyone is happy. They move at night to take cattle. It is the first command of the Maasai to be a moran, but the government doesn't like us to have a separate army. Next year I will be a man after my circumcision, and then I can join the moran."

"What about school?"

"I want to do both," he said. "The girls like the moran. If you aren't a moran, it means with the Maasai you are a very poor man. The moran are very brave and beautiful to girls."

A few feet away, Noah's grandmother was playing with a mound of wet cow dung. She was tiny and shriveled-looking, and wore long beaded leather earrings, like bookmarks, which hung to her shoulders. "Her mind is not right," Joseph said. She struggled to her feet, hobbled over and grinned, throwing her muddy hands around me in a hug. Noah's grandfather, apparently finished with his discussion, came over to greet me and told her to sit down and mind her own business, which she did, chuckling.

The old man's name was Sane, which sounded like "sonny," and Joseph said he was the oldest person in the *boma*. He translated as Sane reported that nobody had seen Ndika, the hitchhiker, since my first visit, but the moran were keeping an eye out for him and planned to beat him. Musanka said that if Ndika showed up, they would turn him over to the police since he had killed a Kikuyu man some time ago. The police had been unable to find him. "The police get lost in Maasailand," Joseph said, laughing at the idea. Musanka interrupted and said we should not speak about this any longer since "the man has been cursed, so there will be no more trouble."

When I got home that night, I studied a photograph I'd taken of Ndika and looked for hints of an evil nature. He looked harmless enough, but I also remembered the young moran we'd met on the road that first day who had seemed to shun Ndika even though he said they were his friends.

The area where Joseph and Noah lived was called Saikeri, a Maasai word that the boys told me means "swamp," though when the rains tapered off, the land seemed more like a desert. As my visits continued, I began to learn a few Maasai words, and some time later I enrolled in a Maasai language class in Nairobi with two anthropologists who were also trying to learn. The language, called Maa, is difficult; a tone of voice can change the meaning of a word, and I never became a fluent speaker. The tribal name means "speakers of Maa," and Maa is related to the language spoken by the Bari people of the Sudan. It has no future tense, though constructions can be made to indicate the future. Some of the Maasai knew Swahili, a phonetic language that was easier to learn than Maa. But mostly, in the beginning, I relied on Joseph and Noah to translate.

I wasn't sure exactly what my relationship was to the people in the *boma*. I showed up, often unexpectedly, and asked a lot of questions, which nobody seemed to find unusual. The Maasai have a high opinion of themselves; they took my curiosity for granted. When friends in Nairobi asked me the purpose of my trips to Maasailand, I couldn't really say. I felt drawn to the people, to the openness of the land, the look of the plains. Chuck's newspaper job covered much of Africa, which kept him traveling most of the time, so he was able to visit the Maasai with me only a few times. Some of my friends from Nairobi came with me on other occasions, but few of them shared my enthusiasm. To me, Maasailand was a magical world, but my friends complained about the filth, the smoky huts, the flies.

Later, I began taping my conversations with the Maasai, thinking I might one day write about them. They were surprised to hear their own voices played back to them. At ceremonies they asked me to record their singing. When I told them I might write about them, they were agreeable, but I wasn't sure they understood, since only a few of the children and one of the women knew how to read. I tried putting it different ways, finally telling them that I would make a story about their lives so other people could learn about them. Sane ran his fingers over his whiskers while I explained; then, speaking for the others, he said it was important for outsiders to know more about the Maasai. From that point on, they worked tirelessly to give me a crash course in their culture.

I brought my camera and made a photo album of the *boma* for them. It was entrusted to Joseph's mother, Nterue, who brought it out on special occasions. When I began taking pictures, they instinctively lined up for portraits, stiff and somber. But they were pleased; the women insisted on wearing their best necklaces and capes, disappearing into their huts to primp for these sessions. A few of the elders were superstitious about the camera, but when Sane took part and the others saw the first batch of snapshots, they began posing too, and even asked for copies.

Some days the *boma* seemed indeed a bleak place. Often the women insisted on talking inside their huts, which were thick with smoke. There were thousands of flies, and the repellents I tried made no difference. They fed off the corners of the children's eyes, and nobody bothered to brush them away. In the rainy season, the children all had rashes, runny noses, coughs, bronchitis, and often malaria or serious stomach problems. Eye infections were chronic among the old people. The women carried their babies in slings on their backs, and there were no diapers. Mangy dogs were employed for the cleanup operations. There was a fair number of flea-ridden cats, which seemed a nuisance to everyone except for a few women and children who regarded them as pets.

People at the *boma* complained about the filth, but there wasn't much they could do about it, given the circumstances of their lives.

"Maasai *bomas* are so dirty," Joseph said, as we went trudging together through the muddy cattle kraal. "Once a person goes to the university and then comes back to Maasailand, all he can see is dirt and mud. He won't even want to stay here, just visit his mother and then go back to the city." The boys listened to me complaining about the crowds and traffic in Nairobi, the problem of finding a parking space, the long lines at the post office and the growing urban crime. But it had no impact. Noah told me he wanted to live in the city after he finished school because "it is so beautiful."

In Maasailand, attacks by wild animals were almost routine. The lions, leopards, hyenas and buffalo, which were the common subjects of Maasai nightmares, were a real threat in their daily lives. Yet they spoke about the menace of these beasts with the casualness of suburbanites bemoaning garden pests. Since my first visit, eight sheep had been killed by hyenas, and the moran had killed a lion that was stalking the cattle.

On one of my early visits, I was disconcerted to find two African missionaries at the *boma*. One of them carried a Bible, and the other, in a leather jacket, was strumming hymns on a guitar. The women stood around them singing and clapping. Their husbands were away tending cattle. The elders, wobbly and frail, protested this unseemly disturbance of their naps, drew up their blankets and moved to a shade tree outside the *boma*. One of them, a witch doctor, held his fly whisk across his face, like a cross held up to a vampire.

Joseph said the missionaries were Presbyterians who traveled throughout the valley, like old-fashioned circuit riders. They cast a dismissive glance my way, perhaps suspecting I was a Methodist who might demand equal time. In their reaction—and in mine—was an assumption of exclusivity. It was the same proprietary attitude I'd noticed in the old white hunter who spoke of "real Maasai," and in the anthropologist I'd met in Nairobi who described the people in her study as "my Maasai."

"The old men hate these missionaries," Noah told me.

"All the women in this *boma* have become Christians," Joseph added, "but nobody believes in it." The Maasai have their own religion, and afterlife does not conform with the tribe's fatalistic outlook. Their mercurial God—Engai—lives in the air, the grass, the rain, on the tops of mountains and in the clouds. They use the feminine gender prefix (*en-*) for God, as they do for many words relating to nature, and speak of Her two aspects, red (denoting anger) and black (denoting benevolence). The vengeful side of Engai is appeased through animal sacrifice and prayer. Some of the women, including Joseph's and Noah's mothers, had given their children Biblical names, but this seemed to have no special significance. Noah's mother started calling herself Agnes because it was pretty, she said. Other children in the area were named Livingstone and Japanese, and one was named Moi, after Kenya's president Daniel arap Moi. Parents rarely called their children by name—it was unlucky—but instead referred to them by such endearments as "my legs" or "my eyes."

I easily made friends with the Maasai women since one of them, a nineteen-year-old named Mary, had been to school, spoke English and could translate for the others. They were candid about their lives and welcomed my visits as an opportunity to pour out complaints about their aging polygamous husbands.

Early on, I brought Joseph's mother a new teapot and Noah's mother a pair of canvas shoes. These small gifts had pleased the women. But when Noah's grandmother asked me to bring her a new *shuka*, a packet of tea, medicine for her eyes, and shoes, I was afraid I was in line for endless demands. The next visit, I came empty-handed, and was ashamed when the women presented me with necklaces they had made, and measured my waist for a beaded belt.

"Where's my *shuka?*" the grandmother shrieked.

"Be quiet!" Noah's mother said.

From what I saw, the women's lives held few pleasures. Maasai men are often twice the age of their wives; marriages are family arrangements involving transactions in cattle, blankets and honey beer. Joseph said that some girls were "booked" for marriage when they were infants. The young girls were allowed to stay in moran camps called *manyattas*, and most began "playing sex," as Mary called it, when they were ten or eleven. For a brief period, a year or two, they enjoyed carefree lives of flirtation, singing and dancing, and making beaded bracelets for the moran. But at the first signs of puberty, girls left the *manyattas* to be circumcised and married.

Pregnancy is taboo before circumcision, although some of the women told me they were pregnant by their moran boyfriends at the time of their weddings. The practice of clitoridectomy—the cutting away of the clitoris and outer lips of the vagina—is a requirement for marriage, a brutal surgery done with a razor and no anesthesia. (The women were amazed to learn that I was not circumcised, some of them having assumed it was a virtually universal practice.)

I had understood that the purpose of female circumcision was the sexual control of women, to reduce the possibilities for their sexual pleasure and therefore insure fidelity. But apparently it did not work that way. Married women were permitted to have sex with other men if they were of their husband's age-group, but not of their same blood clan. If a husband brought home a guest, he might even offer one of his wives to him for the night, but the women had the final say. They were not allowed to have sex with moran, a rule the elders had devised to keep the bachelors away from their young wives, but one that was commonly broken. "Having moran boyfriends is the only thing that makes us feel good," Mary told me. To maintain the semblance of dignity, husbands overlooked all but the most blatant indiscretions, but wife beating was an accepted practice for the slightest mistake in the carrying out of duties, which included hut building and repair, animal and child care, laundry, cooking, and the fetching of water and firewood.

The Maasai calendar includes more than thirty different tribal ceremonies, among them circumcisions, which are family ceremonies attended by many guests. The preparations include the brewing of honey beer and the collecting of sacrificial animals. Much of the meaning of the various ceremonies—in which blessings and sacrifice are key elements—concerns fertility or the regulation of relations between males and females. Some of the symbolism, which originated in the distant past, is unfathomable—obscure even to the Maasai. Before I had been invited to a ceremony, I asked Agnes to describe the women's fertility rite she had just attended.

"It's such a good ceremony," she began. "It happens in one day. The men come out first and pour milk over one shoulder and traditional honey beer over the other. The women wear certain leaves around their necks and smear their faces with white chalk. They walk in a line; the first woman carries a child, followed by a man with a fly whisk, and the last woman should always be a barren woman. Then the men pour milk, cow dung and beer over them. The women usually scream and cry. Some of them fall on the ground shaking. They crawl under a big ram, which is also given beer. Then a small lamb is slaughtered, and each woman takes a piece of woolly hide to wear around her neck."

"I see," I said.

"We never allow Christians at this ceremony," she said.

When I asked her the meaning of these acts, for example, why the women crawled under a ram, she said, "It was that way from the beginning."

Of "the beginning"—or the past—the Maasai know only the stories passed down through generations. There are no documents or artifacts of their past. A migration of Maa speakers is believed to have started from the Nile region before the sixteenth century. By 1650 they were well established in what is now central Kenya.

The tribe's oral history begins with the mythic account of its escape out of a deep, dark crater. As Sane told me the story, a ladder was built, and men, women, children, cattle, goats, sheep and donkeys began to climb out. But the ladder broke, leaving half the people and animals behind. Those who got out first were said to be the "pure" Maasai who lived by cattle alone. Eventually the others escaped, and they became the Somali, Borana and Rendille peoples. The Maasai consider themselves superior to these other tribes, especially those that practice agriculture. A modern twist on the story suggests that the people who left the crater last have become the inferior classes—the farmers, fishermen and city dwellers.

The devotion of the Maasai to their cattle verges on a cult. Their cattle are zebu or boran, tough humpbacked breeds more resistant to disease and drought than high-grade beef cattle. During a drought, the Maasai watched their cattle die (with the steady hope that rain would fall to relieve their problems) rather than sell them to the Kenya Meat Commission.

At a neighboring *boma*, I once noticed a mutilated cow tied up to a tree. The cow had been attacked by a hyena and was in agony, but no one thought to put an end to its misery. Everyone believed it would recover. People went about their business as usual.

Cattle are the basis of Maasai self-sufficiency. Milk is central to the Maasai diet, hides are used to make ropes, sandals, bed mats and ceremonial clothing, dung is plaster for the huts, even cow's urine fits in with the tribal pharmacopoeia, but my comprehension fell short at understanding the deep, almost religious feeling the animals seem to inspire. The Maasai consider it unlucky to count their cattle but recognize each animal, the way we might account for a group of children on a field trip. They indicate numbers by an intricate finger-signing system. (A teacher in Maasailand later told me her students liked to add up numbers but faltered at subtraction. The concept was linked in their minds with cattle loss and upset them.)

The cattle motif was everywhere. The popularity of a particular style of canvas sneakers with the women was due to its mottled vinyl trim, a pleasing reminder of the markings on cattle. The bobbing of heads and shoulders in Maasai dancing seems to mimic the movement of cows to pasture. The leather bags in which the women stored their ornaments were shaped like cattle horns; bib necklaces were a representation of a cow's dewlap.

Elaborate sacrificial rites are observed in the ceremonial slaughter of cattle. Beef is eaten only for special occasions or by moran in special camps. The preferred method of killing is to intoxicate the animal with home-brewed beer, then smother it with a piece of soft hide, a procedure by which not a drop of blood—later to be drunk—is lost, and the hide remains unspoiled. Agnes once offered me a taste of a curdled blood pudding, a treat I could not bring myself to try. For a while I ate other things with them—roasted goat meat, sour milk. The consequence was amoebic dysentery, which took a year of repeated treatments to cure. After that, I often came with fruit or cashew nuts, which I offered to them.

The sight of penned cattle at the Kikuyu-owned Ngong slaughterhouse—where rougher means of slaughter were employed—made Joseph and Noah queasy. They considered their deep affection for cows the norm and were astounded by my ignorance—and insensitivity—about cattle. They knew thirty or forty specialized words to describe a cow, which to me was only brown. They had words that described various types of "honorable cows," and other words that succinctly summed up defects, such as broken tails and horns or missing eyes. There were words relating to cattle that had no direct translation, such as *linka*, which had to do with conditions of driving cattle at dawn.

"Don't they have cattle where you come from?" Joseph once asked me. The truth was, I had never before been close to a cow. I refused to stand in the middle of a herd. Unlike them, I did not find cows especially lovable.

6

SCHOOLBOYS

JOSEPH OLE MEYOKI and Noah Kipetuan ole Semoi (the "ole" means "son of") were best friends, and their families had lived together as long as any of them could remember. They were handsome boys with high-boned faces and enviable straight teeth. Joseph, the older and taller of the pair, had an identity card that indicated he was fifteen. He wasn't sure if it was correct. Noah thought he was probably about fourteen. Joseph was the more talkative one. Noah's dark, deep-set eyes often seemed sad. His slight build and thinness exaggerated the quality. Both attended school, which was not always common among the Maasai.

Whenever I brought magazines, the boys would flip through the pages, their eyes racing over photographs of a mysterious outside world.

"What's this?" Joseph asked, pointing to a photograph that showed thousands of New York City marathoners dashing across the Verrazano Bridge.

"These people look hungry," Noah said.

"Are there *harlots* in America?" Joseph once asked. He'd seen the word in a book, but was not quite sure what it meant.

My meeting with them had been by chance, but Joseph took it for destiny. He made no attempt to conceal his fascination with the modern world. He called it "the new life." He delighted in discoveries such as ice cubes. When I took him and Noah to see *Jaws* 2, it was the first time either of them had been to the movies, and neither had ever seen a fish. They asked when we could go again.

Joseph liked every type of gadget and quickly mastered the use of my camera, tape recorder and shortwave radio. I refused to teach him to drive but gave him rides on the back of my motorcycle. While I was drinking tea with his mother inside her hut, however, he found the instruction manual in the glove compartment and figured out how to start my car.

Noah tagged along on whatever adventures Joseph dreamed up. He seemed to act as Joseph's conscience, a counterweight to his friend's smooth confidence. He also spoke of "the new life," but with less conviction, his eyes filled with uncertainties. In their conversations I overheard allusions to Noah's family problems, but those details he kept to himself. As if to compensate for his friend's quietness, Joseph acted out for me the story of how he and Noah had saved his father's goats and sheep from a leopard attack. Noah was amused by Joseph's performance, proud that the account gave him proper credit.

I offered to take Noah and his younger sister Penina and her girlfriend to Nairobi to show them the tall buildings. The little girls, who wore their best necklaces, had never been to the city, or in a car. The engine fumes, undetected by me, and the motion of the car made them sick. We stopped several times along the way so they could stand by the road and vomit, and, finally, we abandoned the outing.

Not far from the *boma*, on a bare stretch of plains, the Kenya Army had set up a rifle range to train its recruits. A red flag was hoisted to warn off the Maasai when the army men were in camp. When the flag was up, small boys painted in red ocher, pretending to be moran, crouched in the big volcanic rocks to watch the soldiers fire their noisy automatic rifles. When the soldiers left, the boys became amateur anthropologists, sorting through the debris of the campsite, collecting empty soda bottles, bits of blasted plastic and metal, and printed targets that showed a cartoon of a sneering, helmeted soldier, a bull's-eye drawn across his chest. Sometimes they came up with a real find, a rusted pocketknife, a sock, some broken sunglasses.

Joseph and Noah felt a kinship to the soldiers. With the red flag and sound of gunfire, they cleared the plains with no less terrifying authority than Maasai warriors a few generations back. Joseph quickly made friends with them. Indeed, it was a soldier who had given him his first copy of *Newsweek*, and he already recognized the Mercedes-Benz symbol on the Kenya Army trucks as an emblem of modern power. He knew that the man who represented the Maasai in the Kenyan parliament drove a car with the same symbol, called by the same name, as did other rich men in government. His oldest brother, Kureko, a fearsome-looking moran, pointed out the car to me in Ngong. "Mercedes," he said proudly. It was the only foreign word in his vocabulary.

Joseph's personality and energy were so captivating that at first I didn't pay as much attention to Noah. I was surprised when one day I received a note from him that he had mailed at Ngong. Others followed. The neat penmanship—the style and slant varied from letter to letter—suggested that he had labored to make the notes perfect. They all began: "Dear Friend, much and pleasant greetings to you from me, your friend Noah Kipetuan ole Semoi." The messages were usually brief, sometimes newsy, inviting me to an upcoming Maasai ceremony, or telling me of a birth, or if there had been rain, or the latest on his grandfather's failing health. The longer notes were formal compositions discussing a tribal proverb or some Maasai folklore about the Keekonyokie Maasai, the section of the tribe to which he and Joseph belonged. He once sent me a list of all the trees in Maasailand with their Maasai names and the medicinal properties of their bark. The Maasai word for tree and medicine is the same, he told me. Sometimes he asked me to bring things for his grandfather—a can of cooking fat, sugar, tea—or a ruled copybook for him. The notes created a private friendship between us.

A teacher at his school told Noah about an agricultural show at the Nairobi fairgrounds, and Noah sent a note asking if I would take him and Joseph to see the cattle exhibit. Even in school uniforms—cotton shorts, blue sweaters, black vinyl shoes—the boys were recognizable as Maasai. Waiters at a coffee shop were amused by them. But if a stranger's behavior was fawning, the boys would stiffen, attuned to the slightest indignity. A smiling waiter asked me if they were Maasai. "Yes, we are the Maasai," Joseph said. What struck me was the assertion that they were "the" Maasai.

At the fairgrounds, Joseph wanted to ride the Ferris wheel, to taste cotton candy, to ask questions of the men tending each exhibit. His brash charm made him friends everywhere. Noah stuck with me, a little overwhelmed, explaining fine points I had not known about raising cattle, sheep and goats. Joseph ran into some soldiers from the rifle range who immediately recognized him and treated him to an orange soda. They were not sure if they'd met Noah before or not. But Noah was no less observant of the wonders of the modern world.

When I took Noah to visit a sick Maasai boy, it was the first time he had been to a hospital. What immediately impressed him was that most of the doctors wore eyeglasses. He assumed that the eyeglasses imbued their wearers with magical abilities to diagnose and cure diseases. Another time, he asked me to help him fill out a school form. It asked the color of his eyes. Did they mean the brown part, the white part or the black ring? he asked. He had written down all three.

Joseph and Noah told me about an older friend, then in his third year of secondary school, whose family lived near them. His name was Dickson Leponyo ole Ntikoisa, and he was the most highly educated Maasai—outside of their teachers—whom they knew. "He speaks perfect English," Noah said. They thought he might be able to answer my more difficult questions. "Why do the Maasai drink cow's blood?" I once asked. "It tastes good," Noah replied.

Dickson's family were recent arrivals in Saikeri. They had come from a trading center called Euaso where, two years earlier, Dickson had scored the highest mark in the Maasai district on the national primary school exam, earning the coveted Certificate of Primary Education (C.P.E.). Joseph and Noah were due to take the same test, and they spoke of Dickson's achievement with awe. Maasai children usually did poorly on national exams, and few found places in the nation's overcrowded secondary schools. There were 4.3 million primary school students in Kenya, but room for only 500,000 in the secondary schools. Dickson was a student at Oloolaiser Secondary School, a government boarding school in the Ngong Hills.

I met him when he came home one weekend to help his father look after cattle. It was late afternoon, and he and his older brother, Stephen, had just returned with the cattle and were examining them for ticks. Dickson was wearing a *shuka* to please his father, but he had on socks and shoes. He was at least six feet tall and muscular in a way that suggested he had participated in school sports. He had spaces between his teeth, a long, broad nose and was a Laikipia Maasai, a part of the tribe that almost became extinct during tribal wars of the last century. He'd spent enough time in the modern world to find my interest in cattle odd but welcome.

I asked him how he had learned to look after livestock.

"The first thing you learn from your father is that the cow is the basis of your life," he said. "You believe this with all your heart. If you lose that feeling, you lose the sense of your life. When I was about five years old, my father started taking me along to graze the animals. My mother would give me a small gourd of milk to last the day. When I got tired my father would carry me on his back. My father told me you have to like the appearance of the cow in order to look after it properly. But some are very friendly, and they will come up and lick you and become your friend. So that gives you courage to love them. When you are small, you learn to whistle. There are different whistles to let the cows know if you have found water or grass. You learn to look for certain types of grass. There is one kind of grass that makes the cows shiver and become sick. Usually there is one cow that moves faster, or a bull that leads the others. With goats you have to take more care since there are more of them, and they can easily be lost or eaten by wild animals."

"Goats are lazy," Noah said. "You have to push them to move."

"Another thing you learn is to travel long distances, to carry supplies on your back, how to milk the cows, and to make thorn fences for nights when you can't return home," Dickson went on. "Sheep need a higher fence to keep leopards from jumping on them. When cows smell a wild animal, they start running in the opposite direction. When that happens, one herdboy runs after the cows, and the other one goes after the wild animals. You don't feel afraid, you know you are going after the enemy, and you have no other choice. Your whole body feels excited. A wild animal can jump on you before you even see it. But some wild animals are frightened and run away. You always walk in their direction but not as if you are going to fight.

"You shout at a lion. If you make a certain deep sound in your throat—the way the moran do—they know you want to fight. Lions are more easily scared off than leopards. A leopard will attack a human for no reason at all. But a lion will attack only if it is very hungry or if it has been attacked. We make traps around the *boma* using wires and rope tied with a reef knot. You tie it to a post and put meat near the wire. We usually put poison in the meat. When the animal is trapped the knot tightens like a noose. The wire cuts the flesh to the bones. During the last drought I took our animals to a hill on the other side of the Ngong Hills. I was with a younger boy, and we built a fence, but not a very proper fence. That night a leopard came inside, and we heard the sheep running. The leopard was trying to push the sheep away from us. I tried to spear it, but it ran away.

"That happened three days in a row, and on the last day it killed two goats and a sheep. The next night I injected a syringe of Coopertex—that's a tick medicine—into some meat and left it out. In the morning I found four dead leopards, a mother and three cubs. Usually the males and females travel in pairs, so I think the male must have gone to look for food and not come back.

"It's easier to kill a leopard than a lion. I killed my first leopard when I was thirteen, with a friend. We were just grazing the herd when the leopard leaped on one of our goats. When we went near, it started to growl. We were not afraid because we had been taught how to kill it, and that is our work, to protect our animals. I threw the first spear and it hit the leopard in the shoulder and came out the hip. Some people are experts at spearing. That is why I am one of the best at school with the javelin."

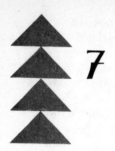

7

SEKENTO

One Sunday I met Joseph and Noah outside the post office at Ngong. Joseph's older brother William, who had recently quit the moran to enroll in school, was with them.

"How is you?" he asked, showing off his English.

All three of them wore school uniforms. Their legs were dusty from the long walk. We were going to visit their teacher, William ole Sekento, a modern Maasai, whose *shamba* (farm) was on the eastern slopes of the Ngong Hills.

Joseph climbed up in the front seat of my Range-Rover, so he could give directions. Noah kept his eyes on the road, pointing out potholes.

"Turn here! Turn here!" Joseph shouted, waving his arms when we had passed the Craze Hotel—a popular landmark—and reached a junction off the Ngong road. We headed up into the hills. "Slow down!" Ahead of us, a herd of cattle lumbered across the road. The boys knew immediately from the way the cows' ears were notched who owned them, and they began an accounting of the fattest, the most beautiful, the most aggressive. "That one is sick," Noah said, pointing to the straggler.

I did not dare honk the horn at the cattle or the shepherd, who was old and feeble. It seemed forever before the cows were gently prodded off the road into the adjoining field. The boys turned to look back long after we'd passed them.

We followed a dirt road that cut across overgrown fields and narrowed to a steep, twisting, rocky trail. We passed a dozen small *shambas* and tin-roofed shacks set in a cozy disarray of fields planted thick with corn. "People here always get rain," Noah said enviously. Each farm compound exhibited a pile of junk, a chair with missing legs, a broken bicycle, a rusted wheelbarrow, scraps of timber, things that might one day be repaired or given some other use. Nobody was around.

Sekento's *shamba* stood beside a windbreak of eucalyptus—a mark of colonial times—with an immense view over the surrounding countryside. Nearby were his father's and brother's houses, backed up by thick forest. We found Sekento in his field, sitting on a log, lost in corn. He was about thirty-five, tall and bone-thin with a finely chiseled face and long, tapered fingers that cut the air when he spoke. The boys watched anxiously, hoping we would become friends. I asked him how the boys were doing at school. Joseph, he said, was among the brightest, but easily distracted. "He could be number one, if he tried," Sekento said reproachfully. "Noah is moderate, but a hard, steady worker. As for William, it is too soon to say."

He began to tease them.

"William, now that you see how tough the job is at school, are you ready to go back to the moran?"

"No, those works are a waste," William said.

"Joseph, do you think you can still run fast enough to steal Kikuyu cows?"

Joseph laughed.

"And what about Noah? Should we cut the holes in your ears today?"

"Never!" Noah said, clamping his hands over his ears. "I can never spoil my body."

Traditionally, the tops of a Maasai child's ears were pierced with a small hole at the age of eight or nine; several years later, the lobes were cut and gradually stretched, using wads of leaves and wooden plugs. It was now a matter of choice, and Joseph's and Noah's ears were not pierced. Recently Joseph's younger brother, Tareu, had insisted—out of tribal pride, he claimed—on having his earlobes cut. He also refused to go to school. Lost in a shuffle of brothers, he was upholding tradition, perhaps to catch his father's attention.

From the house, Sekento's wife, Rahab, called us for tea. A Kikuyu, she was also a teacher and taught at the nearby school where her sons were among the students. Sekento and Rahab had once taught together at another school, a few miles from the farm, but after several women teachers whose husbands were important officials in Nairobi were assigned there, he had been transferred to Saikeri.

Joseph and Noah raced ahead to join Sekento's children. There were six, five of them boys. William hung back to talk with us. He was tall and gangly, twice the age of the boys in his class; he looked overgrown in school shorts. But at school he was respected, and the smaller boys pestered him to find out what moran life was like. He had put that life behind him. The loops of his ears were now undecorated, and he wore no beads.

"So how is school, William?" I asked.

"I like." He went silent, struggling to think of a few more English words. I tried my Swahili, and Sekento shook his head. "You both need practice."

Sekento introduced his sons, Edgar, Alex, Daniel, Jeremiah and Gideon, who bowed their heads in the traditional Maasai child's greeting of an elder. They watched their father's every move, recording details that might be recalled later, in his absence. Because of his teaching job, Sekento was at home only on weekends. It was too far to go back and forth to Saikeri every day. He scooped up the youngest, Grace, who'd been napping on a foam mattress spread on the ground. She squealed and threw her arms around him.

"Let me hear you count," he coaxed.

"One, two, three, three, four . . ." she said, keeping track on her stubby fingers.

"Five, six, seven," Sekento finished. "That's all we've done so far."

The house was a small mud-plastered cabin made of rough timber with a corrugated tin roof. Sekento said he was so short of funds when he built it that he'd used a rock to hammer the nails. Then one day he'd found a hammer on the road—his great find and someone else's loss. There was no electricity or piped water; the children hauled water from the creek. An outhouse stood in the back. Next to the house was a cooking shed where Rahab was frying doughnuts in a pan set over a charcoal brazier on the ground. She wore a floral-print dress and plastic sandals, and her hair was wrapped in a bright scarf. "Welcome! Welcome!" she said. She had dimples like her daughter, Grace, and despite her pregnancies, she was as slim as a teenager.

The cabin had three small rooms, two of them crammed with metal beds. The middle room was a living room, where Joseph and Noah and I sat on a vinyl couch draped with hand-embroidered cloths. Sekento and William took seats on wobbly chairs that sat unevenly on the dirt floor. Chickens, roosters, kittens, a stray dog and barefoot children wandered in and out. The dog, twisted in a pretzel contortion, chewed at fleas until Sekento's mother, Joyce, a tall, heavyset woman, lifted him with the tip of her shoe and flung him outside. She gave me a sack of tomatoes picked from her garden and said she was on her way to the Kiserian market, where she sold vegetables. Grace crawled into my lap, played with my hair and fell asleep. Rahab brought in a teapot and a plate piled high with steaming doughnuts. The boys were pleased and on their best behavior. Their hands were unsteady, spooning sugar into their cups.

After that, I often visited Sekento and his family. I was learning Swahili, and he and Rahab drilled me with flash cards. Years before, a young man from the Peace Corps who had worked at Sekento's college helped him improve his English and introduced him to rock and roll, which Sekento did not especially like. Since then, he hadn't known any Americans, but lately he had observed another one, a middle-aged man who went running in a sweat suit. Sekento knew the man was too old to be a serious athlete; he struggled on the hills and became thinner each week. He thought the man might have some problems at home with his wife. "Why a man who can afford to own a car wastes his energy running, I will never know," he said. After I explained about recreational jogging, he still shook his head.

The area where they lived was called Kerarapon, a Maasai word that means "we are increasing in number." Sekento had been born here. Some of the first educated Maasai, including his father, Edward, had used the name since settling here in the 1930s. Edward Sekento was a retired school inspector, but his education had come by colonial force. He was put in a boarding school, ran away a few times but eventually stuck it out, later joining the civil service. He had two wives and ten children, six of whom worked, as a teacher, a tax clerk, an agricultural extension officer, a messenger, a health inspector and a bank clerk respectively. Two of the children were still in school; one was an art student. Edward had also sponsored the education of several Maasai children whose families either refused or were too poor to send their children to school. One youngster he had boarded was now head of the physiology department at the University of Nairobi.

As a small boy, Sekento knew little about traditional Maasai culture, but he was fluent in the tribal language. When he was ten, his father sent him to his grandfather's *boma* for a few weeks' instruction. Until then, Sekento had seen warriors only from a distance. Up close they were no less frightening. By the time he returned home—his arm broken after falling into a well— he had concluded that tribal life was too primitive for him. Now, with the rising cost of school fees and children's shoes, he wondered sometimes if he'd made the right choice. As teachers, Sekento and Rahab earned a combined monthly salary of 2,500 Kenya shillings, equivalent to about $120.

I told Sekento that I was thinking about writing a magazine article about the Maasai, but I needed to learn a lot more before I could begin. He offered to help as a translator and started telling me more about Saikeri and his work at school. Once I asked him if I could go with him, at least part of the way, to the school. I wanted to see what it was like. I had clocked the distance by road from Ngong to Saikeri. It was twenty-six miles. Even with shortcuts—Sekento had mentioned a cave—it was not much less than marathon distance. *Matatus*, the local bush taxis, stayed out of the Rift Valley. Sekento had once tried to ride a bicycle to school. He ended up carrying it most of the way after the tires went flat and he ran out of patches. Occasionally he got a lift in an army truck. Most times he went on foot.

He described his routine. On Mondays, he was up before dawn. He strapped a small knife under his jacket, stuffed a bag with a cabbage, some potatoes and a tin of cooking fat, and set out for the Rift Valley. The cross-country walks had given him an angular, awkward gait, so even on pavement he walked as if he were picking his way over jagged rocks, his narrow shoulders tensed at an angle.

When he was away at school, Sekento worried about his family. Once, in his absence, a prowling leopard had kept them holed up inside for two days. Another time, wild pigs had devoured his entire corn crop. Crime was a growing problem. His brother George had been attacked by a gang of robbers while walking home from a bus stop, a beating that had left him partially crippled. His uncle's *duka*, a small shop on the same road, had been ransacked. Sekento had bought bow and arrows from a fellow teacher, a Kamba, whose tribe specialized in making them. The arrows were dipped in poison, and he showed Rahab how to use the bow. She laughed at the idea.

The day Sekento and I set off for school, he decided to walk through Ngong rather than take the shorter route through the forest behind his house. Occasionally he ran into buffalo in the forest. "Buffalo can sense you from a great distance," he said, "and they will charge you for no reason at all." In the valley he sometimes encountered leopards or hyenas on their breakfast patrol. A sudden movement in the grass was fair warning for a quick detour. Once he'd met up with a leopard in a cave. The leopard, as startled as he, backed off.

At this hour, the air was damp and chilly. Sekento pulled his cap down over his ears and lit the day's first cigarette. Above us, a thick fog caught on the peaks of the Ngong Hills. The town, gloomy in the fog, was a strip of road with small *dukas* on both sides, an arrangement that reminded me of a frontier town in the Old West. During the rainy season the ground was thick with mud, and the shopkeepers, many of them Indians, did a booming business in cheap gum boots. In the dry season the hills turned brown and seemed to shrink, and a gritty red dust settled everywhere.

Around Ngong, I was becoming a familiar character to the Maasai, though two undercover policemen once questioned Sekento about my business. He bought them some beers and roasted meat and told them that I was a Bible student interested in Maasai culture. Neither of us was a churchgoer, but after that, we had no trouble.

By day Ngong was lively, with an undercurrent of shady dealings. I knew people at Saikeri who had never been to Ngong, and who had no interest in the goings-on. To them, Ngong teemed with an urban sleaziness, the way I felt about Times Square. But to some, like Joseph and Noah, it was exciting. Kikuyu farmers were buying up land around Ngong as fast as they could convince the Maasai to sell it. The constituency had changed so quickly that John Keen, the local Maasai member of Kenya's parliament—one of five from the two Maasai districts—was expected to lose his seat in the next election. Stone houses had started to replace wooden shacks. A small branch of Barclays Bank was soon to open. Long lists of people waited to buy land. Bribery and skulduggery lubricated the procedure. The town's Maasai government "chiefs"—Pulei and Sayo—often sat on a heap of rocks at the Ngong road junction, their *rungus* (clubs) resting across their knees, watchful players with a hand in the action.

The town was still asleep when Sekento and I passed through; the only sounds came from a cattle pen outside the slaughterhouse. A woman at Saikeri had asked Sekento to bring her some cow's hooves, which she used, somehow, to treat snakebites. Sekento shuddered at the idea. He was sure the men who worked at the slaughterhouse eventually went mad.

We continued on a winding dirt road toward the escarpment, past small farms that haphazardly quilted the hills. Curls of bluish smoke from cooking fires rose from each house. The farmers were Kikuyu recently moved to the area. Already the women were in their gardens, bent from the hips, poking at weeds with digging sticks. Other women with *pangas* (machetes) headed to the forest to cut firewood. The farmers had strung barbed wire to keep out the cattlemen. The changes disturbed Sekento. Each year, the farms pushed farther into Maasailand, to the very lip of the Rift Valley. Since individual title deeds had been handed out— land redistribution became a necessity after independence—the Maasai had already given up much of their best grazing land; they seemed not to realize the long-term consequences of land sales.

8

SAIKERI

THE HEADMASTER at Saikeri Primary School was a balding Kikuyu who wore glasses, which were hard to keep clean here. He'd been in Saikeri almost two years. Sekento and I met him when he was returning from Ngong on his motorcycle. "These roads are a disgrace," he said, beating the dust off his pants. "By the way, Sekento, your friend Joseph came to talk to me the other day. He told me he is going to be circumcised in December, and he has to go kill a lion and birds and all this."

"Birds?" I said.

"It's to make a headdress they wear after circumcision," Sekento explained.

"It's a lot of nonsense," the headmaster said, turning to me. "Do you know Joseph Meyoki?"

I said I did.

"Joseph is a brave boy—he's famous for it," he said. "His brother is a big moran. This is a sort of family tradition—all the Meyoki boys have to be tough. Whenever one of these lion hunts is organized, they don't want to leave Joseph behind—they want him in the front line. We go out of our way not to interfere in the culture here, but every day we have to compete with it."

Sekento said he would talk to Joseph.

• •

We walked over to the school. It was not much to look at: a dilapidated, dirt-floored shed divided into classrooms with benches and small blackboards. ("Lake Turkana—a former territory of Maasailand," a teacher had written on one blackboard.) There were no maps, books, or teachers' desks. A gritty wind blew across the courtyard, and Sekento picked up a stub of chalk rolling on the ground. For miles around there was nothing but empty plains. A teacher who had since left had planted some cacti around the flagpole and made a stone border. Every morning the children lined up to pledge allegiance to President Moi. It was a routine followed throughout the nation. The sun heating the metal roof made a steady ping, like rain. It seemed a cruel joke. There had been no recent rain here.

About five hundred Maasai lived in Saikeri. American missionaries had built the school, the first in the area. There were two kinds of primary school in Kenya: *harambee* ("pull together") schools, which were supported by community fund-raising, and schools fully operated by the government. Saikeri was now government-run but not entirely free. Parents were required to contribute to the building fund and to buy their children's uniforms and books. Last year Joseph had been made to sit outside the school and could not attend classes because his father had failed to contribute. He was not the only student in that situation, but when the measure failed to shame his father—and others—into paying, it was dropped, and the children were allowed back in school.

Saikeri Primary School had marked the small beginning of a town. A Swedish aid program financed the building of a health clinic, and the government drilled a well. Several entrepreneurs with an eye to the future had put up wooden kiosks to sell sugar, salt, tea, soap powder and newer items, like maize meal, for which the Maasai were developing a taste. But there were problems, Sekento said. Often, there was no diesel fuel to run the pump, or there were mechanical breakdowns. Several months before, the man sent to fix the borehole for the water well had mangled his hand trying to repair it. Since then, nobody had come. The cattle sometimes trampled the earthen walls of the dam, which the missionaries also had built, and fouled the water intended for human use. (The Maasai claimed the "strong water" made them tough. Few had need of the dispensary.) The missionaries had given up the idea of building a church. A truck carrying building stones made one trip to the proposed site, but the dirt track was so rough that the driver refused to haul in the rest. The stones now lay in a heap on which some goats were basking.

The school had been in operation three years when Sekento arrived. Then, there were only two grades and sixty Maasai students, including Joseph and Noah. Sekento called them "the pioneers." There were few girls among the students. Since most were married by the age of fifteen, parents saw no need to educate them. The school had got off to a shaky start. Sentiments hardened when the police were called in to force parents to enroll their children, and many still spoke of their children in school as "lost." But, gradually, attitudes were changing. School enrollment now approached 130—about one child per family, and there were now 34 girls in the lower grades. Most of them, however, were expected to drop out once they were circumcised. Dickson's father had recently taken his youngest daughter out of school and arranged for her marriage. But Sekento said she was not angry; marriage was all that was expected of girls.

There were five teachers for the seven grades, called "standards." Sekento was the only Maasai. Morale was low, and the turnover high. To keep teachers, a new row of cement cubicles, which held the heat like ovens, had been recently built for them to live in. But few could tolerate the remote location, the bleak landscape and the frustrations for long. Maasai culture was also alien and disorienting to outsiders. Some teachers asked for transfers or quit teaching entirely if they were refused. Sekento himself wanted a job nearer home, but his requests for a transfer were turned down every year. He was needed for the younger children who spoke only the tribal tongue.

Joseph and Noah were about to enter standard seven, then the final year of primary school. There were six boys in their class, the first Saikeri graduating class. During the next year, they would take the C.P.E.—the national primary school exam—the first ever given at Saikeri. If they made a passing mark, they would receive a certificate. It took a much higher mark to secure a place in secondary school. Some might be accepted at Maasai Technical School near Kajiado, the only school in the country that catered to the tribe. But it was a small school, and the competition was stiff. Private secondary schools, a growing industry in Kenya, were a new alternative, but tuition was expensive, and Sekento said some of the teachers who worked in them could barely read and write themselves.

For Joseph and Noah, a low mark would mean the end of their schooling; whatever their dreams about "the new life," they would have little choice but to become cattle herders like their fathers. The exam was a major test for Saikeri. The parents of other children would be watching to see how the boys did, to see whether school was a waste of time. Sekento, aware of what was at stake, had volunteered to tutor the boys and arranged for them to sleep at the school on weeknights so that they could study. The huts in their *bomas* had no lights for reading, and their fathers would always think up some chore to take them off their schoolwork. Sekento showed me an old exam he was using as a drill. The questions, in English, covered math, science, religion, music and grammar. A sample question: "What metal is used to make coat hangers?" Would the children even know what a coat hanger was?

There were also distractions outside of school, about which little could be done. The boys had missed half the previous term helping their fathers move cattle. There were lion hunts and cattle raids—far more exciting ways to spend the day than sitting on a hard bench learning multiplication tables.

Joseph and Noah were further preoccupied with convincing their fathers to circumcise them. Because they were not yet circumcised, they were still children in the eyes of the tribe, obliged to greet elders with a bowed head rather than a dignified handshake. Circumcision was a major event in Maasai life, the test of a boy's character. It was performed in public, without anesthesia, before judgmental witnesses. Girls were allowed to cry out during their circumcisions. But for boys, any display of pain or emotion, even a blink, would leave a lifelong blemish on one's reputation. Such cowardice was regarded as a slight to the tribe, and the family would be obliged to pay a cattle fine for their shame. Joseph and Noah practiced for their circumcisions by pinching each other, learning to withstand the pain, neither daring to flinch.

Most of their friends had been circumcised the year before, and some had already joined the moran. All Maasai males were grouped by age-sets determined at the time of circumcision. For schoolboys, moranship was out of the question, yet the idea of it loomed powerfully in their fantasies. Joseph's brother Kureko, who had been a moran for six years, had tried to convince him to give up school and join in the fun. Joseph had resisted so far, but obviously the temptation was strong.

Sekento had hoped the boys' fathers would arrange for the ceremonies during the previous school vacation, which would at least put the distraction behind them, but the plans had been changed. Joseph's father was entangled in a land dispute that took up his full attention. Noah's father had decided to move his family to a new *boma*, a chaotic undertaking, since he was drunk much of the time. Sekento, aware of Noah's discomfort, was too polite to mention it when we first met. Instead, in Noah's presence, he told me that Noah's father, Semoi, was a famous leader. He was the *olaiguenani*, the chief spokesman for his age-set. He was selected for this job at the time of his own circumcision and was expected to carry out important duties throughout his life. Sekento described him as a spellbinding orator. "People have always respected him," he said. Noah looked sad as Sekento described his father, and I had thought at the time that the sadness was because his circumcision had been postponed.

• •

Sekento called from Ngong one weekend to tell me that the cochairman of the Saikeri land committee had been eaten by a lion.

"*Eaten?*" I echoed in horror.

"Not completely, but he's dead, and so is another man."

On Monday, I drove out to the Saikeri clinic, where the two men had been treated. There were two full-time nurses, Matthew Kivuva and Titus Kimilu, both Kamba. Matthew had been on duty when the two men were brought in. While we were talking, a Maasai girl hopped in. She had a thorn in her foot and asked Matthew to remove it. Two moran stood in the doorway watching as he swabbed her foot, then pulled out the thorn. The girl screamed. The moran snickered. Matthew, wearing a white lab coat over his jeans, handed her the thorn—it was two inches long—and put a bandage over the wound. She stood up tentatively, then skipped out the door.

"It would help if they wore shoes," Matthew said.

The small clinic was spotless. There were wall posters promoting sanitation and measles vaccinations, which few of the Maasai could read, and there was not much business. Titus had worked at clinics in Maasailand for eight years and had been in Saikeri for three. "I don't know why the numbers of patients are reducing," he said. "At first there was a lot of curiosity from the women. Now it's kind of tapered off."

"Sometimes it seems like a losing battle," Matthew observed. He had been in Saikeri less than a year. The lion incident illustrated his point. The lion had attacked a donkey at one of the *bomas*. Some men had chased it off and then laced the remains of the donkey's carcass with poison, figuring the lion would return for it. The lion did return, but the poison deranged rather than killed it. The next morning an old woman grazing her goats spotted it. She shouted for help and ran for her life. Two men came to her rescue and fought the lion with swords. It took them an hour to kill it, and they were badly bitten and clawed. The right arms of both were nearly chewed off, their chests were ripped, and they lost a great deal of blood. Both were "spear bleeding," hemorrhaging internally. It had taken several hours to carry them in to the clinic.

There was no vehicle at Saikeri to remove them to the hospital. The school headmaster rode his motorcycle to Ngong to summon help. He arrived at five o'clock, but there were no vehicles available that could manage the rutted dirt roads. He drove to Kerarapon looking for a Maasai named John who owned an old battered Land-Rover. John had helped out in the past. But on the last trip to Saikeri, he had overturned his truck. He had no insurance and could barely drive. This time he wanted payment, in advance, and named a price. The headmaster had little cash with him, and more time was squandered convincing John to accept a smaller fee. By then it was dark, and John's headlights were smashed. He said he'd have to wait until morning.

Meanwhile, the family of one of the wounded men had carried him from the clinic to their *boma* to be treated by the local herbalist. Matthew worked throughout the night, trying to keep the other man alive. In the morning, when John arrived, the families argued against taking the men to the hospital. By the time they finally reached the hospital, it was too late. Both men died within hours.

"The lack of vehicles is our greatest problem," Titus said. "When the headmaster is not here with his motorcycle, we have to rely on runners. And very few people in Ngong have these sturdy trucks that can handle the roads."

"There's also selfishness," Matthew said. "People in Ngong just don't want to be bothered. They don't want to take the risk. We had a child who got very sick one afternoon. There was nothing I could do for him, and nobody was around, so I went to Ngong myself, on foot. I couldn't find anybody to help, so I went back to Saikeri. By then the child was cold and dead. That is just one example. I could tell you other stories just as bad."

"Even though we're close to Nairobi, this is still the bush," Titus said.

Sekento came into the clinic with a Maasai named Joakim ole Mereu. "Here's the man who can tell you everything about Saikeri," he said to me.

"I'm a field enumerator," Joakim said. "I've been out here almost two years making a study for the Central Bureau of Statistics."

I asked him what he had found out.

"The main problem is alcoholism," he said. "I'd say seventy-five percent of the men are alcoholic, and about thirty-five percent of the women. It gets worse every day. Assaults are up. The main health problems are VD, tuberculosis, bronchitis, eye infections, dysentery and malaria."

"The VD situation is improving," Titus said. "Malaria is getting worse."

"About half the children here die before the age of five," Joakim continued.

"From what?" I asked.

"Everything you can think of. They fall into fires in the huts; they fall out of trees; they die from snakebites, whooping cough, measles, even diarrhea. They eat diseased animals."

"A lot of these things are treated at home, and we see only the worst, when the witch doctor gives up," Matthew said. "There are a lot of problems with births. The pregnant women are underfed to make the deliveries easier, and also because the men are stingy. They make the women look after cattle right up to the last month. Most of the babies are born at around two kilos. They look like premature babies, even at full term."

"In general the nutrition is bad," Joakim continued. "The women and children get about a quarter of the calories they need. The men go off to town and eat a kilo of roasted goat meat with their friends, then come home with a packet of sugar for the family. Most of the kids get by on milk."

"But we've made progress on the babies," Titus said. "We've reduced infant mortality to about one in four. Quite a few women bring their babies for checkups now. We talk to them about vaccinations. One thing they're up to date on is breast-feeding. They nurse for three or four years. It works well for family planning—it's why Maasai women don't have as many children as other tribes. The husbands don't sleep with them when they're nursing. I think that's one reason the women nurse their children for so long, to avoid having sex with these old men."

"But sometimes the women don't want to let us examine them because we are not Maasai, or because we are of a different age-set than their husbands," Matthew put in. "It is discouraging. I try to remember that my tribe—the Kamba—used to live like the Maasai. It's all a matter of development. But there's no leadership out here. We have Chief Sayo. He has no house, no toilet, how can he be an example, a leader? The blind leading the blind. We try to teach the Maasai not to eat diseased animals. And what happens? Chief Sayo goes around boasting how he can eat anything!"

"The only time the politicians come out here is to display themselves right before elections," Sekento said.

"Then they get elected and forget where they came from," Titus added. "And the leaders who are supposed to be helping the Maasai are the very ones who have engineered all the problems with land selling. The Kikuyu are going to move in here like locusts if something isn't done. The land committee is totally corrupt. The best man on that committee was the one who got eaten by the lion."

"If you want a plot of land, bribe," Sekento said. "If you want a job, bribe."

I asked if they couldn't expose the corruption.

"It's everywhere—it's normal now," Sekento said.

"People who try to expose it are bribed to shut up," Matthew said. "They cool you down fast."

"And once a Maasai gets educated and takes a job in Nairobi he doesn't want to come back here," Titus said.

I asked Joakim if as a Maasai he felt any special commitment to help his tribe.

"Not really," he said. "I feel proud to be a Maasai. But I don't feel that *nini* [thing]. The Maasai have no aim for the future. They don't want to listen to you. They think if you are educated you'll cheat them. It's like they're living in 1850."

9

THE CHIEF

THE SUBCHIEF of Ngong and Saikeri—in effect, the local sheriff—was the man the Maasai called Chief Sayo. I knew his youngest wife, Mary, the only woman in Saikeri who had gone to school. She had completed primary school at Euaso before she married. Sekento had asked her to teach an adult literacy class after the previous teacher was killed in a motorcycle accident, but Chief Sayo, who was jealous of her literacy, refused to let her take the job.

Mary was nineteen and had one child, a baby she had named Louise, who had the same broad, cherubic face as Mary. "Louise doesn't look anything like Sayo," I observed, and Mary smiled coyly.

Mary had not wanted to marry the Chief. "When he first came around to talk to my father, trying to marry me, I disliked him so much I would cover my eyes so I wouldn't have to look at him," she said. He was persistent and brought her parents cattle, blankets, honey beer, even cash. She once threw a bucket of water at him. He smiled and told her, "You could throw blood on me, and I would still marry you!"

The Chief was an imposing figure, more than six feet tall, and one of the few overweight Maasai—outside of the politicians—I had seen. "He's so fat!" Mary complained, puffing out her cheeks. He walked with a confident, menacing swagger and carried a fancy wooden club, which was sometimes put to use.

At government ceremonies, like President Moi's coming to the Ngong Hills to plant trees, Sayo wore his government-issue khaki uniform with a black felt beret. Sometimes he added an ascot. He carried an address book in his pocket and asked visiting officials to write their names and telephone numbers in it. He memorized every entry in his book so he could point to any and pretend he was reading. But to keep up with politics, he made Mary read him the newspapers.

"What do you think of the situation in Chad?" he would ask.

Often, when I was on my way to Saikeri, he would flag me down, waving his club, and demand that I drive him somewhere or else buy him a whiskey in Ngong. I had little choice; it was clear he could make trouble for me. He told me once he'd like to marry me. I could get a divorce from my husband, he said. He liked educated women. When we drove out to see some land he owned in the Rift Valley, he told me he was going to build a shop and a "proper" house to live in out there. Then, he said, I'd change my mind.

On the way, he asked me to stop when he spotted some Tanzanian cattle traders. He said he could always recognize Tanzanian Maasai because their skin was darker. The border with Tanzania was closed, though the Maasai went back and forth, dodging the police. Sayo got out of the Range-Rover and stood silently, his club held high, like a scepter. His uniform caught the Tanzanians' attention. They froze in their tracks. "You are not allowed here!" he bellowed. "Go back to your own country! *Get lost!*" The Tanzanians fled.

The Chief was not popular with the Maasai. He was a civil servant, a government chief, without any real authority within the tribe. Often he called meetings in Saikeri to discuss development projects—road grading or repairs on the borehole—and demanded beer and roasted goat meat. When he was drunk, he heckled the Maasai about their filth and backwardness.

"Education is the most important thing!" he told the

people at Saikeri. Every year, at the start of the school term, he called a meeting of parents and advised each family to send at least one child to school or face a fine. He set a poor example, however, keeping his eldest son, Kintolel, a friend of Joseph's and Noah's, at home to look after his animals. His two younger sons were in school, but he refused to educate his school-age daughter. The parents usually mocked his order, showing up at the school with two-year-olds to enroll. "Here, take this one," mothers would say of the babies slung on their backs.

Chief Sayo asked me to lunch and told me to pick him up at noon. Mary said he was jealous of our friendship, but she was allowed to come along as a translator. I met them in Ngong with another man, a Maasai elder who was wearing an orange plaid blanket, a purple knit cap and dangling earrings. I assumed we were going to one of the local butcheries where roasted goat meat was served. But Sayo, wearing his ascot and looking smug, had something else in mind. We ended up at the Carnivore, a trendy tourist restaurant just outside Nairobi. Some of the kitchen staff were sitting in the parking lot taking a break and smoking. Recognizing the Chief, they came up to greet him. Sayo led us into the restaurant and told the maître d' he wanted to see one of the owners, a white Kenyan named Martin.

Martin, looking a little harassed, came out of his office wearing a powder-blue safari suit. He seemed surprised but happy to see the Chief and shook his hand. I had no idea what this was about until Martin explained that recently he had been married in an outdoor ceremony in the Rift Valley, below the Ngong Hills. Chief Sayo's permission had made it possible. Sayo was now collecting his free lunch.

As Martin showed us to a table, the tourists all turned to look at the Maasai. Our host ordered a round of rum drinks. When they arrived, Mary did not like the taste and asked instead for a Coke. Skewers of chicken, pork, beef, venison and impala were brought to the table. "Chicken—for Kikuyu," Sayo said, motioning the waiter to take it away. He preferred well-done roast beef. When it was brought, he took a bite, said he had never tasted "such sweet meat" and belched loudly. None of them would touch any game meat, the house specialty. The Maasai eat game only in dire emergency. The old man warily eyed his plate, unfolded his napkin and spread it across his lap, following Mary's example, but he had problems coordinating the knife and fork. (I thought of my own squeamishness eating their food at the *boma*. The Maasai, watching me gnawing a bone, had said my teeth were not very strong.) The old man ate a small portion and began picking meat from his teeth, spitting it on the floor. Only then did the curious diners around us turn away. Sayo's eyes were bright from the punch. He ordered a whiskey. On the way back to Ngong, he was in a boisterous mood, pointing out suburban estates in Karen, which once had been the site of a *manyatta*. "The only things left now are some of the trees," he said. "I remember some of them." Sayo and the old man decided to spend the night in Ngong. The Chief told Mary to walk home.

Sayo stayed mostly in Ngong, though sometimes he would show up at Saikeri in the middle of the night, bursting into his wives' huts and yelling (according to them), "I am the Chief!" He suspected his wives of sleeping with moran and hoped to catch them at it. Sayo had three wives, including Mary, but the first wife, Nanta, had run away. She lived with her brother at Empaash, where Noah's father was moving his family. Nanta's three sons had stayed behind with Sayo, which was the custom in a Maasai divorce. But the oldest son, Kintolel, had told Noah he planned to run away and join her.

Many afternoons, Mary and I sat outside the *boma* in a thin strip of shade, our backs leaning against her hut, while she nursed Louise. She liked to practice speaking English with me. She said her life was boring and resented the fact that her husband would not let her teach at the school. "Sayo is trying to make me into a foolish woman like his other wife," she said. "He wants me to sit at home and do nothing."

The other wife's name was Lenkenwua, and after a while she joined us. Mary made a face. Sayo had also campaigned hard to marry Lenkenwua, since her father was rich and a good number of cows came in the bargain. Lenkenwua had three children and was also looking after Nanta's sons. There was some friction because Mary did not help her much. Lenkenwua wished that Nanta would return. "Mary and I don't get along," she told me privately. "Somehow her education makes a difference."

Chief Sayo and Nanta were a chief subject of gossip in Saikeri. The women admired her spunk, since few women ran away for good from their husbands. Everyone was waiting to see what would happen next. Sayo and Nanta had married out of love, which was thought to be highly unusual.

The problems between Sayo and Nanta, the women told me, had begun when her father died. Nanta's dowry had not been fully paid, and her brother, Tingisha, asked Sayo to give him a cow as a gesture of goodwill. Sayo's refusal was complicated by the fact that Tingisha was married to Mary's younger sister. Tingisha's dignity was at stake. The two men had argued over the cow, and Nanta, forced to choose sides, decided her first loyalty was to her only brother, so she had run away. The Chief now forbade Mary to visit her sister.

Mary said that Sayo had started out a simple cattle herder. But after he married Nanta he went to work for some game hunters as a tracker and hide skinner. When he knew the business, he bought a gun and a license and began to hunt on his own, selling skins and ivory to dealers in Nairobi. "There was good money in that business, and I was an expert," he boasted to me. "I never wasted a bullet."

When the Kenyan government banned hunting, Sayo continued and was arrested for shooting a zebra. Through the ivory business he had political connections, and he was soon out of jail. Almost immediately afterward, he was put on the government payroll and was made a subchief.

Since he was supposed to promote development among the Maasai, I asked him why he refused to send his oldest son and his daughter to school. "I am a leader of the Maasai," he said angrily, "and I will decide when to educate my children." Later he told me he had promised his father to raise his first son traditionally. "Maybe I am a little sorry about that now," he said, "because times have changed, but since my father is dead, we can't discuss it. My son Kintolel will be like me. I did not go to school, and today I am a government official."

"And what about your daughter?"

"We will find a rich husband for her."

Mary smirked when she heard the story. "The only reason he keeps Kintolel at home is because he won't spend money to hire a shepherd," she said. "It also makes Nanta angry." Kintolel was the last bargaining chip in their unfinished business.

I asked Sayo if he wanted Nanta to come back. "I wouldn't take her back for a million shillings," he replied shrilly. "Nanta has another *friend* now, and I hate her completely. She had two men before me. She is not a reasonable woman. If you became my wife and went with another man I would cut your neck!"

Nanta came to Ngong secretly to meet with her two younger sons when they were competing in a school sports day, and I met her with Sekento at one of the tea shops. Kintolel had run away to live with her only the week before, and Sekento, who was acting as my interpreter, warned her that Sayo would make trouble. But she only shrugged. She seemed to enjoy showing up on Sayo's turf, greeting her old friends from Saikeri. Her confidence was dazzling.

She was a tiny woman, with high, broad cheekbones and a sprinkling of gray stubble on her shaved head. She asked for a cigarette and smoked it daintily, like a socialite. I had never before seen a Maasai woman smoke.

"Sayo is a fool," she said. "I don't care what he does."

She had a baby girl by a boyfriend from Euaso, a man who was also involved in politics, and who had once been elected as a local councillor.

While Nanta's feistiness was a source of amusement and inspiration to her friends, her divorce was regarded as a desperate measure in that it required her to give up her children and to rely on her brother. But she did not seem to mind.

"I am free," she said gaily. "I do everything on my own, and I like it."

"Do the other women envy your freedom?" I asked.

"Yes, some of them admire my position," she said. Then, with a mischievous grin, she added, "The way it goes, there's always one wife who is loved most. You cannot equalize wives. Some husbands like the youngest wife, some like the eldest, the one they started with. Number-two wife is the hard position. So wives compete. To win you have to be looking after the animals, caring for the husband, giving him everything he wants, taking care when he is away. That is how to win. Otherwise, you are neglected and your children suffer."

"It sounds like being a slave," I said.

"Yes, like that," she said, "but what can a Maasai woman do? She can't even sell a cow to get medicine for her children. Everything is the property of the husband. Some women get so angry they put a curse on the husband."

"How do you do that?" I asked.

"While the husband is away you invite the *oloiboni* [ritual expert] to tea," she said slyly. "You tell him your problem. I might say, 'This man has bothered me, and I want to finish him.' He gets some herbs and crushes them and makes the curse. The *oloiboni* decides the right curse for the problem." Her eyes narrowed, and she laughed. "Other people see you are having tea with the *oloiboni*, and everybody understands what you are after. The men become very scared."

"Does it work?"

"Of course," she said. "And it is the safest way, with no mistakes."

Nanta said there was a woman at Kaputei who had tried to poison her husband by putting a cattle-dip mixture in his milk. But he smelled it and refused to drink. "He didn't beat her, but he sent her away," she said. "She went to a man she loved, but now nobody will marry her daughters. I'm sure she would like to hang herself."

"You mean actually kill herself?"

"Yes, it is becoming more common, with both men and women. There was a woman near Empaash whose husband took another wife, and she tried to hang herself with a rope, but somebody found her still alive. There was a woman who heard her brother had died, and she hung herself because there were only two left in the family. Sayo has a blind stepbrother who is unable to do much, and he has no children. One day his wife went out to get firewood, and she came home very annoyed. She drank some milk, then took a rope and hung herself. Sometimes when a man finds out his wife is sleeping with many moran he will hang himself. This is especially common if the husband beats the wife, and she still continues to see the moran."

But Nanta did not plan to curse Sayo, and certainly not to kill herself. Her strategy was psychological warfare, at which she was expert.

10

NOAH

JOSEPH CALLED from the post office in Ngong to tell me that Noah was sick. "Can you come to see him?" he asked, adding that he had waited in line all morning to use the only coin-operated telephone in the town. I knew it must be something serious, since the boys were generally cavalier in regard to illness. They endured recurrent bouts of malaria, shivering without complaint, and bridled at the suggestion they visit a clinic. "This is a normal disease," Noah had told me stoically. Joseph once limped around for weeks with a thorn stuck in his thigh until his leg swelled so he could hardly stand. Only then—with urging—did he agree to see the Indian doctor in Ngong.

But the day Joseph called, Noah was in terrible shape. I hardly recognized him. He was covered with sores, and his eyes were swollen shut. He had trouble holding up his head. When he tried to talk only a squeak came out. He made louder squeaks when I insisted on taking him to Kenyatta Hospital in Nairobi. Joseph headed back to the *boma* to tell his mother.

We drove to the hospital, and Noah seemed to shrink into his seat as we got closer. Treatment was free, and the reception area was crowded. Hundreds of people milled about, and every bench was filled. Some people

▲ 77

sat on laps, while others spread out on the floor or camped on the grass outside. A doctors' strike had recently ended, but apparently not without bitterness. A notice was posted at the nurses' station:

PLEASE ASK THE PATIENT IF THERE ARE PREVIOUS X RAYS. DO NOT RELY ON WHAT THE DOCTOR WRITES ON THE FORM. THAT IS OFTEN WRONG.

I found a corner and Noah sat down on the floor to wait while I joined the registration line. People who were unfamiliar with the queuing system elbowed their way to the front of the line and arguments broke out. Some were country people who seemed genuinely ignorant of how to form an orderly line or wait their turn. They looked suspicious when other people pointed them to the end of the line.

A few feet away, there was a sudden commotion. A woman shouted, "*Mwizi!* [thief!]," as a young man sped past clutching a woman's basket. A crowd was soon upon him, wrestling him to the floor. The mob went at him with fists until two policemen arrived, pried him loose and dragged him away, screaming.

"Chicken pox," the doctor said, when Noah was finally examined. "He's badly infected; you'd better leave him here." Noah looked stricken. In a hoarse croak he said he was feeling better now, and maybe he should just go home. The doctor shook his head.

The children's infectious-disease ward, far more organized and cleaner than the main hospital, occupied a separate building across the street. Bright crayoned drawings were taped to the walls. It was a sunny day, and some children were playing in the grassy courtyard. Many of them had chicken pox or measles. A young Indian doctor with long, dark hair wearing a turquoise sari and a red dot on her forehead met us. "Oh, you poor thing," she said when she saw Noah. He did not seem to mind when I left.

Within a few days Noah looked much better. He asked if I would bring him some novels. At the bookshop, I picked out *Robinson Crusoe*. He liked that and asked for more books. The doctor said he should stay a while longer, but I began to wonder if he would ever want to leave. He had never before slept in a bed with a foam mattress and sheets, and he had made friends with the other children. He even liked the food. He asked if I would bring his father to visit.

I had never met Noah's father, Semoi. He seemed to be away most of the time, making arrangements for the family's move, or drinking in town. Joseph and I found him in Ngong. He had come there, having heard about Noah's illness, and was anxious to see him. Joseph was shy around him, introducing him as *olaiguenani*, the age-set leader. He did not look well. He was tall and gaunt, with severe features, his face narrow and hollowed like the carving on a totem pole. He wore an orange blanket that accentuated his thinness. But his manners were gracious and dignified. He shook my hand, thanked me for looking after Noah and promised to give me a goat when I visited the new *boma*. In the car, he was silent and preoccupied, running the tips of his fingers across his upper lip, absently staring out the window. When he asked Joseph for news about Saikeri, it seemed only a politeness, and he did not pay any real attention to the answers. At the hospital, he drew his blanket around him with a flourish and strode ahead of us into the ward. The other children, none of them Maasai, stared at the stern and exotic visitor. Semoi glanced across the room and unexpectedly reached out to tickle the toes of one of the children whose bed he passed. There were giggles, and other children stuck out their toes playfully, on a dare. Noah looked momentarily horrified, as if the situation might suddenly spin out of control. Then, realizing his father was not drunk, he relaxed and made room on his bed for him to sit down. Joseph and I waited outside. When it was time to leave, Noah looked happy, even, I thought, proud.

A few weeks after Noah left the hospital and returned to school, Noah's grandfather Sane asked Sekento and me to meet him on the rifle range. He was watching from the top of the big hill overlooking the empty army camp, and when we drove up, he climbed down, leaning on a whittled stick. He was close to ninety, we guessed.

He had been born near Kinangop, the southernmost peak of the Aberdare Range, not far from Mount Kenya, but had grown up in the Maasai reserve after the British evicted the tribe from the highlands. The record of his tribe was still vivid in his mind. Whenever I had questions about the past, he would say, "Ask me everything now, before I am such an old fool I have no memory left at all."

His childhood memories were a grim recollection of tribal downfall—of diseases, drought, cattle plague, war, the arrival of white men and the treaties that led to the tribe's resettlement. When his family left Kinangop, around 1913, he had watched his father burn down the old *boma:* they left nothing behind. His father told him the Maasai were being punished for "greed," for the excessive bloodshed of cattle raiding. His grandmother died on the way to their new home.

Sane had arthritis and walked slowly, his sandals dragging, kicking up little clouds of red dust. We sat under an acacia tree on some rocks arranged around an old campfire, which the soldiers had left. When Sane sat down, his blanket settled like a tent on the sharp points of his knees. He rubbed his legs. "Old age is a misery, no matter what anybody says," he observed.

Sekento and I swatted at flies. A swarm of them hung in the air, and no amount of waving would drive them off. I asked Sane how he put up with them. He was philosophical: "One fly is annoying, but you get used to so many."

He was still a handsome man. A fine, silvery bristle covered his head. His skin was leathery, a tawny color that matched the plains. His teeth were crooked and chipped, but very white from frequent polishing with green twigs. His eyes were pale and clouded, but his vision was still good. When he was a moran, he told us, a Hindu trader had given him a small mirror. It was the first time he had seen his reflection, and he was surprised by his own good looks.

He showed me a long claw mark on his thigh, the scar of a lion hunt. "*Eyeeiiii*, it was all foolishness," he said, and quickly covered it. Until recently, he had still dreamed of those days, but now he had nightmares of being old and useless, trapped in his own troubled sleep. He had two wives, Noah's grandmother, who had become senile and often ran away, sometimes getting lost, and another who looked after him, though her health was also frail. Most of Sane's friends had died, and a loneliness for them filled his memories. I had brought him a blanket that I hoped would cheer him. He ran his fingers across the satin binding and said, "I think I will die in this blanket." He took my hand and spat on it. This was a blessing, he said, and I should not wash my hand right away, to insure the potency.

As a senior elder, Sane had three jobs. One was to reflect on life, he said. Another was to look after the children tending goats and sheep, and to pass on lore from the past. The third was to help settle disputes within the *boma*. Lately, the disputes had revolved around the drunkenness of Noah's father, Semoi.

Semoi's behavior was increasingly erratic, and the changes in him, which seemed to be the result of his drinking, bewildered and frightened the entire family, not just Noah. Other men in the *boma* watched him with disapproval, but they remembered him as a great leader and were intimidated by his position. Some of them said Semoi was "cursed," and not entirely responsible for his behavior.

Sane could not reconcile his son's current behavior with what he had once been. "When Semoi was a boy, he was as brave as fire," he said. "He was number one and respected by everybody." Just before his circumcision, he had been selected as the leader of his age-set. He was expected to lead the group throughout his life, but in recent years he had succumbed to drink. It started when Semoi's admirers first brought him beer. Sane hardly drank himself, and he thought his son's drinking was an unavoidable hazard of his job. It would be impolite to turn down hospitality.

As the drinking got worse, Semoi vented unpredictable rages on his family. There had been recent violent episodes with his two wives. These incidents were unprovoked and beyond the bounds of acceptable wife beating. The younger wife, Kipeno, had threatened to run away after one brutal beating. Semoi had attacked

Noah's mother, Agnes, with a stick and then disappeared for several days. When he returned, he acted as if nothing had happened and announced that he was moving the family to Empaash.

In the past three years Sane had sold more than twenty cows, trying to find a cure for Semoi's alcoholism. He had taken him to many traditional healers, including a witch doctor who made a cut in his stomach and sucked out eight devils, which he had determined were the cause of the problem. The witch doctor had advised Semoi to quit drinking. He had tried, but his short-lived sobriety ended with a binge in Ngong. He had acted so wild—chanting loudly, talking to imaginary beings, picking fights—that a barman had called the police, who took him to Mathari Mental Hospital in Nairobi. Several weeks later, Semoi came home, claiming to have escaped, and for a while he seemed better. Then he started drinking again. He had become irresponsible and sometimes failed to show up for meetings to discuss ceremonial matters. Recently, some of his duties as *olaiguenani* had been quietly shifted over to another man.

The day Sane met us, he asked if we knew of any cure for alcoholism that his own search might have overlooked. He did not mind what it cost, he said. We told him there was no cure and probably nothing he could do to make Semoi stop drinking.

"People stop drinking only when they want to," Sekento said.

"I have seen so many families fall apart because of this drinking," Sane said softly. "I can't imagine what will happen to us."

Sane was especially concerned over the repeated postponements of his grandchildren's circumcisions. The preparations for the ceremony—in which Noah and his younger sister Penina were to be circumcised—could not go ahead without Semoi's consent. In the case of Penina, the delay was especially troublesome. She was about thirteen, and the family was worried that she might become pregnant before her circumcision, ruining her prospects for marriage.

Semoi had long ago made arrangements for Penina's

marriage to a man now in his mid-forties. She had met him only a few times and was too shy to talk with him. Agnes said he was a kind man. He had two other wives and had made a down payment on Penina, which had brought the family nine head of cattle. He was pressuring Semoi and had offered to put up the full costs of the ceremony, if that would hasten things. But Semoi could not seem to get organized. Sane tried to talk with him, but he would not listen.

After a while, Agnes and Penina appeared at the edge of the rifle range, bent over, with loads of firewood harnessed to their backs. They waved and trudged up the hill in the direction of the *boma*. After they had unloaded, they returned bringing a steaming pot of tea and tin cups. Penina, whose dark eyes held the same look of uncertainty as Noah's, greeted her grandfather with a bowed head, then left to join her friends. Agnes watched her run off. "How can you control a girl that age?" she said. "What do they understand?"

Agnes, a plump woman with one crooked eye, coped with her husband's drinking as well as she could. Most of the time she was cheerful. She spoke of Semoi's problem as an "illness," and tempered her criticism. She and Kipeno, the younger wife, acted as supports for each other in low moments. At first they had not discussed Semoi's drinking, as if each secretly hoped the problem would disappear if nothing was said. Agnes had not thought it appropriate to gossip, even with a co-wife, but now the difficulties could not be ignored. Both women talked of leaving Semoi, but not before the circumcisions of the children.

Agnes had three younger children in addition to Noah and Penina, and kept busy. She was an expert at beadwork, and I had sold some of her necklaces to shops in Nairobi. When I gave her the money, she tied it into the corner of her cape. The money was for Noah's schooling, she said, and asked us not to mention it to Semoi. If he knew, he might take it to buy beer. She was dreading the move to Empaash. The name meant "open plains," and she pictured a desert. Kipeno was already there with her baby daughter, building new huts. "I will be leaving behind all my friends," Agnes said. She and Joseph's mother had organized a Saikeri women's cooperative to sell milk and vegetables. Sekento had helped them plant their first garden, and now they were watching eagerly for signs of growth. "Where Semoi is taking us, people are not so developed," she said. "But maybe Semoi will improve when he gets away from Ngong."

11

GIRLFRIENDS

CURIOUS TO LEARN more about Maasai girlhood, I tried to talk with Penina, but she always answered my questions with a shake of her head or mumbled, "I don't know." Her timidity was not uncommon; none of the little girls I met showed any confidence or sense of self-worth.

One thing Penina enjoyed was beadwork, making wristbands for her boyfriends, but she was flustered when I asked about them. Of the time she had spent at a moran *manyatta*, all she would say was "I liked the singing and watching the moran dance."

Mary ene Sayo and her best friend, Njisha ene Meyoki, the younger wife of Joseph's father, were more forthcoming on the subject when we met one day at the Craze Hotel near Ngong town. It was a risky meeting for them, since they came without their husbands' permission. I had sent the invitation through Sekento, and they had walked from Saikeri, though Njisha was about six months pregnant.

They ordered tea, saying they were not hungry when I offered to buy lunch, but later they asked for bottles of beer and wanted to try my cigarettes. At first I refused, worried that Chief Sayo might walk in and catch them, and also I was not anxious to spread the habit.

Mary ordered the beer herself, begged me to let her smoke, and finally I gave them each one cigarette. Neither had ever smoked, and they coughed but were soon blowing puffs of smoke at each other, laughing. The dingy restaurant was empty except for us, and the Kikuyu waiter stared at them in disbelief.

They had dressed up for the occasion, wearing matching print capes, green sneakers and fancy necklaces. Njisha had a doll-like quality about her, even pregnant, and the waiter soon fixed his gaze on her. Not missing the attention, she became more animated, throwing flirtatious glances his way. I'd noticed before that she enjoyed taunting men. She was in her early twenties and had four children, the youngest of whom was named "Baby" because that was what a nurse had called the infant when Njisha visited a Catholic mission clinic.

When I asked them about their girlhoods, Mary said hers was unusual in several aspects. She was the youngest of nine children, six of whom had died. I'd met her parents once when they came to Ngong to visit an herbalist for her mother's intestinal problems. They were a delightful couple who walked arm in arm, with Mary's father leading the way with his staff. "My father is famous because he had only one wife and doesn't beat her," Mary told me, adding that he had planned to have several wives, but found himself satisfied with one.

When she was four, the *askaris* (policemen) took her away to school. Her older sister, who had wanted to go to school, stayed home to help her mother, and Mary remembered both of them crying when she left with the other children rounded up in the *boma*. Mary enjoyed school, liked her cotton jumper uniform and tried unsuccessfully to convince her parents not to cut her earlobes. The same year her ears were pierced, she took a rolled piece of cloth, lit it in a fire and burned decorative scars on her thighs. There were three on one thigh and four on the other, like vaccination welts. She did not much like the idea, but these markings were attractive to boys. When she finished primary school, her grandmother convinced her parents to bring her home to be circumcised and married.

Njisha had a traditional girlhood, helping her mother

and tending goats and sheep, but her family was poor. Her father had died when she was young, leaving her mother with six children to raise and only minor help from relatives.

They began talking about men—their favorite subject. I told them that one of my friends in the States had taken a lover much younger than herself. Njisha giggled, saying, "That woman must be part Maasai!"

Mary was also giggling and said, "You should see how homely and skinny Njisha used to be—none of the boys liked her. Now she is beautiful, and all the men want her."

Njisha blew a wobbly smoke ring and observed, "You know all men are the same—liars." Mary shrieked with laughter, and I realized that they were slightly drunk.

Their first boyfriends were moran. Njisha said she first had sex when she was about nine. Mary said she was about ten. They didn't remember much about it.

The Maasai practiced no birth control, but the older girls, who did not want to risk pregnancy before their circumcisions and marriages, told them about the "safe days" for sex. When I asked Mary and Njisha which days those were, they gave conflicting answers. I tried to explain the menstrual cycle to them, but they were skeptical and became pensive and quiet.

Finally, Mary, who said she wanted only two children, asked if I knew about a *dawa* to prevent pregnancy. A few months before she was one of several women at Saikeri who had inexplicably had miscarriages, but now she thought she might be pregnant again. Njisha ran her small hands over her rounded stomach and said she didn't want any more children after this one was born. "If we can get a *dawa* it would have to be a secret," Mary said. "Sayo would kill me!" I advised them to visit a family-planning clinic, though neither of them ever mentioned it to me again.

Both had secret boyfriends, unmarried junior elders recently graduated from moranhood who were roughly their same age. "We meet them in the bush when our husbands are away," Mary said. I asked them if they were worried about getting caught and beaten by their husbands.

"Our lives are very different from our mothers'," Njisha said. "The old women didn't dare say or do anything! We do what we like. If we want to come to Ngong, we come. It makes the men angry, but so what. Let them beat us until we are dead."

They told me about a recent party at a *manyatta*. "Seventeen women from around our area went there to sing," Njisha began. "Only four very old women and Joseph's mother stayed home. We painted ourselves with ocher and had a good time. When our husbands heard, they came to the *manyatta* and asked what we were doing. They made us come home and then beat us. We just laughed. Some of the moran came later that night to find out if we were all right. They are much more concerned about us than our husbands are. That was the best day we ever had. Joseph's brother Kureko was there; it was mostly his friends. They said they wanted to remain moran until they died, but they were going to be made elders soon, so they made this last big party."

"The best time of my life was just after I was circumcised, but still not married," Mary said, taking a second cigarette and trying to figure out how to use my lighter. "I was completely free, without any work, and I spent all my afternoons and nights with moran. *Eyeeiiii!*"

I asked them about their circumcisions, thinking of Penina, who would soon undergo the surgery. Njisha boasted that she had felt little pain during the ordeal.

"Oh, Njisha, that can't be true," Mary said. "You know how bad it is. What about the terrible pain in your stomach and how sick you feel afterwards?" Mary took a long sip of beer. "You feel a pain you cannot imagine. It is like you are dying—even your ears and eyes are in pain. There is so much blood. After you are cut, the women put leaves on the wound to stop the bleeding. Then you rest, but you can't sleep because it hurts. The women make you drink sheep fat and you get sick. Sometimes they check and find out that the circumcision was not done properly and more cutting is done. You rest for a month, and your friends visit and you can eat all the food you want, like milk and honey and roasted meat. When I stopped hurting, I was happy during my rest time because I didn't have to work."

Njisha stuck by her story. "I don't think it's so bad," she said. "I was brave and was given four cows."

I asked them how their circumcisions affected them sexually.

"After you are circumcised you still enjoy playing sex every way—on your back, on your side, on top of the man—it's very good with the younger ones," Njisha said. "Do you do it like that? I liked playing sex before I was circumcised and after."

Mary agreed that it made no difference. I later asked Nanta the same question. "It changes everything," she said. "After you are circumcised, everything you feel with a man is in your heart and head, not your body."

12

SHOKORE

JOSEPH'S FATHER, Shokore ole Meyoki, was a peculiar-looking man, short and bulky, with flat forbidding features, a rough complexion and heavy-lidded eyes that gave his face an unexpected Oriental cast. I guessed he must be in his sixties. He always wore the same outfit, a buttoned wool overcoat with the collar turned up. His bare legs stuck out below, the same olive brown as the coat. His expression suggested he was the keeper of some dark, pleasing secret. But the appearance of shrewdness covered a deeper sense of life's disappointments.

He was having problems with his two wives, especially Njisha, whose pregnancy he regarded with suspicion. The other, Nterue, Joseph's mother, was a secret drinker. The two wives had been quarreling lately. He blamed the situation on development. "Before, there were no roads in Maasailand, and a man could keep an eye on his wives," he said. "Now the women go everywhere!"

He told me that men today had to beat their wives more than their fathers ever did—and use a bigger stick. "Women have their own affairs, sons have their own affairs—nobody respects fathers anymore," he said wistfully. Later he told me that his own father, who had been rich and powerful, had cursed one of his own quarrelsome wives, and she had died as a result.

Shokore had recently beaten Njisha for napping when she was supposed to be washing clothes. But it was really jealousy that was making him angry; it was well known that Njisha had boyfriends, one of whom was probably the father of her expected child. Whatever the circumstances, Maasai men accepted all children their wives bore as their own, though there were private recriminations if it was found out that the father was a moran.

Nterue, a dowdy woman with seven children, disapproved of Njisha's frippery and resented the fact that her husband paid so much attention to so troublesome a woman. She had recently turned her energies to helping organize the Saikeri women's cooperative. "We can't depend on the men anymore," she sniffed. "My husband loves all his children, but he treats Nijisha's children better than mine. If he goes to Ngong he will buy potatoes, sugar and ghee for her, but he brings me nothing. He says my children are big and can look after themselves. He wouldn't even bring me a sweet."

She also worried that Joseph was spending too much time in Ngong. "There are some rough thieves there," she said. "He won't listen to me. Children today don't listen to their mothers. Now the children say to the elders, 'Who are you? You are not educated.' But I support education. If our children go to school, then they will become teachers, doctors and big men in parliament. All we can do is pray that they have good behavior too."

The first time I met Shokore, he had pulled me aside and, with a sly glance, reached into his coat pocket and pulled out a dirty, crumpled ten thousand Italian lire note. He had found it on the road, he said; he thought it had been dropped by a tourist. He was certain it was worth a fortune, the answer to his recent setbacks. The last drought had reduced his herd by half, and he now had only fifty cows. When I told him the value of the lira and what the note might buy—some roasted meat for his friends—he threw it on the ground and kicked it away with his rubber sandal. But he quickly recovered his composure. He was certain his luck was due to change, if only by some other dramatic turnabout.

Lately, his hopes centered on the outcome of a land case, which Joseph said had been dragging on for years. The dispute involved Joseph's elderly, blind uncle named Njamba. In the 1940s, Njamba had married a Kikuyu girl who, with her young brother Paul, came to live with him on a piece of land near Kiserian, just beyond Ngong. The girl's parents were dead, and Njamba had accepted her brother as a stepson and seen to his circumcision. After a while, Njamba decided he preferred to stay in the Rift Valley with his cattle and two other wives, a not uncommon arrangement. The Kikuyu wife was content to farm the land and sent her brother to a mission school. At the approach of independence in the 1960s, the land around Ngong was demarcated, and Njamba was given a title deed to the fifty acres on which his wife and her brother lived. As he got older, Njamba's visits to the farm were rarer and rarer. Paul grew up to become a teacher and was made a district supervisor of Catholic schools. His sister eventually died, but Paul remained on the land and built a stone house.

In the early 1970s, when pressure was mounting for farmland, Paul had helped Njamba sell twenty-six acres to two Kikuyu farmers. A few years later, Njamba decided to sell the rest to raise money to help out Shokore. Njamba was old and in poor health, so Shokore went by himself to talk with Paul about the sale. Paul was furious, saying that he already owned the land and had paid Njamba for it, producing documents with Njamba's thumbprint to prove it. Shokore could not read the papers, but when he told Njamba about them, the old man flew into a rage and said they could not be genuine. Over the years Paul had given him money, but he believed it was the money due him from the two Kikuyu farmers. The only documents he remembered putting his thumbprint on were the papers relating to the land sold to the farmers.

Njamba and Shokore took the case to a local council of elders, accusing Paul of taking advantage of Njamba's blindness and illiteracy to swindle him. The elders said it was a serious matter and advised them to consult a lawyer. Shokore knew nothing about lawyers and was annoyed to find that it would cost him money to hire one. No one in the family except Joseph could speak English or fluent Swahili, and there was a good chance they might be cheated once more. It was because of the land case that Shokore allowed Joseph to stay in school, realizing that his knowledge of English—Kenya's official language—would be useful.

When Njamba's health deteriorated further, Shokore sent Joseph to Ngong to inquire about Maasai lawyers, but the nearest one lived near Mount Kenya. The family was informed that Paul had hired a lawyer—one of the top criminal lawyers in Kenya—and immediately Joseph was sent to Ngong again to ask the shopkeepers about lawyers. "Any lawyer, but not a Kikuyu," Shokore instructed him. A barman gave him the name of Kiraitu Murungi, a young Meru lawyer, recently out of law school. Joseph telephoned him from the post office and made an appointment. Then he took the bus to Nairobi. Kiraitu was surprised that his client was only a boy, for his voice had sounded older. He told Joseph to bring his father and uncle the following week, explained his fees and wrote them down for Joseph. Shokore reluctantly sold three cows to pay the retainer.

Early one morning, while Chuck was away, I looked out the window and saw Joseph and some of his friends sitting outside on the lawn, waiting to be noticed. When the Maasai came to my house, they never rang the bell or pounded on the door, considering it rude. I recognized the older boys, whom I had seen with Joseph before, in Ngong. He said they were cattle traders, but Sekento privately called them "Joseph's bodyguards." One of them, in a wide-brimmed leather hat and bell-bottoms, had once asked to borrow money from me. I hastily dressed and went out.

"Joseph, why are you here so early?" I asked.

"My father is waiting in town," he said. "Today we are moving on the land case. We are going to see the advocate, and maybe you want to come with us." Joseph was to act as his father's translator, a role that explained his new air of self-importance.

I was curious, and after a few gulps of coffee—sweetened tea for them—we set off. Before we did, I asked Joseph's friends to put their cattle sticks and clubs in the back of the truck. They looked to Joseph for a nod before agreeing. In Nairobi they wandered off, planning to meet up with him later.

Joseph's father, his brother Kureko, and his blind uncle, Njamba, were waiting outside the lawyer's office. Kureko was short, like his father, and powerfully built, and he had a fierce expression. Among his fellow moran, he was known as a specialist with the *o-rinka* (club). The watchman at the entrance to the building was suspicious of the group. Seeing me, he asked, "Are you in charge, memsahib?" Kureko, sensing insult, pushed him aside. The watchman raised no objection.

Kiraitu, the lawyer, wore black-rimmed glasses and a pin-striped suit, the uniform of Nairobi's young business elite. He put some folding chairs around his metal desk, motioning us to sit down. Joseph helped his uncle to a chair and arranged the folds of his dirty blanket around his knees. The old man was disoriented and already fatigued.

Kiraitu told me that his interest was constitutional law. With a mixture of defiance and youthful pride, he mentioned that he had turned down a Harvard fellowship "to avoid further Western brainwashing." This reminded me of a day I had gone to court with a friend and been surprised to see the judges in robes and wigs, like British barristers. I mentioned it now to Kiraitu, who immediately opened a desk drawer and—as if handling a dead rat—held up a curly white wig and laughed. The Maasai looked at the wig without comprehension. "They are not impressed by our modern ways at all," he said. "Isn't it refreshing?"

He asked Njamba to start at the beginning and tell him everything that had happened with his land up to the present. Njamba began a long, rambling discourse, interrupting Joseph's attempts to keep up with the translation.

"The old man says he trusted that Kikuyu like a son," Joseph began. "The boy used to look after him. . . . He says that boy changed very much, and he is very annoyed at him."

"Joseph, ask him to be specific, about the land," Kiraitu said.

Joseph shouted to his partly deaf uncle, who tried again. "What he says is that the problem is the boy is a Kikuyu." The old man's memory was spotty. He could not recall events by year. He kept talking of the "time of the red moon," and "during a drought, when hyenas ate six sheep."

Shokore listened calmly to the long interrogation, his cattle stick balanced across his lap, his hands folded. There was a peaceful smile on his lips. I imagined he was thinking of how he would spend the money, once the case was settled. I was less confident about the outcome. Kiraitu said there was a court backlog; it would be several months before we got an answer. Meanwhile there was nothing to do but wait.

13

WILSON

"LAND SELLING is a disease," Semoi said one day in Ngong. "Before land demarcation, everybody was friendly." He had a cut over his right eye and a swollen lip, the result of a fistfight with Wilson, the chairman of the land committee. It was Wilson's job to make sure the local Maasai were registered and given individual title deeds to their property. Some parts of Maasailand had only recently come under a plan to divide the land for private ownership.

At first, the Maasai opposed the idea. Land was a communal asset that allowed for seasonal grazing. Private ownership, which implied boundaries—fences—threatened that time-honored system. But after the government took large parcels for national parks, the Maasai realized that deed registration was necessary to secure their land. The government promoted the idea by offering loans (in cattle, not money) that required title deeds as collateral.

It was no secret that the committee, which was supposed to protect Maasai interests, was rife with corruption: healthy bribes bought the best plots of land. There were complaints that Wilson, a Maasai himself, was bypassing rightful claims and selling land to the highest bidders. The sudden appearance of outsiders—"foreign-

ers"—who'd moved into the area seemed supporting
evidence to the claims of graft.

The situation got worse after the co-chairman—a man
the Saikeri Maasai had trusted—was killed by the lion.

Semoi had invited Wilson for a drink to discuss the
problems, and Wilson refuted all charges. After a few
beers, the conversation turned into a shouting match.
Other men in the bar took sides, and a brawl followed.

Semoi saw no immediate remedy to the situation. He
believed, as many Maasai did, that Wilson was conspir-
ing with other local officials, all of them taking kickback
profits off illegal land sales.

"Everybody is greedy now," he said. "People will lie
and cheat to get money." However obvious this might
seem to the rest of the world, it was a new concept to
the Maasai, who relied on a bartering system and had
little experience with a money economy.

The earlier demarcation of Ngong might have served
as a warning. Ngong was ideal agricultural land, and
much of it had been set aside to belong to the Maasai.
Once they were given individual title deeds, there was
tremendous pressure from Kikuyu farmers. The Maasai
were not interested in farming, and the hilly country
was not suited for cattle. Many had sold out, agreeing to
long-term monthly installments. A good deal of the
money was spent in bars. Now the same thing was going
on at Saikeri, where a kind of boom mentality had over-
taken reason.

Shokore was among the land sellers. He had held a
deed to some two hundred acres. Bit by bit, he was selling it off. He planned to sell Njamba's land too, if the
court decided in the family's favor. There was no convincing him otherwise. He said he was selling land because he needed money. He wanted to buy cattle to
make up for those he'd lost in the last drought. He needed
money for Joseph's circumcision ceremony. He was
thinking of building a *duka*, maybe buying a truck,
though he did not know how to drive. The list was endless, and depressing.

He seemed unconcerned at the suggestion that one
day the land would run out and with it his way of life.
Now he had money, and he enjoyed buying rounds of

beer for his friends. He hadn't bought any cattle yet. He was waiting for lower prices.

In his sober moments, Semoi—surprisingly—was one of the few who realized the potential dangers of selling off Maasai land to outsiders, and who made efforts to discourage the land sellers.

"To me there's no difference between somebody who sells land and somebody who sells cattle," he said. "The land and the cattle are God's property. We only look after them. If you sell, you suffer. It is a big question that God asks you: 'Why did you sell me, when I am not yours?' Before, the Maasai did not sell animals for money but only exchanged, maybe a heifer for an ox. When the heifer came to the *boma*, the other animals would ask where it came from, and why it came here. That heifer might say it was an exchange for the ox, so please be kind to me, be social, since I am with you now. Even animals know something. When a cow that is bought, not exchanged, comes to the *boma*, the same questions are asked. It says, 'I was bought.' Then it will be told, 'You are bought because you are liked more than we are, and since you are bought you are going to make it more overcrowded.' Animals that are bought do not multiply as well as the ones you have inherited from your father. The bought ones are foreigners."

I asked Semoi what he thought would happen to the Maasai.

"We will end up with no land, no cows and no money," he said. "Then we will be finished."

To stem the land selling, the government was promoting an alternative plan for the Maasai. In 1969 foreign development experts, mostly American, had come up with the idea of setting up Maasai group ranches in arid areas where there was less pressure from farmers. According to this scheme, elders would be given land under a common title, and no individual could sell out. The ranches varied in size and were to be made up of anywhere from sixty to three thousand members. The government agreed to provide access roads, water points and cattle dips. There was talk of developing subsidiary industries, including canneries and dairies. On paper, it seemed sound. Typically, however, no one had asked the Maasai what they thought.

When the first officials went out to explain "group ranch," the Maasai did not seem to understand. Their language had no words to describe the concept, and it became impossible to proceed until the linguistic problem was worked out. A large enclosed area did not exist in Maasailand. How could it be described? The closest they could come was the term "*ol-okeri*," a stripe, like a zebra's, a word they used to describe small tracts kept aside for grazing calves. The verb *a-ker* (to occupy), from which it was derived, implied selfishness.

The initial discussions between the officials and the Maasai ended agreeably, thanks to the customary politeness on the part of the elders. They had listened, gone home, and thought no more about the idea. The officials might as well have proposed the introduction of chopsticks.

After the first ranches were set up, the Maasai continued to move their herds wherever they pleased, ignoring the yet-unfenced boundaries. The government, blaming worsening economic problems, backed off its commitment to provide service facilities and training. Following the traditional lines of authority, record-keeping duties at group ranches fell to elders, most of whom were illiterate.

The Maasai then raised the question of inheritance rights. The planners had not thought of it. Would the sons of group-ranch members be given land when they came of age? Even if subsidiary industries evolved, eventually there would be a surplus of unemployed young men. Now there was talk of dismantling the project. Meanwhile, in Ngong, Wilson was lining up buyers for individual title deeds.

I went to see Jeanne and Denny Grindall, the American Presbyterian missionaries who had built Saikeri Primary School. They also complained about Wilson, who had once been an evangelist connected with their project.

"The change in Wilson is one of the saddest things we've ever seen," Jeanne said. "We've known him since he was a young man still in school. It seems that when some of them get educated, they turn against their own people. It's every man for himself."

"Wilson maintained the first school we built for a year," Denny added. "He was a good man. I think the drinking started when he became head of the committee, right after his father died. It was just too much for him."

Sekento was among those who had applied for a deed. He said he had given Wilson a goat and seven cases of beer, just to get on the registration list. Two years later he was still waiting.

"Don't hold your breath," Denny said.

"We've seen a lot of selfishness come out of this land-demarcation business," Jeanne said. "Some men get thousands of acres, and some get a little four-acre stony patch. I don't know if the idea ever was to divide the land equally. We just put up more windmills to get water over to the Maasai in the next valley. The people who live there used to live nearby, but they were pushed out because they weren't rich enough to bribe the committee for better land."

"It's a puzzle to me why the Maasai are selling land to the Kikuyu," Denny said. "There's no question they are very intelligent, but they seem to lack vision. I look at the land problems and ask myself, 'If they're so smart, why can't they figure it out?' They go from season to season, always believing the rains will come, the land will be there. I just don't know."

The Grindalls, now in their mid-sixties, were originally florists from Seattle, Washington, and had worked with the Maasai since 1968. In that time, they had built a model village—Quonset-style huts made from cement and chicken wire ("wind-, rain- and termiteproof")—and taught the Maasai to grow vegetables. Fifteen acres were under cultivation at Olosho-oibor, at the foot of the Ngong Hills, where the Grindalls were headquartered. An African minister took charge of evangelical duties.

The first time I visited the Grindalls, we talked at the

kitchen table inside one of the Quonset huts, which served as their home. Not much larger than a trailer, the hut was neatly arranged, with food carefully wrapped in plastic and stored in antproof canisters. Jeanne made chicken soup and tea and apologized for the stale crackers. She had not been to town for a couple of weeks.

Denny, spry and deeply sunburned, wore a golfer's hat on his balding head. Jeanne, who had studied home economics in college, was also trim, with loose curly hair and fine pale skin. She was "allergic" to sunlight, so she worked indoors, teaching the Maasai women how to cook vegetables. Many of them had never tasted vegetables and had no idea of what to do with them. Denny had meanwhile built a 1,250-foot earth-fill dam at Olosho-oibor, a second dam at Saikeri, and several water tanks and schools elsewhere in the valley.

Sometimes anthropologists or development experts came to visit them. "Academics really gall me," Denny said. "Their attitude is usually, 'Why not just leave the Maasai the way they are?' I call it the 'Kodachrome-warrior syndrome.' The whole idea is, it seems to me, 'Look, pretty soon we won't have these primitive, starving people to look at.' So I don't argue. I take them to the *bomas* and let them see the kids with worms and eyes full of flies, and I say, 'What about that?' They have to admit we might have something. Most of them have no idea what they are talking about.

"Then you have celebrities," he went on. "Shirley MacLaine was a case—a movie actress who walks into a *boma* and figures she knows everything about the Maasai. She wrote all sorts of nonsense about them in one of her books. Some doctor in Chicago once wrote how the Maasai are immune to malaria. They *all* have malaria. We've had a real hard time keeping out famine relief during droughts. I tell the Maasai there is no reason they should go hungry if they will just learn how to grow and store their own food. If they would grow hay or alfalfa, they could hold on to their cattle during droughts, but it hasn't caught on yet.

"The famine-relief people were here with milk powder during the last bad drought. We've had researchers from the university asking the Maasai what they were doing for future droughts, and they said, 'Nothing, somebody will feed us.' We've seen what's happened with the American Indians up around Puget Sound—the government took the incentive right out of them. The same thing could happen to the Maasai."

A tall Maasai in a *shuka* rapped on the window, and Denny went out to see what he wanted. Jeanne confessed to me that she missed her eight grandchildren. "I struggle with the loneliness," she said. "The missionary movement seems to be in decline. Most of our friends have gone home in the last few years. We know a Scottish couple who live near Nairobi. They buy manure from the Maasai for their garden. We had one friend who was teaching Africans to fly 747s, but he's left. Most Sundays we go to the Baptist Church on Ngong road, but these days, my goodness, there's hardly a soul we know. We try to get into town once a week for supplies, but when it rains, the black-cotton mud is really a problem. This year they actually sent trucks to grade the road and even put down some merrum (gravel). But we hear it's a training program, and I guess when they get it perfected they'll stop. It means so much to have a passable road. The hardest thing for Americans is to be patient, as patient as the Africans are. We see so much we want to do right now. We'd like to build this type of hut all over Maasailand, but we've always insisted that the Maasai pay for them. They raised almost half the money for the dams. The huts cost about three hundred dollars to build—three good cows. The women really want the houses, but the men are reluctant to sell their cattle. You know their thing with cattle. Denny says it's like a man who keeps three Cadillacs in the garage. The women are more for development because they do all the work. The men just wander around and then come home at night and say what a hard day they've had."

After a while, we went outside to tour the vegetable gardens. Jeanne waved to a Maasai woman who was pulling up weeds. "That woman has had a lot of trouble," she said. "She started a garden at her *boma*, and now there's a man who claims the land is his. He doesn't want cultivation on that land. Every time he sees her gardening, he throws rocks at her. The chiefs are trying to settle it. With land, it's always the same story. They sell the land, get the money, buy a vehicle, let it fall apart, and end up with nothing. There's a lot of land selling around here. Pretty soon I'm afraid it will be all Kikuyu living in here."

Denny was hoeing, his arms bright pink from the sun. Some Maasai women were sprinkling newly planted rows with a watering can. A group of women with babies slung on their backs was enjoying Denny's jokes.

"Look at this," Denny said. "We've got Swiss chard, carrots, onions, broccoli—the Maasai love broccoli!" His enthusiasm was irrepressible. "The soil here is good, and you can grow four crops a year." He wiped the sweat off his face. "It's volcanic soil, a little low in potash, but with all the manure we overcome that. See that girl—it's her first time using a tiller, and she was scared to death at first. She's doing just fine now. There's no reason for anybody in this valley to go hungry. See that woman with the sprinkling can? The first time I saw her she was carrying a bag of onions from the market in Ngong. I said, 'So you let the Kikuyu grow your food.' A week later she came here with her baby and asked me to teach her how to grow. We water with cans so there's no waste, and they learn how to use their hands. In the dry season we use about eight thousand gallons a day from the dam. Those windmills"—he pointed to four of them—"pump water three miles over to the next valley. We now have about seventy-five people cultivating. There's never been anything like it in Maasailand!

"I'm training some of the young men to start projects like this elsewhere. But you make one area a success first. These people are steeped in a culture that says it's beneath their dignity to dig in the soil. See that old man there—it's his first day. He said to me, 'I thought what you were doing was wrong, and I used to laugh, but I think you are right now.' The men get mocked for cultivating, but I tell them it doesn't hurt me to to do it. Keeps me young, in fact. If I wasn't here, I'd probably be back home sitting in my rocker."

Walking me to the car, Jeanne said, "I think Denny is probably happier here than I am. He really loves it." She brightened at my invitation to lunch the following Sunday. "That would be lovely," she said.

14

TWO WORLDS

I MET DICKSON one afternoon, after classes, at Oloolaiser Secondary School, in the Ngong Hills. He had telephoned earlier and asked if I would come, explaining that he had a serious problem to discuss. He was wearing gray slacks and a short-sleeved cotton shirt, the school uniform, but his lanky height, beaded bracelets and belt easily distinguished him as a Maasai among his mostly Kikuyu classmates.

We walked down the dirt hill to town, past a general store blaring disco music and an Indian tailor's shop whose hopeful signboard showed a smiling bridegroom in a tuxedo. In this town, however, the typical groom wore a *shuka* and rubber sandals. Dickson suggested we get a soda in the Ngong Hills Bar, but it was too crowded and loud to talk there. During the day the upstairs rooms were used by prostitutes, whose children ran up and down the hallways.

We stopped at a tea shop whose walls were freshly painted with murals depicting local scenes of farms, cows and menacing lions. Two Kikuyu businessmen were in deep conversation over a platter of goat meat. A Maasai moran was standing at a sink in the back, admiring his face in a mirror. Another was waiting his turn.

Dickson ordered a Coke but said he wasn't hungry. He got straight to the point: he needed money for school fees. The headmaster was threatening to expel him unless he paid up. His father had refused. He was planning a circumcision ceremony for his youngest son, which would entail slaughtering a number of cattle to feed the guests. He had no extras to sell to raise money for Dickson's tuition. "You can't go to school forever," his father told him.

"I've had this problem ever since I started school," Dickson said. "I've always gone to my relatives for help, but since the last drought they are tired of me asking them to sell their cattle. They can't understand why it takes so long for a person to become educated. They say they are wasting cows for nothing. Sometimes I feel like I'm living in two worlds. At school I concentrate on the books, and the teachers encourage me. Then, when I'm at home, it's a serious matter if my father catches me loitering with a book. Sometimes I'm sorry I got into all this. I think about working in Nairobi, earning money, but sometimes it seems useless because that way of life is so expensive—buying a house, food, furniture and beautiful decorations. But I also have this idea about education—that I must go forward.

"The old men say the boys who go to school are losing respect for the elders. It's partly true. I respect my father, but I don't want to live like him. Now I'm studying to take my O levels, and I told my father that if I do well on my exams next year, the government will pay for the rest of my education. There aren't so many Maasai in the colleges, so I think I have a good chance."

I asked him why his father had let him go to school in the first place. "He was forced," he said. "It happened when we were living at Euaso. The *askaris* came and made the children go to school. They told my father they would put him in jail if he didn't send me, so he agreed. We didn't live very near the school. I used to walk through the forest early in the morning, when it was still dark.

"At first, my father went with me halfway because of the dangers. All the way he would talk about how this was a waste of time. Then I started going by myself.

Once, I met a leopard, and I ran home. After that, I carried a small spear. I used to hide it near the school compound, because the teachers didn't want weapons around the school. At first, I hated going to school. I was frightened because the teachers wore Western clothing, which I had never seen. My father told me that when the teacher was away, I should run home. I thought it was a good idea. I remember one day we were all sitting on the floor practicing writing, and the teacher went out for a while and all of us ran away. I ran away a lot, but I was always forced to go back to school. People at the *boma* said I was losing a lot of energy for nothing going to school. My mother was the only one who wanted me to be educated. But my father said we should shift our *boma* and get away from the school. I agreed, but after we moved, another school was built near us, so I had to go again."

During a serious drought, the Maasai children were allowed to go home to help their fathers move the cattle. They stayed home for two years in the mid-1970s, happy to resume their traditional duties. When the drought ended, the *askaris* took them back to school.

"When I returned to school the teacher saw that the long distance I had to walk to school was affecting my schoolwork," Dickson said. "So he invited me to live with him. I stayed with him for about a year, and it influenced me very much. He told me about some Maasai who were learned men and who had built good homes. He told me how their lives were, how many cows they had, and said if I continued with school, I would become an important man. He said I could triple the number of cows I owned if I got educated. That's what impressed me. So I worked hard and became the top student in my class. I started wearing a shirt and pants in standard four, and I felt very proud. But when I went home I had to put on the *shuka* for my father.

"My family moved again, but I stayed behind with another family so I could continue at school. But then the man's wife got tired of me because I was not her son. So my mother convinced my father to move back near the school, and she built me a little hut so I could study. I was getting ready to take my C.P.E. exam, and my father thought, Good, soon he will finish and come home and join the moran. I had a small paraffin wick so I could read until eleven o'clock every night. My father didn't like to see me with a book during daylight. On weekends I looked after the cows, and I liked doing that.

"I was circumcised right before I took my exam," he continued. "I was of two hearts, wanting to follow tradition, but also I wanted to do well on my exam. It was hard to study because the men were drunk around the *boma* all the time, getting ready for the circumcision ceremony. I was prepared to look for a job after I took my exam, but then I got a very high mark and a letter came saying that I was accepted for secondary school. It cost twelve hundred shillings [about seventy-five dollars] and my father said I couldn't go, so I had to tell him a lie. I told him the letter about school was very official. I showed him how I wrote with a pen, and then I showed him the letter, which was typed. I told him it said if he didn't send me to school he would be jailed for seven years. So he thought about it, and then he sold a cow. I felt bad about lying to him, but I didn't see any other choice.

"I got to school late the first term. It was a shock coming from Maasailand. There were students of all tribes. The students in the upper classes harassed the ones in the lower classes, and we had to fight to survive. This harassment of the younger boys is a custom learned from the British, but it made the first year very difficult. We were forced to wash the dormitories, the classrooms, the dining hall, to do the laundry and make the beds. If you refused, the older boys beat you. I just wanted to go back home, but then two students were suspended for beating the younger boys, and it discouraged the others.

"When the teacher told us to write 'biology' in our notebooks, I had no idea what it was. Now I have learned biology, calculus and physics—my best subject. We also have Christian religious education and Bible study. We studied the Old Testament and St. Luke's Gospel. But we also studied about Muslims and Jews, about Confucius, Hindus and the old African religions. Did you know that the Kikuyu and the Maasai had God before the Christians came? We have always believed in God. When Maasai women milk the cows, they always pray. When there is a drought, the men make animal sacrifices. In the Old Testament, the men sacrifice rams, the same as we do.

"The Maasai and the Jews have some customs that are the same. We don't drink milk with meat, and we have always had circumcision. The Maasai have never believed that you went anyplace after death. They believe that when you die you are finished. Death to the Maasai is not such a bad thing. Even when the moran raided cattle from Europeans who had guns, they did not fear death. The Maasai know that when you die you become like the soil. When I was young, the Maasai would take a dead man and smear his body with sheep fat, put a clean *shuka* on him, and leave him on the plains to attract wild animals. I remember when an old man died in our *boma*. The women were crying, shouting and screaming. The children kept playing, but then everybody else became quiet, nobody talking, nobody eating. After about two days they recovered. It was normal. The Christians fear death very much."

I told Dickson that the Kikuyu mechanic who fixed my car after the brakes failed had told me he didn't fear death either. As a result, I hired a new mechanic.

A few days later, I went to visit Dickson's headmaster. The school fees were not very much, and I asked the headmaster if it was true that he planned to expel him. "We have to be tough," he said, "otherwise some of the parents would never pay a shilling, and the school would fall apart. In Dickson's case, because he is a Maasai, the father is very stubborn. These old Maasai men will fight you all the way before they sell a single cow. But I would have found some way to let him stay."

I told him I would pay the fees, but he was apologetic and insisted on splitting them with me. Dickson was relieved, and his father thanked me. I suspected that the old man had had this plan in mind all along.

15

PROFESSOR MALOIY

Several times when I was in Ngong, I noticed an elderly Maasai man hobbling around with a walking stick, wearing a tan felt hat with a chin strap, a sports jacket and trousers. His face was deeply lined, and his eyes were clouded with cataracts. It seemed odd that a man his age was dressed in Western clothing. Whenever he saw me, he always tipped his hat. Intrigued, I stopped one day and greeted him in Maasai, *"Ira supat?* [How are you?]," but he answered in English.

He said his name was James ole Torome and that his son Tom owned the Ngong Hills Bar and Restaurant. Another of his sons, Clement, owned a bar near Narok and served on the county council. I asked him how he had learned English. In 1910, he said, he had been sent with a group of Africans to study languages in England, France, India and South Africa. It seemed hard to believe. That was about the time the British began forcing the Maasai from the highlands.

"There were quite a few black men studying in England then," he said.

"So how did you like traveling?" I asked, still doubtful.

"Comme ci, comme ça." He gave a Frenchman's shrug.

"You speak French too?"

"*Mais oui!* I happen to be fluent in many languages—English, French, all the tribal languages in Kenya, of course, and also Somali, Arabic, and the Indian dialects." He spoke a few sentences in Hindi.

"The Indians in Nairobi always say to me, 'You can't be an African!' But I tell them, of course I am an African. I just use my brain." He said he'd seen me around, sometimes with Sekento, and he asked me if I was also a teacher. I told him I was a writer and invited him to tea. We went to his son's bar and found a quiet corner.

"Most outsiders can't understand the Maasai," he said when I mentioned my interest. "Even now some ignorant people will say the Maasai are primitive. The British always underestimated our culture. You know why the Maasai did not develop? Because they had millions of cows and were rich in comparison with other tribes. They were content. The Kikuyu were poor, and when the British came, they took their chances and went to work for them. But slowly the Maasai are changing. They are starting to realize that power today—financial power—lies in education."

I told him that most of the Maasai I knew still didn't want their children to go to school, and that his view sounded overly optimistic. "It's true, we have problems in that area, but most of the younger ones are changing," he said.

His own education, he explained, had come about almost by chance. After his father died, his mother married a Kikuyu. When the colonial police came to collect children for the mission school, his stepfather proposed him, as he did not want his own children taken away. "Nobody understood then what education was," he said. "My mother was very bitter and cried. The marriage was never the same after that." At the time, he said, other Maasai cited her case as an argument against mixed marriages.

"I was seven years old when I started school," he went on. "All of us feared the whites. We didn't know what to expect from them. But the missionaries were kind. The only reason I stayed was because they had a lot of food at school. I learned to read and write English and Swahili, and I became a Christian. Christianity is a little more elaborate than the Maasai religion, but the idea of God is quite the same. The missionaries let me go home to be circumcised. I went with the moran for a couple of years, but I really had none of the requirements. My ears weren't cut, and my brother said I should have them done, but I refused. I let my hair grow long, but basically I thought moranship was a waste of time. With education you have an assignment to do. After that I went to England, and so on."

He winked. "It's impressive, I know, but it was not so easy. When I started out, I had some psychological conflicts. I did not associate with the whites, but they gave me a house and good money. In 1920 I was a government chief in Nyeri. The Maasai didn't like it until they saw that I used my money to buy cattle and start a family. But I didn't like what was going on. The British tried to force the Maasai to pay hut taxes. This was a trick to try to force the Maasai to work for the whites. When they refused, the *askaris* took their cattle, and it became very violent. I remember the Maasai killed a provincial commissioner and some others too. Some of the Maasai died in jail until the British stopped that practice."

Torome worked as a translator for the British Army and in the High Court. Later he became a road-building foreman in Kenya and South Africa.

"During World War Two I was a second lieutenant, and I visited all the regiments—Kikuyu, Indian—as a translator for the British," he said. "I picked up quite a few languages, including Zulu and Afrikaans, building the roads; I worked on all the first roads built in Kenya—as far as Kisumu and Mombasa. Then I was sent to South Africa to teach the Africans how to build roads. After the war, I was taken to the High Court to try out as a translator. The British judge asked me if I could speak English. I told him, 'It is not my native language, but I shall try.' I said this a bit sarcastically, but the judge said to the European who brought me, 'You have brought a nice boy.' So he gave me a job and a suit to wear."

At the same time, Torome became active in preindependence politics. When the Mau Mau uprising began in 1952, he smuggled guns to the Kikuyu fighters. In 1953 he was arrested and tried in the High Court. He hired four lawyers—two Europeans and two Indians—to defend him from being hanged. "It was very unusual for an African to have advocates then," he said. "It took them by surprise." He was acquitted for lack of evidence, but soon after he was put in a detention camp. The British detained more than twenty thousand Africans before defeating the Mau Mau in 1956. More than thirteen thousand five hundred Africans and ninety-five Europeans died in the struggle.

Earlier, Torome had opened a bar and restaurant. He was the first African in Kenya licensed to sell whiskey. While he was in detention, the British bulldozed his bar and confiscated his life savings from a bank account. When the "Emergency"—as the British termed it—ended, he was sick and penniless.

Torome's son Tom, who was tending the bar, joined us for a while and confirmed all that his father had told me. He was forty-two and had also studied overseas, going to Denmark in 1964 on a scholarship to study agriculture and economics. That was fifty-four years after his father had been to Europe. "I must say I was surprised at the Europeans' reactions, because my father seemed to have met more civilized people in his time," Tom said. "The people in Denmark were so ignorant, many had never seen an African, and they thought we lived in trees and caves and were very hostile people. I remember children would touch my skin and then rub their fingers, as if they expected dirt to come off."

After college, Tom worked at a number of Kenyan government jobs and ran unsuccessfully for parliament. But now he found the present situation in Kenya "messed up" and preferred to remain a private businessman. He said he had bought the bar and restaurant from some Indians in 1971. "A few years ago I was interested in helping the Maasai to get started with a cattle cooperative and growing wheat, but it's just too frustrating, there's so much jealousy. It's easier to work on my own."

His father asked me if I knew Professor Maloiy, a

Maasai who was chairman of the physiology department at the University of Nairobi. "He is a very interesting fellow," he said. "A bit stubborn, but ahead of the others. You should talk to him."

I'd heard a lot about Professor Geoffrey M. ole Maloiy, who was possibly the most highly educated Maasai in the world. He was from Saikeri and had been born in a traditional *boma*. His father had four wives, but none of the other children in his family was educated. Sekento's father had boarded him as a youngster so he could attend school. Chief Sayo boasted that he was a relative of his. Other Maasai, including his brothers and stepbrothers, said he was "aloof" and "acted superior" to them.

"The only thing he cares about is living in the suburbs and having the best hi-fi equipment," one of them told me.

I went to see Maloiy at his university office. He was a large, bulky man with glasses and a deep, booming voice. His desk was covered with stacks of papers, and he seemed very busy, though the university was closed for vacation. I explained that I was a friend of the Sekento family, doing research on the Maasai. "Has it been approved?" he asked sternly.

"What?"

"You need government approval to do this kind of research, you know." I said I was unaware of that, but he waved his hand in the air. "Don't worry. I'm on the president's review board; I'm sure this is all right." In fact, he said he'd been hoping to find someone to write a serious history of the Maasai since he was too busy. "Our history is going to evaporate; pretty soon all these old people who know everything will be dead. You'd think some Maasai would be working on this, but nobody is."

I mentioned the criticisms I had heard about his aloofness to the tribe.

Irritated, he handed me a sheet of his letterhead. Across the bottom was printed: "Maasai Elder, Physiologist, Consultant in Tropical Animal Ecology and Agriculture."

"You see," he said indignantly, "I am very proud to be a Maasai. Proud of the history and proud of our culture. My wife is Maasai. My children already have a strong sense of being Maasai. If they greet you, they will never shake hands; they will greet you the Maasai way, respectfully, with a bowed head. I normally tell my friends that if you don't speak Maasai, you are not truly educated. If I were born a non-Maasai, I think I would hang myself, because life would not seem worth living."

"I guess it's a misunderstanding, or just jealousy," I suggested.

Maloiy nodded. He was forty-four and successful. Of the children that Edward ole Sekento had boarded, he was the most accomplished. After secondary school, he was given a scholarship to study physiology at the University of Aberdeen in Scotland. He completed his Ph.D. there and spent a year at the Institute of Animal Physiology at Cambridge. Returning to Kenya, he worked with the East African Veterinary Research Organization. In 1973 he became head of the animal physiology department at the University of Nairobi. In 1975 a National Science Foundation fellowship and a Fulbright grant allowed him to do research at Harvard University. In 1979 he returned to Harvard as a visiting professor. His specialty was comparative physiology. "I'm interested in human adaptation to the environment," he said, "and I'm working on something about the Turkana [a Kenyan tribe] now. I haven't done any work on the Maasai as yet."

I asked him what he thought of the present situation of the Maasai.

"I tell my Maasai colleagues—including Chief Sayo, who is a relative of mine—that the end of the road is in sight for the Maasai," he said. "I think a lot of people would tell you there is no hope for the community."

"Is that what you believe?"

"I would say things are . . . How should I put it? *Grim*. The land is being subdivided very hurriedly, without consideration of the fertility of the land, the rainfall and what each person is interested in doing on it. It would have been ideal to subdivide it in a very systematic manner. It now depends on who you are and how you entertain the people on the committee making the decisions—in other words, bribery. Now the Maasai are starting to think in an individualistic way, and they are no longer interested in the welfare of their neighbors or their section. It is common for neighbors to quarrel now. Today, if a fire breaks out on your land, nobody will let you take your animals onto their plot to graze. I have a ranch about fifteen miles from Kajiado, and all my neighbors are traditional Maasai. We have a system where we share facilities, even though everybody's land is individually owned. But don't ever underestimate these traditional Maasai. They are stubborn, and they can just as easily move the demarcation post. They can really pull a fast one on you. There was a successful rancher living near me who was murdered two years ago. I am certain the neighbors engineered it. He controlled the Kiserian town slaughterhouse, and people felt it was wrong for one person to own it. So they shot him dead. The whole situation is disturbing, and it's getting more awkward every year. I see more of this coming—murder, fighting over land ownership."

I asked him what he thought of the Maasai working in Nairobi.

"The Maasai will never succeed working in Nairobi," he said. "The reasons are so petty I don't think I need to go into them."

"What do you mean?"

"Well, they are given all the chances in the world to succeed, and they don't take them. They lack self-discipline and sometimes determination. Also, they have a bit of empty arrogance. It is very frustrating to me. I have a lot of contacts all over the world. One of my Harvard friends at the International Laboratory for Research in Animal Diseases would like to help Maasai students study overseas, but I can't find any Maasai with the ambition to do it."

"Maybe it's Western ambition they lack," I said.

"It's too late to criticize Western values. Almost every Maasai has a transistor radio or wears a film canister in his ear. They've all been exposed, and now it's up to them to be selective as to which of these values they want. Edward ole Sekento knew education was of value, and that's why he helped me and the others. But there are not so many like him."

When I mentioned Dickson's situation, he said he knew about it. "The headmaster talked with me about his case and three other boys who also need help," he said. "So a meeting was set up to raise funds, but nobody except me showed up."

I told him that I had paid a part of Dickson's tuition.

"You see—that's what I mean," he said. "The boy has to rely on foreigners."

"Do you feel detached from other Maasai?"

"I'm sure *they* would say . . ." He stopped himself. "I feel a certain detachment because . . . I feel they are so goddamned lazy. They don't seem to realize that they should have defined goals and defined values. They should look at life in present-day Kenya and not be sitting around talking about how once they were great moran and killed a lion. They should forget this. A lot of them are wealthy compared to other Kenyans, and yet they haven't utilized the resources available to them. Chief Sayo has ranches everywhere, but no resources to develop them. Most of the Maasai are involved in the very lowest level of cattle trading, and they get no benefit from it. If I decided I wanted to work on cattle development, on forming a cooperative, people would immediately say I was exploiting them. And there is jealousy. Some of the young men are working in Nairobi as watchmen. What kind of thinking is that? The Maasai are experts at security. They should be running the private security companies. Instead, they let themselves be exploited, and they will continue to be exploited in employment, cattle trading and wheat growing. A Maasai could make a fortune if he had land and not a single cow. After the rain, he could cut hay, bale it and sell it. He could supply a research institution, like this one, which is working on experimental animal feeding. The Maasai need to be more aggressive and adventurous. They have an aggressive attitude in the wrong direction, like stealing animals from the Kikuyu. And this is where the educated Maasai fail. We haven't been involved in extension work. It doesn't mean we have to preach, but we can use our land as a model for others. That American Denny Grindall has done a lot at Oloshooibor by being involved in physical work himself. He showed them by example how to build better houses. This is the failure of our educated people, not educating others by visible example."

A few weeks later, the headmaster at Oloolaiser Secondary School sent me a letter saying that Professor Maloiy had offered to pay Dickson's tuition if future need arose.

16

EMPAASH

Noah's mother was getting ready to move to the new *boma* at Empaash, but she was also stalling since she was not anxious to leave her friends. Semoi suggested that I drive Noah, Joseph, Sekento and him out there, to take a look at it. We headed for Naivasha one Saturday morning on an old, bumpy tarmac road that ran along the escarpment. It was a picturesque route, through tea plantations, but the morning fog was too thick to see much of the scenery. With the headlights on, we crept through the high country. When the fog lifted and the pines thinned out, we caught glimpses of the Rift Valley like flashes of light. Where the forest ended abruptly, the view became dizzyingly wide; the valley floor appeared perfectly flat, bare except for the acacia and a few candelabra trees that resembled giant cacti. Sekento, who was not usually impressed by big landscapes the way I was, put down his newspaper and let his gaze linger on the vast country.

"Esidai-o-ling! It's very beautiful," Noah said. "More green than Saikeri." Joseph was oblivious. He had my cassette-player headphones planted over his ears and was humming loudly to Michael Jackson. We slowed down for some baboons sitting on the road picking fleas out of one another's fur. They scampered at our ap-

proach, but a few cantankerous elders held their posts and bared their fangs.

At the turnoff for Narok, we followed the road that led to Maasai Mara and the game lodges. The old disfigured volcanoes, Suswa and Longonot, towered on either side. Suswa—Oldoinyo Onyokie, the "Red Mountain," the Maasai called it—featured in tribal lore. It was where Joseph's brother Kureko camped with the moran. During Eunoto, the junior-moran graduation, secret rites were conducted on its rocky ledges. The caves were famous for housing leopards and bats.

Semoi said some Europeans were studying the crater, and he had heard they had discovered two very big snakes—one white and one red—and another unidentified creature with only one eye. Some of the Maasai had gone to investigate, but it was too dark inside the crater to see anything.

"Sometimes we hear voices of people from crater, but we have never been able to see them," Semoi said. Sekento's eyes did not lift from his newspaper, but Noah leaned forward with interest.

"Who are they?" he asked.

"They might be people of God," Semoi said. "I have gone up to the crater many times in the old days, but now I hear the park people charge money."

"What's *that* thing?" Joseph asked, removing the headphones and pointing to two massive white satellite dishes set in the middle of the plains. A watchman at the satellite station who lived at the new *boma* had told Semoi the dishes had "eyes" to spot enemy aircraft. But Sekento said it was a telecommunications station and had to do with the relay of international telephone calls. We stared at the big dishes, as incongruous in this setting as a space station from Mars.

We drove another twenty-five miles across flat scrubland. A few Kikuyu were farming without apparent success. Most of their fields lay crumbled and bare. A woman was pulling out stunted corn, tossing it into a pile. "Foreigners here too," Sekento said.

Semoi said part of the land belonged to the wildlife department, but beyond the satellite station it belonged to the Maasai. There had been rain on the Maasai side, and the plains were grassy, filled with Thomson's gazelles, impalas, zebras and a few ostriches. Noah called out their names in Swahili and pointed out the giraffes for my benefit. We slowed down as three giraffes crossed the road in front of us, like giant bobbing hobbyhorses. Semoi said he liked the area because it was flat and easy for grazing cattle.

We waved at a few Maasai herdboys tending sheep, drove farther and came upon the only signs of settlement: a forlorn grouping of tin-roofed *dukas* set off from the road. "The *boma* is there," Semoi said, pointing to a huge pile of boulders that concealed any sign of it. It seemed an improbable location—treeless and unprotected, except for the rock wall. For a drinking man, the location had advantages. Semoi suggested we stop at the *dukas* first for refreshments. His friend owned the bar.

Joseph and Noah jumped out of the truck and ran across the road to find the *boma*. Semoi told them to pick out a goat for me to take home, then he led us to the bar. Sekento also knew the owner, Sha ole Leperes, a short, wiry Maasai with balding gray hair whom he introduced as "Mr. Sha." He was the watchman at the satellite station and was wearing a blue guard's uniform with a wide green tie and trousers that bagged over his desert boots. He was obviously an important man in the neighborhood and had been trying to convince Sekento's father to let him marry his oldest daughter. Since he already had four wives, Sekento's sister Janet, who was the object of the negotiations, considered the whole thing a joke. She worked as a clerk in Nairobi and had a Kikuyu boyfriend. But the discussions continued because Sekento's father did not want to offend the amiable Mr. Sha.

Mr. Sha's bar was a rough shack with a slanting metal roof that extended over a narrow cement veranda. The porch posts were painted with zebra stripes. The view held miles and miles of empty plains. Several elders in blankets were sitting on benches, drinking beer. They greeted Semoi, offered him a bottle and asked what was new in Ngong. While they talked, Mr. Sha gave us a tour of his establishment, including a battered truck without wheels that he had just bought. Once it was fixed, he planned to start a *matatu* business. The bar, a small, dark front room furnished with two picnic tables and benches, had a service counter caged in with chicken wire. A picture of President Moi was nailed to the wall. There were no customers. Next door was a room with a counter and shelves that Mr. Sha's wives operated as a shop selling packets of soap powder, tinned cooking fat, safety pins, small mirrors, hard fruit candies and tea. When we went in, a group of Maasai women were examining a stack of *kangas* (printed cotton fabrics). Mr. Sha's wives, who looked no older than teenagers, were patiently unfolding them, one by one, holding them up so the women could check for imperfections.

Mr. Sha was watching Sekento's face. "I think your sister would like it here," he said proudly. "Since none of my wives can read or write, she could take charge of the *duka*."

"Maybe, but it is not my place to interfere with my father's decision," Sekento said tactfully.

Off the back of the bar were four small rooms that served as a hotel. Mr. Sha said we could talk there, and asked one of his wives, who was peeling a bucket of potatoes, to bring extra chairs while he went to get sodas. In one room a Maasai was sprawled on a metal cot, snoring.

"So how is Janet?" Mr. Sha asked when he returned with bottles of orange soda. Janet had asked her brother to put in a few discouraging words. "She's very busy with her job," Sekento said and let it go at that.

Semoi joined us, ordered a round of beer and proposed a blessing. He spat on my hand. "Grow up! Be rich!" he said. He smoked a cigarette, watched the ash grow long, and blew it off. He commended me for being a punctual person. It seemed a funny thing for him to say, but the Maasai were punctual themselves and always showed up when they said they would. They complained if I was a few minutes late for an appointment.

"You are welcome here any time," Semoi said. "When

I make a ceremony to circumcise my children, you will be the guest of honor."

Sekento reminded him that Noah was studying to take his primary school exam that year, and he hoped the ceremony could be arranged around that.

"Everything depends on the rain," Semoi said, "and first we will make another ceremony for the elders. Then we have more preparations for the children. But, Sekento, I support you, I support development, and I think we can rhyme on this."

A Maasai stuck his head in the doorway to greet Semoi and did a double take when he saw Sekento. "Naisiawua?" Sekento said, recognizing his uncle. The two men embraced with exclamations of disbelief. They had not seen each other for several years. Naisiawua sat down, took a pinch of snuff from a leather tube hung around his neck, inhaled deeply and asked for a soda. Mr. Sha yelled to one of his wives to bring it. Naisiawua wore a bright pink *shuka*, which looked suspiciously like a bed sheet. He had crooked teeth, a round face, and the same long, narrow eyes as Sekento's father. Sekento looked at him as if he were seeing his father in another life.

Naisiawua and Sekento caught up on family news. Naisiawua was living on a large group ranch beyond Empaash, had three wives and sixteen children, and was renting six hundred acres of private land to a European wheat farmer. He had previously rented some of it to Kikuyu, but they had not paid him for a year, so he had kicked them out. He was thinking about building a *duka* and his youngest son was in school. From a leather pouch tied to his waist he took out a bank savings passbook. "You see, I am not educated, but I am no fool," he said. When Sekento asked how he had managed to get a deed to six hundred acres, he winked. "I know all the shortcuts," he said.

Semoi told them about the fight with Wilson. Naisiawua nodded emphatically. "You have to smear these committee people with bribes to get their attention," he said. "Once people get a little money, they become selfish and proud." Mr. Sha said it was the truth.

The beer was making Semoi restless, so he got up and said he wanted to talk with Mr. Sha, alone. He told us to meet him at the *boma*.

When the two men had left, Sekento asked his uncle what was wrong with Semoi. Naisiawua leaned back in his chair and looked outside the door, to make sure nobody was listening. He said that Semoi's problems had started when he failed to take charge of a ceremony for junior elders. He had been in Ngong, drinking, and the elders went ahead with the ceremony without him. When Semoi found out, he was enraged. He got drunk and argued with the elders and finally threw a club at them. Unfortunately, it was the *o-kiuka* (a special black club) that had been blessed by the *oloiboni* and presented to him by these same old men when he had become age-set leader. The elders picked up the club and started blowing on it, which was a way to make a curse.

Naisiawua whispered, "They said to him, 'If this man is not yet a fool, now you will see it!'" Since then Semoi had been acting very peculiar. His younger wife, Kipeno, had found him sleeping with the cattle one night. He sometimes sat alone, talking to himself. He wouldn't listen to anybody. "The problem now is very serious," Naisiawua said. "The two old men who cursed him have died, and there is no way to get rid of this curse. But Semoi knows that is the cause of his troubles."

We walked over to the *boma*. Kipeno had gone to fetch water with Nanta and one of Mr. Sha's wives. Joseph and Noah had picked out a goat and tied it up with a leather strap. Chief Sayo's son Kintolel, who had run away from his father, poked the goat's ribs to show me how fat it was. He was remarkably good-looking, with bright, mischievous eyes like Nanta's and a quick smile. He wore a red *shuka* with a beaded neckband and bracelets around his wrists and ankles. Sekento asked him if he was going to school now. He said he was not but would like to. The roof had blown off the nearest school, and the teachers had run away, so the school was closed. He said he was just looking after goats and sheep, but he was glad to be living with his mother.

He asked us to bring him a ballpoint pen on our next visit.

I asked Noah what he thought of the new *boma*. He said his mother wouldn't like it. "The huts are all crooked, not like Saikeri," he said. "And this is a bad place, by the *dukas* where my father can drink."

Semoi was inside one of the huts with an elder, and more blessing was going on. We could hear the elder's voice and Semoi's responses, which Sekento translated.

"For God to give you children!" the elder said.

"Naai! [Oh God!]" Semoi said.

"For God to give you animals!"

"Naai!"

"For God to make you loved by all people!"

"Naai!"

"For God to help you wherever you go!"

"Naai!"

The two men came outside, spat, and the elder limped off without greeting us. Meanwhile, a man and his son arrived on their way home from a ceremony. Their faces were painted with white chalk and red ocher. The father wore a beaded hide cape. The boy had leleshwa leaves stuck in the holes in his ears. He spoke English, and asked me about a job. "I have completed my primary school two years ago," he said. "I have a certificate, and now I lead an aimless life because most of my father's cattle have died. So I want a job. What is your advice?"

"What kind of job do you want?" I asked.

"I hear about Maasai watchmen in Nairobi, but I don't want that," he said. "I can read and write. I want to work in an office."

"But you should continue your education first," Joseph put in. "It will help you find good work."

"My father cannot afford the school fees. So myself I want to work. I would like to be a messenger for an office. If you hear of a job, you can tell the people here, and I will come."

"Okay," I said. "I'll try."

It was getting late, and Sekento said we should head back to Ngong. He had a long walk ahead of him in the morning, taking the boys back to school.

Noah and Joseph lifted the goat into the back of the truck and tied its legs. It thrashed and tried to break loose. I thanked Semoi, who spat on my hand once more. He took Noah aside to talk privately. I watched Noah nod his head repeatedly, but he was frowning.

Mr. Sha gave Sekento a necklace that one of his wives had made to give to Janet. Naisiawua asked Sekento to bring his father for a visit. He would make a party, he said. We could let Mr. Sha know the next time he came to Ngong.

Noah was quiet as we drove home.

"What did your father say?" I asked.

"He was drunk, talking nonsense," he said.

When we reached Sekento's *shamba*, Noah and Joseph unloaded the goat. Sekento had offered to look after it for me.

I asked Noah if it was true his father was cursed.

"Yes," he said. "It is a bad thing."

"But do you believe in such a thing?"

"My father believes it," he said. "What you believe comes true."

17

RIPENO

An old Maasai named Lekashu, who lived at Empaash, asked if I would take him to Nairobi to have his eyes checked. He was an untidy man with a whiskered face and badly discolored teeth and was almost blind from cataracts. His wife had goaded him to have a checkup. Sekento suggested the Presbyterian eye clinic at Thogoto, just outside Nairobi, where one of the medics was a Maasai named Francis.

When we arrived, Francis was sitting on the veranda of the staff dormitory with the orderlies, shelling peas and listening to a cassette tape of religious pop music. He took us over to the clinic, where he examined the old man. At first, Lekashu balked at the strangeness of the optometry equipment used to test his vision. The eye drops made him uncomfortable. But Francis was experienced with such cases and gently reassured him, explaining what cataracts are and why they reduced his vision. He told Lekashu that minor surgery, which would cost him practically nothing, could fully restore his sight. There was a German doctor who would perform the surgery. Lekashu agreed to try it. Francis was pleased, since it is difficult to convince the Maasai to undertake any treatment more complicated than eye drops. Glaucoma, trachoma and cataracts are widespread problems among them, and many accept blindness as a natural stage of aging. When we left Lekashu, he seemed completely relaxed about the operation scheduled for the next morning. Francis said he would call me with the results.

The following afternoon, Francis called and said with some exasperation that Lekashu had jumped off the table just as the doctor was ready to suture his eyelids and begin the procedure. "He told us he was tired and wanted to go home," he said. "He's still here, if you want to collect him."

I drove to the clinic and found Lekashu sitting on the grass, straight-backed, as if excellent posture might compensate for the wound to his dignity. But he seemed depressed. While waiting he had talked with several old Kikuyu men who had had the same surgery, and now they could see perfectly. There was a reason why he had resisted. The only other time he had "come under the knife" was at his circumcision, he explained. While that operation was performed, two elders held him in a sitting position. When the German doctor told him to lie down on the table and tied down his arms he knew something was wrong and broke loose.

"We explained everything to him," Francis said. "I don't know why he is acting this way." He asked Lekashu if he'd like to give it another try. The old man said he would prefer to go home. He added huffily that he would look elsewhere for "proper treatment."

Driving back to Empaash, Lekashu didn't say a word. He was probably afraid of what his wife would say. She seemed surprised to see him back so soon and smiled, thinking he was cured. Realizing that was not the case, she called him "an old fool." I felt sorry for him. Francis said that without surgery he would almost certainly go completely blind.

Kipeno and Nanta were at the *boma*, sitting on the boulders with their babies. "Hello, my lover!" Nanta called teasingly to Sekento. "When I saw your vehicle I thought it might be Sayo coming to harass me." Kipeno giggled. She was tall and broad-shouldered, had dark, smoky eyes, and was wearing a beaded neckband with a large white button attached to the front and narrow bracelets on her upper arms. Her *shuka* was yellow and orange and was tied in a way that showed off her figure.

Nanta asked Sekento how her sons in Saikeri were doing at school. Sekento said they were fine, but that Chief Sayo was still very angry about Kintolel's running away.

"Who cares what he thinks?" she scoffed. She added that a wild animal—a lion, they thought—had eaten one of her brother Tingisha's cows. Another cow had been attacked the week before. Tingisha was grazing the animals illegally on game-department land, so he could not report either incident without risking a fine. Since Tingisha's cows had been killed, she was nervous taking the sheep and goats out to graze. "Lions can come any time and grab the animals—or even me!"

I asked Nanta what she did on a typical day. "I get up early, when it is still dark, and milk the cows," she said. "I use calabashes to collect the milk, and before I cap them I spill a bit of milk east and west and say a prayer. Then I fetch water, not too far from here, and I make tea. Then I look at the sheep and goats to see if anything is wrong. I give some milk to Kintolel, and he takes the cows out, maybe ten miles away. I keep the calves here. The women with husbands make tea and porridge. The men sleep until the tea is ready, and then they go to the middle of the *boma* and start talking to other men, and they try to wash their cattle sticks with cow's urine, which is good luck. The work of men is one thing: to command the wives to do this, do that, look after the sheep, the goats, the calves, the children, clean the huts. The men just sit around and think what to tell the women to do next.

"In my case, my brother tells me what to do," she went on. "So I also have to try to please him, so he will help me, feed me, be kind to me, and give me the cows and goats I need. But it is a fair exchange, and at least he doesn't beat me. He is very polite. Once the men are up, I take my goats and sheep outside. I give them salt, if there is salt, and let them rest. I mix the salt with soil. I clean out the place where the sheep and goats sleep, so it won't be muddy if it rains. Then I take the animals to drink water. If it is a dipping day, we do that. Then I have to fetch water to wash clothes. I have to find firewood. I have to make repairs on my hut. Then Kintolel returns with the cows, and they are milked. We check all the animals to make sure they are all there, and to see if there are any problems. That all happens in one day. Of course, if I were married, any little thing that went wrong, I would be beaten for."

I said that in America a wife could have a man jailed if he hit her.

Kipeno and Nanta were impressed. "If a Maasai woman had that kind of power, do you think she would carry firewood on her back?" Nanta said. "If Maasai women had that kind of power they would tell the men to get the firewood!"

Kipeno was giggling so hard, listening to Nanta, that tears ran from the corners of her eyes. When Nanta left to fetch water, Kipeno said, "Nanta is my best friend because she is always so happy. She is not really as settled as she seems, because her other sons are still at Saikeri with Sayo. But she can laugh about her problems."

Kipeno hoisted her daughter, two-year-old Resian, up onto her back and said we could get some sodas at the *duka*. Semoi was off with the cattle, so she was free to talk with us. We went to one of the empty back rooms at Mr. Sha's bar. Mr. Sha was on duty at the satellite station, and his wives were tending the bar. A Kikuyu mechanic was working on the *matatu*, which now had wheels. Kipeno sat down on a sagging bed, dangling the baby over the dirt floor to let her urinate.

I asked her if it was true, as I had heard, that her father was a rich man. "Yes," she said. "But the life of a rich girl is no different from the life of a poor girl, except that more men want to marry you. I used to hate that practice that somebody would marry you because your father was rich. But later I didn't mind it because it meant that my husband would have a lot of cattle. Now I think it is better when a man marries you for your father's wealth. If he marries you for your beauty,

Noah's uncle Musanka,
the man who first brought me
to the boys' boma

PHOTOGRAPHS BY THE AUTHOR

Joseph ole Meyoki,
June 1981

The family:
Semoi, Noah, Agnes
and Kipeno's baby

Semoi with the cattle

Penina and her mother, Agnes

Joseph's mother, Nterue

*Noah's grandfather Sane
and his wife;
Ngong Hills in the background*

Joseph's father,
Shokore ole Meyoki

Joseph's brother Kureko,
a moran

Chief Sayo in uniform

Mary

Nanta

Nanta's son Kintolel

Nanta's brother Tingisha

*Mr. Sha and
William ole Sekento*

Kipeno and Noah, June 1986,
after Noah left his job
and returned to the boma

when you get older, the love will change, and you can be neglected. Look what happened to Nanta! Love can easily turn to hate." She had seen it happen with her own mother. Her father had three wives, and he disliked her mother. "I don't know why," she said. "My mother is very beautiful, but my father always loved his youngest wife the most. That is why I am happy to be the youngest wife myself."

I asked Kipeno if her father beat her mother.

"O-ling! [Very much!]. He was very wild, and he beat my mother the most. She used to tell me things you could be beaten for: if the thorn gate is worn out when the husband comes home; if the animals get ticks, and the women don't take care of them; if it rains, and the hut leaks while the husband is sleeping. The women should go out quickly to cover the leaks and repair the huts. Whenever I saw my mother unhappy or annoyed it was after she was beaten. My father beat me too, and it made me think that men are not very kind. I think when Semoi first came to talk to my father about marrying me, I hurt his feelings. I did not want to talk with him. I did not think he was attractive."

The morning of her wedding, Kipeno continued, she painted herself with red ocher and put on a beaded cowhide with a wide belt, leather sandals and a special necklace with long trails of beads. Then the elders blessed her. She strapped two calabashes of fresh milk on her back and left the family *boma*, walking very slowly out of her mother's gate, as tradition required. Noah's grandfather Sane and another elder escorted her to Semoi's *boma*. Usually the groom and a best man joined the escort. But Kipeno was told that Semoi was sick. The two old men walked ahead of her, but they never spoke with her, which was also custom. They walked for several hours and spent the night at Kisemes trading center. The next morning they crossed the valley to Saikeri. Everyone was happy to see her. "I remember that Noah's mother was especially nice to me," she said. "But it all seemed very strange to me. My mind was still back at home."

When a Maasai bride enters her husband's *boma* for the first time, the other women line up and taunt her.

They accuse her of being ugly and worthless, or even a thief. The women understand that the new bride is nervous, and the insults are aimed at further upsetting her so she will have a good cry and get rid of her anxiety. Afterward, she is given gifts. "I remember the women shouted at me that I never slept at night because I was out stealing," she said, giggling. "But when I got inside the gate Noah's mother gave me a cow. Semoi had another wife then, Rimas, and she also gave me a cow. Noah gave me a sheep. Penina gave me a cow. Sane gave me a cow. Semoi had already given my father blankets, cows and some beer."

After the animals were presented to her, she went inside Noah's mother's hut, where Semoi and several women were waiting. Semoi left and sat outside. The women tried to remove Kipeno's calabashes from her back, but she refused to let them. This was also custom, and she demanded additional gifts before letting them have the milk. That night she slept in Semoi's mother's hut with his mother and Agnes's youngest daughter, Hannah. Semoi slept in Rimas's hut. Kipeno said she felt so homesick she cried all night. In the morning she milked nine cows. Nine was considered a lucky number. It corresponded to the number of openings in a man's body. The third night Semoi slept with her. "I hated it in my heart," she said. "I was thinking about my boyfriend, but I had been given to this man, so I had no say."

Shortly after Kipeno arrived, Rimas ran away. "We didn't know her very well," Kipeno said. "But she was a good dancer, and we were told she works in a place dancing for tourists. Semoi has heard she has a child, and it might be his."

One night, Semoi got drunk, quarreled with his mother and hit her. Kipeno and Agnes heard her crying all night. The next morning, the old woman left the *boma*. Nobody knew where she went. Semoi was nervous that she might be planning to curse him, as cursing was a privilege of elders. He headed for Ngong to console himself with drink.

The first time Semoi beat Kipeno she ran home to her father. But a few days later Semoi followed her, and her father made her return to him. While Kipeno was pregnant, Semoi hit her with a stick. She went to another *boma* and stayed with friends. Noah's grandfather came to talk with her, but she refused to return to Semoi for three months. When she went home, Semoi apologized.

"The problem is that everybody fears Semoi because he is the age-group leader, and he used to be very good at that job," she said. "He could always speak very well about development and settle quarrels. But when he changed, nobody wanted to talk publicly about his drinking. But we all knew anything might happen. I used to cry by myself. Sane was afraid. Agnes and I could talk with him about it. We like that old man very much, and he tries to help us. Semoi has also talked about his drinking. He talked about it before we dared to. He knew it was beer that made him act wild."

When Kipeno was pregnant, the old women who looked after her warned her to expect a difficult birth. They came every night and rubbed her stomach with fat to try to "squeeze" the baby into a better position for delivery. Semoi had been kind to her in the final months. He brought her meat and looked after the animals by himself. The labor, as predicted, was long and painful. Kipeno remembered it was raining, and the woman who cut the umbilical cord said to the infant: "You are now responsible for your life, as I am responsible for mine." That was customary. She named the baby Resian after her father's mother. Soon after the birth, Semoi began drinking heavily and was taken to Mathari Mental Hospital. When he came back, he never talked about it. "Agnes has told me what Semoi used to be like, that he was gentle and respected," she said. "But I never knew him then." Kipeno said she tried to stay out of his way. But she was worried that Noah might grow up to copy his behavior.

Once, after Resian was born, Kipeno had taken her daughter and again gone home to her father. Semoi had been drinking and burned her arm with a stick. She showed me the scar. "I told my father I was never going back," she said. "But then Semoi came, and he acted very happy, like a good man. He brought my father two cases of beer and a blanket. He denied ever beating me. My father asked him what this scar was from. Then he admitted he had done it, but he said it was an accident, and he only meant to scare me. I was angry, but my father said, 'You take her, but never beat her again.' I feel some bitterness, but there is no way out. I try to think of the good things in my life. There are so many things I love, especially animals when they give birth. And my baby. She is the only personal thing I have."

18

WARRIORS

CURIOUSLY ENOUGH, it was from Dickson that I first learned about the life of the moran. At his father's *boma*, one weekend, he showed me how to throw a spear I had bought from Joseph. It was standard length, nearly six feet long, with a thirty-inch steel blade joined to a narrow metal shaft with a short wooden grip. It weighed about five pounds.

"Try it," Dickson said.

I lifted it to my shoulder and heaved. It fell a few feet in front of me.

"Don't twist your body; do it like this," Dickson said. He held the spear at hip level, his shoulders squared. In one quick, smooth movement, he sent the spear sailing into the air. "It's something you have to keep at to get perfect," he said.

I tried it a few more times, until my shoulder started to ache.

"That's better!" he said, watching the spear take a wobbly course and thud to the ground.

He picked it up and wiped off the blade. "We usually practice with the blunt end, so we don't wear out the point," he said. "But I don't want you to slice off your ear."

Dickson's father and older brother had taught him

to hunt. "I started out with my friends, killing hyenas, wolves, and giraffes," he said.

"Giraffes!" I said.

"A giraffe is a good animal to learn on, because it can't fight back," he said. "In a few minutes a giraffe falls dead from spearing because it bleeds to death. A giraffe has a very tough skin. Spearing it in the ribs is hard, so we aim for the pelvis, where there is a lot of blood, which comes out like from a water tap. There is a big artery that passes through to the legs. We didn't know about arteries as boys; we just knew that was the best place. I learned about arteries in school. The first time we killed a medium-sized giraffe. We took turns chasing it and resting until the giraffe got tired. I was the second one to spear it. We slaughtered it and ate the meat, just to see what it was like. It was very sweet-tasting, but tough. We left the skin."

Without meaning to, I shuddered.

"You don't want to hear about it?"

"No, it's okay—go on."

"If you had to live with wild animals, you'd have a different opinion," he said. "After giraffes, you start on leopards. They wait in the bush, and you have to sur-round them and move in close to spear them. If you get very close, you use the sword. Leopards have a soft skin, and it is easy to spear them. The lion's skin is not very tough either. Some animals are very clever. The leopard uses its front paws to protect itself, and it can even push away the spear. You try to hit the leopard in the forehead, using a stone or a club or a spear. You can kill a leopard with a rock. If it is not facing you, you try to spear it in the ribs. It is very hard to kill a lion just attacking the head because the head is very hard. Usually we hunt leopards only if they attack. But the Maasai will attack a lion for no other reason than that it is number one."

"What about zebras? Are they safe?"

"Zebras are a problem because there are so many now, and they use up a lot of water that we need for the cows," he said. "But zebras are not usually attacked. Some Maasai hunt them and sell the skins in Tanzania. Nobody eats zebra meat, but if you drink a soup made from zebra fat, it will cure any problem of the thorax. The oil of an ostrich is also very good for healing, and you can drink it like water. An ostrich is very mean, and it can fight fiercely with its legs and wings. It can slap you with the wings. I saw an ostrich attack some wild dogs that came near its young. It slapped the dogs down, then kicked them. If you try to take an ostrich's eggs, it can even strangle you under its wings. When a lion attacks an ostrich it is a very tough battle. I have been told that the ostrich can sometimes defeat the lion."

Dickson hunted lions with the boys he had grown up with, who were now moran. None of them had gone to school; some had never been to Ngong. They had tried to recruit Dickson but eventually gave up.

"In primary school, I thought about becoming a moran all the time," he said. "I used to put red ocher on my hair and body and pretend to hunt lions. Once you are circumcised you can join the moran, and that's why boys are always begging their fathers to circumcise them. Every Maasai boy wants to kill a lion and be known as a hero in Maasailand. Even now, when I finish my O levels at school, I might join up for a few months. I usually go with the moran during school vacations, but I've never been a moran for longer than two or three weeks. You want to try throwing a sword?"

"Not really," I said.

"The thing with the sword is to be careful not to cut your arm when it comes down," he said.

Before the spring break, Dickson sent me a note from school informing me that he would be spending his two-week school vacation with the moran. "Life is a zigzag line, and one must learn to cope with every part of it," he wrote. He signed the note "The Desert Wanderer."

Relations between moran and schoolboys were sometimes strained. The moran tended to regard schoolboys as weak and cowardly. The schoolboys considered the moran "illiterates." But Dickson was careful to avoid acting superior about his education and was welcomed into the warrior ranks whenever he had time off. He worried that school life was making him "soft" and looked forward to his forest sojourns, explaining that being with the moran was "another kind of school."

From Dickson's description, the life of a moran was idyllic from a teenage point of view. The Keekonyokie moran numbered more than a thousand and ranged in age from about fifteen to twenty-five. The older moran lived in the *manyattas*, which their mothers built. There were elders around to give instruction on the social order, and mothers to act as chaperons for the uncircumcised girls who stayed with the boys. The moran competed at wrestling and club throwing and practiced with spears, swords and shields; at night they danced and sang with the girls. Hairdressing was another preoccupation; the upkeep of a moran's hairdo required long hours of tedious work. Bits of wool had to be twisted into the hair to lengthen it for styling into the moran's distinctive plaits. Dickson's friend Runges, a senior moran, wore a tight plait that hung to his shoulder blades.

Dickson once wrote out for me a list of rules for moran, most of which were designed to instill discipline and group spirit. Moran were not allowed to eat or drink alone, or to drink milk at their family *bomas*. I asked him about the rule that forbids moran to have sex with circumcised women—or to eat meat that the women have seen or handled—and he acknowledged that the sex prohibition was not strictly followed. The moran referred to their secret affairs as "night traveling."

The traditional duties of the moran were to defend the tribe and restock the herds through cattle raids. But since there were no more wars to fight, except an occasional border skirmish, he said the moran mostly roamed about in small competitive bands, stealing cattle, hunting lions and building up reputations.

The organization of the moran was structured like an army, with junior and senior divisions, hunting regiments, which Dickson called "teams," and field commanders. Each age-group was presided over by an *olaiguenani*. Boys circumcised within a certain period of time, as stipulated by the Keekonyokie elders for the benefit of the whole tribe, formed an age-set and would serve together as moran. As younger boys entered moranship, the senior group was retired, and the junior moran moved up to make room for the new initiates. Dickson's friends belonged to the "right hand," the older group, while Joseph's and Noah's age-mates comprised the bottom ranks, or "left hand." The senior group held the ultimate prestige, and the younger moran were competitive with them, anxious to see them retired. The turnover took about seven years and was marked by an elaborate graduation ceremony—Eunoto—during which the older group's hair was shaved off by their mothers.

Dickson said the highlight of moran life was *olpul*, the meat-feasting camps at which the moran gorged on meat to build up strength before a lion hunt or a cattle raid. To bolster their courage, the moran also drank a special "soup" made from herbs, roots and bark that acted as a narcotic to rouse their aggression. High on this soup, they were ready to face lions.

Once, at Saikeri, I happened to see several moran who had taken the brew. They behaved as if they were having seizures, flew into fits of hysteria, made strange choking sounds and foamed at the mouth; two of them fell on the ground rigid. At first I assumed it was mere acting, since all the moran have a theatrical air about them. But Joseph, Noah and Dickson assured me the soup was powerful, and the frenzy was "real." In severe cases, often at ceremonies, little girls were made to sit across the fallen moran's legs, an act that generally restored them to consciousness.

"Once you start shaking, you can't stop," Dickson said, and added that drinking the soup also brought on sweating and headaches, and sometimes a hangover.

After his circumcision, Dickson was invited for the first time to attend an *olpul* in the forest with his older brother and his friends. Neighboring *bomas* donated eight bulls for the feast, and the moran had slaughtered and eaten two of them when he arrived from school. Dickson did not drink the soup but watched the others. "First, they started shaking and bragging about how great they were," he said. "Then they decided to go on a cattle raid." He stayed behind to tend the camp. Later that night, the moran returned with seventeen stolen cows. The cows belonged to a high-ranking Kenya Army officer who later sent helicopters to search the bush for them. When the cattle were not located, the officer made a radio plea for the return of four of the cows that had recently calved. Some Maasai elders heard the news in Ngong and relayed the message to the moran, who, for the sake of the calves, complied, leaving the four where they were easily found. They kept the rest.

Dickson had been on lion hunts, the most recent a "fantastic adventure" in which twenty-eight moran took part. With bells strapped to their thighs, they had hiked to a remote area and made camp. Throughout the night they heard roaring; nobody slept. At dawn, they scattered across the countryside. When one group spotted a male lion, they shouted for the others. A senior moran ordered some to hold back, in case the first group's spears missed their mark. But the back-up regiments—including Dickson's—objected: everyone wanted a chance to throw the first spear and claim the lion's mane, or to snare the tail as a prize. Ignoring the command, the moran charged forward. Dickson threw his spear quickly, but the lion jumped out of the way. A second moran hit the lion's chest, and a shower of other spears followed. The lion sprang, and within seconds two moran were on the ground bleeding and groaning. The wounded lion lay beside them, writhing and near death. All eyes were on the unclaimed tail. Several scrambled to hack it off. When it was certain the lion was dead, the scalp and mane, which rightfully belonged to one of the wounded boys, were sawed off. The moran then loaded their injured friends onto their backs, taking turns carrying them, and hiked to a road where they flagged down a passing truck to take them to the district hospital. The wounded boys were soon back in action, proudly showing off their scars.

Two weeks after Dickson sent me the note about his vacation plans, he returned from the bush wearing three new beaded bracelets that his girlfriends had made for him. He said he had five girlfriends but was in love with one named Joyce.

"Did you have a good time with the moran?" I asked.

"It was great—like hanging out in a den of thieves," he said. But he had not taken part in any cattle raids or lion hunts.

"I can't risk it now. I could be expelled from school if I got caught." He had, however, taken part in five cattle raids before giving it up. Only two had been successful. "The failures are always more interesting," he observed. On the last raid, he and his friends had tried to steal some grade cattle from a Kikuyu ranch. They used swords to cut the wire fence around the cattle pen, but the frightened animals stampeded, waking the owner, who came after them with a gun. He fired into the air, and the moran took off. The wife's screams and the gunshots brought out the neighbors, who joined in the chase. "When you hear gunfire, the best thing is to disappear," Dickson said. The owner followed them on a motorcycle. They lost him in a thick forest.

Joseph's senior-moran brother, Kureko, claimed to have killed a marauding elephant that had intruded on his camp. He had also stolen dozens of cows from the Kikuyu, and some of his friends who had been caught at it were in jail. Kureko reported these stories with great nostalgia as he was nearing the end of his service. He was thinking of becoming a cattle trader, but he discussed this possibility without any real enthusiasm.

With Joseph, I attended one of the last in a series of graduation exercises in which Kureko's age-set was retired from moranhood. The largest of these, Eunoto, had taken place two years earlier. The ceremony we went to was Enkang Enkeene (The Village of the Strap), at which a symbolic leather strap, which had featured in the Eunoto ceremony, was cut up and divided among the group. The young men were also given cattle sticks, symbolic of their approaching junior elderhood.

Kureko's ceremony, the last in which his group would be called together, was held on the Kaputei plains where a special *manyatta* had been built. Joseph and I had no trouble finding it. We followed a lurching *matatu* weighted down with crates of beer, met other Maasai walking to the ceremony and gave a lift to some young moran who sang boisterous fight songs. At the *manyatta*, the elders were drunk and bleary-eyed. The festivities had begun days earlier. Some elders had passed out; others staggered past. The younger boys had formed dancing circles and were singing and taking turns jumping in the air. Joseph was on lookout for the arrival of the moran across the plains.

"They're coming!" he shouted, as all who were able rushed outside to witness the parade of several hundred red-daubed, chanting moran marching in single file toward the *manyatta*. Two other lines—one of women and another of elders—approached from opposite directions, and the three lines converged and spread out in a large circle. But the sudden stateliness of the occasion was not to last: one of the drunken men reeled toward me, noisily demanding to know what I was doing there. Joseph tried to explain that I was an invited guest, but he would hear nothing of it. To avoid further confrontation—everyone was staring at us—I left, with Joseph remaining to report the details. I was sorry to go; I had promised Kureko to take a picture of him with his friends.

A week later, I met them in Ngong. Kureko looked miserable. I asked Joseph what was wrong. "He says he's finished," Joseph said. Kureko was mourning the passing of his moranhood. "Now whenever I hear the old songs, I will only remember those great days!" he said. "Even now I wish I could continue for ten more years. I was a *human being* then! *Tough! Strong!*" He pounded his fist on the table. And then—as he often did when he tired of my questions—he put his head down. Today, especially, it seemed that talk was beside the point.

19

A BROKEN STAR

IN LATE OCTOBER 1981, the Maasai began to worry about drought. A haze of dust settled over the valley, and a hot, dry wind blew from morning to night. There was hardly a blade of grass on the plains, and the Saikeri dam was low. Agnes and her friends gave up on their vegetable garden, which now seemed frivolous, and began to pray for the cattle.

Musanka made a sacrifice with a ram. The ram was intoxicated with honey beer that the women had brewed for ceremonies. More beer was poured over it. If the ram immediately shook off the beer, Noah's grandfather said, it meant rain was close. Everyone watched. But this ram did not shake at all. The sky remained cloudless.

Sane thought it might still rain. He had seen enough droughts to know the real thing and said I could check with a mystic named Koimarish, who was a reliable predictor of rain. He was a Maasai who lived on top of the Ngong Hills and claimed to be visited by angels. Sane, like most people, called him "the man who talks to God."

Sekento thought he was a lunatic but admitted he had followers who consulted him on a variety of problems, including marital disputes. By chance, I saw Koimarish one day near the Kiserian market, where Sekento and I had gone to visit his mother's vegetable stand. Sekento pointed him out walking on a narrow dirt trail across the Ngong Hills, followed by three Kikuyu men in sports jackets. Koimarish wore a blanket and was a foot taller than any of them. I wondered what business the Kikuyu—dressed as if they had come from church—might have with a Maasai clairvoyant. Apparently, with a drought impending, everyone hedged his bets.

At Sane's urging, Sekento, Noah and I went to see Koimarish. We climbed the steep path to his broken-down hut. It stood alone except for a few humpbacked cattle and some sheep and goats out front. A tattered green flag—a prayer flag—flapped overhead. Koimarish was used to unexpected guests and suggested we sit outside on some flat rocks arranged for visitors. His wife brought tin mugs of tea—a dead fly floated in mine— and excused herself to go to a wedding.

We sat on a ledge overlooking the Rift's hazy corridor. The view alone was worth the climb. The faint pink outline of Kilimanjaro shimmered above the plains to the south. Toward Saikeri, we saw funnels of smoke where the Maasai were burning off pasture in the hope that rain would come soon.

We asked Koimarish what he thought.

He sat alertly, one finger raised to the sky, like an antenna set to receive distant messages, beads of sweat forming on his long, fleshy nose. Sekento and Noah looked amused. Finally, he spoke. He blamed the stars— in particular one "broken star"—for the delay of the rains. He cupped his fingers over one eye like a telescope and searched the sky. He said if we came at night he could point it out. The "hole" in this star allowed the hot winds to blow through it. But he said the star would soon shift position. The rain would begin in ten days. It would not last long, but it would be heavy.

I asked Koimarish when he had first realized his talent for predictions. "It was when I was a moran," he said. "I began to get feelings in my body—like a heat in my heart. At first I was afraid, and I told no one. Once on a cattle raid I told my friends that we would get eight cows that day and I described their colors. When that came true, I became very popular." Before he was born, an *oloiboni* had told his father that his seventh son would be special. Koimarish was the seventh and last son. "My father told me about it, and everybody in the *boma* watched me," he said. "My father wasn't so sure, but he used to pray that I would become an age-set leader. But I seemed quite normal as a child, and soon everybody forgot about what the *oloiboni* had said until I became a moran. Even then some people said I was mad, but generally my predictions came true."

Noah was curious about the angels whom Koimarish claimed to know.

"Sometimes I have been with them right here where we are sitting now," he said. "But other times they have lifted me"—he raised his shoulders as if for takeoff— "and taken me to the tops of other hills, to pray."

Noah was skeptical. "What do they look like?"

"Like human beings with bat wings," Koimarish said. "And they wear hides, like the old people."

This was too much for Sekento. He got up and walked around, smoked a cigarette and looked at the cows.

Noah, who had seen drawings of silver-winged angels in a religion book at school, could barely keep from laughing.

Koimarish did not seem to notice. He said that some Maasai thought he must be an *oloiboni*. But he was quick to differentiate himself from the traditional ritual experts, the very first of whom, according to tribal lore, was an orphan boy found on these hills. "I don't deal in curses or poison," he said. "My work is happiness, peacemaking."

"Do you believe what he said about the angels?" Noah asked, when we were driving home. "Myself, I think the man is abnormal."

"He's out of his mind," Sekento said.

I withheld my judgment. Even if he was slightly mad, he seemed very kind.

When rain began to fall in Nairobi, I checked my calendar. His prediction was off by a day. But the rain was heavy.

Sekento and I visited Koimarish several times. There were few more pleasant ways to spend an afternoon than sitting on top of the Ngong Hills, and I was curious to find out more about the mystic. He saw the future in dreams, and sometimes voices spoke to him. "Some people say to me, 'How can a poor man who is so skinny and wears torn clothes talk with God?' But I am content with my life," he said. "My heart is very rich, very clean and fat in front of God." Koimarish said he was progressive and sent his children to school. His wife Margaret did not seem to think he was strange, though years ago another wife had run away. "The first wife was frightened," she told me. "I used to wonder if my husband was lying about talking to God, and I was frightened too. But everything he says comes true, so this must come from God. Now I find that some people fear me as they fear him because they think I may share the same thing. When they see me they say, 'There is the woman whose husband talks to God.'"

Once, Koimarish asked me if I was sick. I said I had a stomachache. "I knew it," he said, and went into his hut, returning with a bottle of Coca-Cola, which he opened with his teeth. He gave me twenty shillings and said I should use it to buy medicine in Nairobi. When I asked Koimarish about my future, he said there was nothing worth mentioning. "If you had any problems, I would have told you right away," he said. "Any troubles you have will pass." He told Sekento not to bother asking for a school transfer; he would be in Saikeri for a long time.

A local church was trying to convert Koimarish. It was always good publicity for a church to win over a witch doctor—as some people believed he was—and the newspapers often carried features about such unlikely conversions. A Maasai businessman named Paul, a member of the church, had been making visits to discuss the possibility with the mystic. Sekento and I arrived one day to find Paul reading the Bible to Koimarish, who gazed off into the valley. Paul said he had recently completed a Bible study course and had translated some stories into the tribal language. Koimarish listened with interest and interrupted now and then to add stories of his own experiences with the angels he knew. Paul said when he first came to visit, he had doubts about the mystic's claims, but he now believed that Koimarish was "a deeply spiritual man, a God selection." He had reported his findings to the congregation, and many of his fellow churchmen were afraid that he had come under an evil spell. But Paul continued his visits. He said Koimarish's predictions had helped him to make profitable business decisions. But the mystic refused to convert. He pointed to his head: "Most of what is in the Bible is already up here," he said.

I asked Koimarish if I could bring him anything from Nairobi, and he said, yes, a new prayer flag; his was almost ripped to shreds. It had to be green, the color of grass—God's favorite color, he said. I bought green canvas and sewed him a flag. The day I brought it, he called his family together to admire it and to say a prayer. His wife served Cokes. Then he led his five children in singing some hymns that Paul had taught them.

A short time after our last visit to Koimarish, Sekento and I happened to meet Joseph's father in Ngong, and he invited us to have a beer in one of the bars and told us that if we were still interested in psychics, he knew a Samburu *lais* (a fortune-teller) named Thomas who worked as a factory watchman in Nairobi. The Samburu tribe was related to the Maasai and lived in northern Kenya, and Shokore thought that their *lais* were the best at predicting the future. He had recently consulted Thomas on some secret matter and told us when and where we could look for him.

Sekento and I drove to the factory where Thomas worked and found a group of Samburu tribesmen in *shukas* waiting at the front gate to see him. He was a short, compactly built man wearing a guard's uniform, and when he got off work he led us to a small park a few blocks away where some men were hammering out dented fenders. The Samburu graciously said we could talk with him first, since their business was likely to take a while, and they moved a few feet away and sat down in a huddle.

Thomas sat on the grass and talked above the din of the hammering. He said he had come to Nairobi four years before, after a bad drought. He added that he enjoyed modern life, and that he was helpful to the city's small Samburu community.

"Does your employer know you are a *lais?*" I asked.

"No, I haven't told them," he said modestly. "I just act like a common man."

I asked him how he was different from a Maasai *oloiboni*. "Mostly we do blessings," he said. "I can do a kind of cursing with words, but I don't use herbs. We *lais* are all friendly with one another since we come from the same family."

Sekento asked if he was successful.

"Yes, I rarely fail," he said. "I can make blessings to stop cattle raids and to help people going into business. If somebody has problems with a marriage, or if a wife runs away, I can help. If somebody wants to marry but fails to get a wife, I can help that too."

"How does it work?" I asked.

"I say, 'In God's power you will get your cow back— or your wife back,' like that. You, who are asking, believe you will get what you ask for, and then there is my power. That is the way it works."

"How are you paid?" Sekento asked.

"I charge twenty shillings, then if my advice works you come back and give me a better gift, like a cow."

Sekento asked him about his chances for a school transfer. The *lais* closed his eyes and thought for a while. "No, I don't see it immediately," he said. "But I can give you a tip for the horse races."

"We never go to horse races," I said.

"You should go today," he said and gave us the name of a horse. I handed him twenty shillings. On the way back to Ngong, Sekento decided to stop at the racecourse and try his luck. Later, he telephoned.

"I lost," he said. "But I figured out why. You paid the twenty shillings."

20

REUNION

AFTER THE RAINS started, and everyone was in a better mood, Sekento and I took his father, Edward, to Empaash to visit his brother Naisiawua, whom he had not seen in fifteen years. Edward was wearing a tweed cap, a sports jacket and a vest. We found Naisiawua waiting at Mr. Sha's bar in a pink *shuka* and an assortment of beads. The two men shook hands, hugged and sat down on a bench on the veranda, putting their heads together and holding hands like little children. *"Ai! Ai! Ai!"* they kept saying with tears in their eyes. Sekento and I went into one of the back rooms where Semoi was sitting with an elder named Musei. I recognized him as the old man who had blessed Semoi the first time we visited, and when I said so, he apologized for not greeting us that day. "Normally I am not a rude person," he said, "but I thought you were missionaries. I try to avoid them." Musei was about the same age as Noah's grandfather and a friend of his.

Semoi opened a flour sack on the table and proudly took out a loaf of bread, three shriveled chapati, six greasy doughnuts and a can of Kenya Creamery Butter that he had bought in Narok that morning. He opened the can with his knife and began slathering everything with thick layers of butter. Some flies that landed in the butter had to be picked out. He handed Sekento and me a slice, but Musei declined. "I can't eat that *mzungu* [European] food," he said. Sekento and I took polite bites. I swallowed a large lump of butter.

"Delicious," I said.

"Yes, it's good," Sekento agreed.

Semoi smiled. "We like to treat our guests kindly, and I know this is the kind of food you prefer."

Musei examined Semoi's knife, turned it over, stroked the edges and polished the blade with his blanket. Then he cut the edge of the table, hammered a fly and gave it back to Semoi.

I asked him what he knew about missionaries.

"*Ai!* They always come around to bother people," he said. "They told us once that men could walk on the moon. But how is that possible? The moon is like a piece of glass"—he picked up a soda bottle and pointed to the bottom—"like this. The moon is too small for a man to walk on it. They said the men went to the moon to collect rocks. *Hoooiiiiii!* What's wrong with all the rocks here? Another thing they tell us is that there is life after death. I know that is not true. I have known many people who died, and we never saw them again. The missionaries say there is a soul that lives like a human being up in the sky. We have never seen such a thing. When the white men say there is life after death, I begin to think that maybe they are a favorite of God. It is like a father who has several sons, but he prefers one to all the others. Maybe the black people are not so liked, and we are missing out on something. It is true that we Africans are a little more wild and hardheaded, and we don't always follow what God advises. With us, even a child can kill his father."

"European children can kill their fathers too," I said.

"Maybe, but I can also make curses on people who bother me," Musei said. "If I go to water my animals and I meet another man there and I am annoyed, I curse him. I can even hit him with my club and kill him instantly."

Musei dipped his fingers into the tin of butter and used it to polish his club. "Do you believe there is life after death, Sekento?" he asked.

"I don't think about it," he said.

"My grandfather, my great-grandfather, they are dead and we have never seen them since," Musei continued. "When my grandfather died, we put his body out on the plains and the hyenas ate it. We heard them. There was nothing left, not even bones. When you die, you're gone! Is there a place where these dead people go? *There isn't.* The government tells us to bury the dead in graves. This is what Christians do. Even the ones in the grave rot. What is left to go anyplace?"

Sekento asked him if he wanted to be buried.

"Yes, I do," he said. "If you put a body on the plains, and no wild animals touch it for two or three days, then we say that man was bad—even if he was a good man when he was alive. People will always remember whether your body was taken quickly by the wild beasts, and it will influence the way people treat your family. I don't want it witnessed whether I was good or bad. It is serious if your body hangs around too long."

Semoi told us that Musei had been among the elders who had supervised the ceremony at which he was selected as *olaiguenani*. At the ceremony, a Keekonyokie ritual that marked the opening of a new circumcision period for the whole tribe, the elders made a ritual fire by rubbing together two sticks of olive wood. Musei held a special position with Semoi's age-set, as he had kindled the fire for the group and blessed the boys before their circumcisions.

Musei said, "If Semoi ever refused me anything, I could curse him and remind him of the blessing and of the fire I made for his group." He began to reminisce about the ceremony. "It was a very big day when the boys came very early in the morning to wrestle an ox with their hands. The ox was suffocated, not cut on the throat. The elders then made a cut and took out the blood and mixed it with milk. The new *olaiguenani* was the first to drink it. Then they took out the innards— the lungs, heart, liver, kidneys. The heart must be taken out carefully; if it is just cut in any way it means everybody will die. So the elders use their fingers to carefully remove the fat around the heart. The slaughtering was done inside the *boma*. A plant called *o-seki* was put on the ground so that the meat didn't get mixed with dirt. Then a kind of table was made to burn the meat on. But before the meat was eaten, the boys made a long line, with the *olaiguenani* first.

"The elders cut a special piece of meat and smeared the boys' foreheads with it. The two elders who did the smearing were tied around the waist with a rope that other men held to keep them standing; otherwise, their backs would hurt from all the bending. There were a thousand boys in line! When the meat was ready, the boys who would be circumcised ate first, until they were satisfied, and then the others ate. This ceremony lasted five days, and then the boys went home to be circumcised in their *bomas*."

When Naisiawua and Edward, still holding hands, joined us, we all got into my truck and drove out to a grove on the plains where some men were slaughtering a goat to celebrate the brothers' reunion.

Semoi climbed up on a pile of rocks to supervise. Kintolel was allowed to attend, to help the older men collect firewood. He unloaded his wood, and after the goat was smothered and the men had slit its throat, he got down on his knees and lapped up the blood. The elders watched with approval. It was a great honor for him, and when he finished he wiped his mouth and announced, "You see, I am a pure Maasai." He then sat back on his haunches watching the men carve up the carcass, putting aside various parts for roasting.

Sekento's father watched him with curiosity and asked if he was in school. Kintolel explained that he could not go to school because he had to look after his mother, and Edward seemed saddened, but he made no more of it.

We told Semoi about our visit to "the man who talks to God" and about the men in Saikeri sacrificing a ram before the rain started. "It seems many of these traditions are dying out," he said. "Noah's generation will be the end of many practices, like witchcraft. Today the schoolchildren read the newspaper to find out when it will rain. Some people say they still believe in the old ways, but in their hearts they don't. And today the *iloibonok* are not very powerful. Also, they charge a lot of money before they tell you anything."

Musei's view of the future was even bleaker. "When all the children are educated, then the cows will be finished," he said. "The younger generation is not interested in cows, just money and beer. We don't know what to do about it. But it will be a good thing when we are done with moranhood. In our time, moran stole cows only from the Kikuyu, but the boys today will steal from anybody, even their own people."

Three men were walking toward us. "Those three always show up when there is food," Semoi said. He called out to them, "You can come here, but all you will get are the lungs!"

After the meat had been roasted and eaten, Semoi and Musei used their clubs to break up the bones. Sekento thought it had some superstitious meaning, but Semoi explained, "We don't want to draw the wild animals."

21

POLITICS

KENYA'S TELEVISION news always began the same way: "His Excellency, the president, Daniel arap Moi, today . . ." The verb that followed was usually "declared," "warned" or "blasted." The president, a member of the small Kalenjin tribe—and a staunch anti-Communist—brooked no criticism. His word was law, and his portrait hung on the walls of every shop and office in the land.

In 1982 rumors were starting to circulate of coup plots. "PRESIDENT BLASTS RUMORMONGERS" was a morning headline, but the speculations continued. "Be careful you are not keeping cash in your house next Friday," the Indian greengrocer said to me knowingly. The African butcher with friends in the army advised me to buy extra meat for the freezer. "Have you heard anything?" a neighbor asked. Trouble was in the air. One night the radio announcer signed off, "And that's the end of the war . . . I mean, NEWS!"

I stocked up on canned goods and kept the gas tank full, not sure what to expect; reliable information was scarce. The government owns the country's only radio and television stations and one of the three major newspapers, but even the independent newspapers were careful not to offend the government. There was no official censorship, but journalists who raised questions about Moi's policies risked detention, and several had already been arrested. A free-lance journalist was sentenced to four and a half years in jail for possessing a pamphlet critical of the government.

"My patience is running out," the president warned, and in May he launched a get-tough policy, detaining without trial, under public-security laws, the country's former deputy director of intelligence. Seven other Kenyans were known to be in political detention, including a former member of parliament, several university lecturers and a Nairobi lawyer.

The University of Nairobi and another college were closed following protest demonstrations. Moi accused the students of buying Maasai swords and guns in order to intimidate others to support their cause, and sent them home to report to their village chiefs, like probationers. Police began house searches, looking for "seditious" materials, including any book that mentioned Marx. The crackdown continued with expulsions from the ruling party of two politicians linked with plans to form an alternative socialist political party. Parliament reacted quickly by legalizing the ruling party as Kenya's single official political party, a measure that was passed without a single vote of dissent.

The morning after the vote, I went to Dickson's school, curious to learn the students' reactions. A group of them were standing outside the headmaster's office silently reading a morning newspaper clipping tacked to the bulletin board. When I asked them what they thought, no one dared to express an opinion. They shrugged and walked away. "Students have learned it is not smart to have ideas about politics," Dickson whispered.

At the time, there were five Maasai members in parliament, three of whom were close advisers to President Moi. It was a curious situation, since the Maasai politicians were best known for their jealous feuding, and their records of public service were less than outstanding. They represented the districts of Kajiado and Narok, had minimal contact with their Maasai constituents and regularly insulted one another in public. The newspapers reported their quarrels like episodes in a long-running soap opera. For Moi's purposes they were trust-worthy confidants whose small tribe posed no political threat.

The Maasai paid little attention to national affairs, were cynical about the practice of modern politics and made no demands of their elected officials, whose appearances, nearing election time, were mere formalities. They had no faith in the system and also no urge to change it.

The Maasai politicians campaigned on promises of new schools, roads, dispensaries, cattle dips and water facilities—few of which ever got built. On the eve of elections, they toured the *bomas*, handing out gifts—sugar, tea, even livestock—to influential elders. They hired trucks to haul the Maasai to the polls on election days. The novelty of the ride was the only reason some of them voted.

I asked Semoi why the Maasai didn't boot the old guard from office, since they had done very little to help the tribe. "Why bother?" he said. "Politicians are all the same."

"We get all kinds of characters in politics," Sekento's uncle Naisiawua added. "The ones in parliament do nothing but argue with each other. Our chiefs are appointed, and we have no say. Most of our officials are corrupt. The only reason they go into politics is to get rich."

The best known was the Kajiado South MP, Stanley ole Oloitipitip, a flamboyant and outspoken cabinet minister. The stereotype of the fierce Maasai, he boasted he was "pure Maasai" and "not some chicken farmer." He spoke plainly—even crudely—and sometimes with wit. During a drought, when the government tried to stop the Maasai from grazing their herds on the Ngong Hills where the water table had fallen dangerously low, he said, "Do they want the Maasai to live like dikdik in the rocks?"

Oloitipitip was popular with the Maasai, who appreciated his style, though his boastfulness and lack of sophistication, plus his physical appearance—he was bald and almost unbelievably obese—made him the butt of national jokes. When he appeared in newsreels, often accompanying President Moi on district inspections, audiences howled with laughter.

Born in 1927 in Loitokitok, Kajiado district, where he attended only a few years of primary school, Oloitipitip had joined the King's African Rifles during World War II and served as nurse and sergeant in India, Burma and what was then Ceylon. He later worked for the colonial health department but quit in 1960 to take up politics. He had served in parliament since independence.

He was once accused of being a kingpin in the illegal ivory trade and had accumulated sizable, unexplained wealth while in office. But he was a shrewd politician and retained closer links to tribal life than any other politician. He had twelve wives, and some of their fathers were important traditional leaders among the Maasai.

Until the mid-1970s he concentrated on consolidating his power as the undisputed leader of the Maasai. His longtime rival for that position was the MP for Kajiado North, the assistant minister for works, John Keen. The two men had known each other since primary school, but Oloitipitip let no one forget that Keen was a half-caste with some German blood in him.

Over three decades of quarreling, truces were declared and broken many times, and neither man showed much interest in the more mundane duties of public office while this struggle continued. Once Oloitipitip threatened to relinquish his seat in Kajiado South to stand against Keen in Kajiado North. "I would thrash him without much ado," he said, but later gave up the idea.

Typical of their antagonism was a running battle over Keen's campaign to force the Maasai to wear trousers. It started in the late 1970s when Keen, piqued at the lack of progress among his constituents, issued an ultimatum that if they did not take up farming and start wearing pants within six months, he would quit office. The Maasai considered both stipulations beneath their dignity. A delegation of elders was sent to refresh the MP on the basic order of things. Keen fell silent as the deadline passed. He did not leave office.

Oloitipitip made the most of the situation. "Mr. Keen should be reminded that the men who built up the Roman Empire did not wear trousers. Neither did Gandhi when he terminated the British Empire in India. Whether the Maasai wear trousers or not, the important thing is that they have healthy souls."

Keen countered that Oloitipitip wanted to keep the Maasai "under a thick blanket." Oloitipitip called Keen a "loudmouth."

In 1976 Oloitipitip moved to the forefront of national politics as a leader of a crusade to block a constitutional amendment that would have prevented Moi (then the vice president) from succeeding the ailing Jomo Kenyatta. Since 1978, when Moi took over, Oloitipitip had been rewarded with a series of top posts, serving as local government minister since 1980. This position and his special relationship to Moi gave him considerable power, but his constant squabbling with other Maasai politicians, his unchecked outbursts and his megalomania also made him a growing embarrassment.

"Uhuru [independence] is a sweet commodity," he declared, "because it has enabled me to own several sleek cars, a twelve-room house, twelve wives and sixty-seven children. What else do we want?" Oloitipitip's fleet included a Citroën DS20, a Mercedes-Benz 350SLC and a Range-Rover. At his homestead, near the border with Tanzania, he built a school to accommodate all his children.

He once canceled a district tour because too few dignitaries showed up to greet him. Moi was forced to rebuke him for stirring up tribalism after he accused Luo tribal leaders of disloyalty to the regime. Luo students at the University of Nairobi responded by burning Oloitipitip in effigy. The editor of the leading newsweekly wrote: "Mr. Oloitipitip would be doing himself and the country a big favor if he put an indefinite moratorium on public pronouncements."

In 1982 it came to light that he had "borrowed" more than a million shillings from the city council to pay for his son's lavish wedding reception and then fired the council treasurer who questioned the expenditure. But it was unlikely the scandal would hurt his chances for reelection. Few Maasai would hear about it—or care. Soon after, he was moved to the Ministry of Culture and

Social Services, but he refused to see the shift as a demotion, claiming expertise for the new job as a man with many wives who was knowledgeable in African traditions and culture.

Semoi had known Oloitipitip and Keen ever since he had been selected as age-set leader. At Saikeri, he had lived in Keen's district, and before elections he was handsomely courted. "Whatever was being given out, I always got the lion's share," he said. "But I liked Keen. He was tough. He was a good speaker. I felt he was bright and capable. But over the years he never did what he promised. He was a friend, and you don't blame a friend—so to me he was clean. But he did nothing for Saikeri. We couldn't get the road fixed. He never came out there. Oloitipitip is the one I know more about. He was even tougher. I knew him when he was just a cattle and donkey man. Once he bought about one hundred heifers, and he had a Kamba man who was supposed to sell them in Maasailand. When the Kamba returned with the money and asked for his share, Oloitipitip refused to give him anything. So the Kamba cursed him and one hundred and fifty of his animals died. After that Oloitipitip couldn't look around without finding trouble. He went to an *oloiboni* who fixed the curse, and then he went back to work. He got another hundred cows, but then he went to another witch doctor, near Mombasa, to make sure he was cured. He was getting ready for his first political campaign, and he won. He got where he is today because of the witch doctors."

"All the Maasai in parliament depend on the *iloibonok* for curses," Naisiawua said. "They can remain in parliament forever with the help of witch doctors. That is the secret of politics."

22

NTULELE

KENYA'S GROWING political uncertainties were of negligible interest to the Maasai, who were preoccupied with a divisive tribal issue involving land. I first heard about it while driving Semoi and Naisiawua to Narok to pick up cattle medicines. On the way, we passed a fierce-looking Maasai walking along the road carrying a spear as well as bow and arrows.

"An Ildamat," Naisiawua muttered.

Semoi added, "Those people should be cursed."

During the last serious drought, the Keekonyokie and Purko Maasai had allowed the Ildamat, a smaller tribal section from the south, to graze their herds in an area of Narok district called Ntulele. This was a traditional courtesy, but when the drought ended in 1979, five hundred Ildamat refused to leave and return to their own land.

The land around Ntulele was being subdivided for private and group ownership, and the Keekonyokie and Purko quickly formed a registration committee to issue deeds. Now the Ildamat were claiming a share of the land by historical right. They said the Keekonyokie and Purko had moved to the area after the British drove them there, and that their Ildamat great-grandfathers had originally settled the land. In the past century, the

Purko had fought a bloody war against the Ildamat. The Ildamat lost, and the survivors fled to the south. No one could recall the exact reasons for the war, but the present dispute seemed aimed at settling old scores. There had been several violent clashes, the most serious in 1980 when seven Maasai died of gun and spear wounds and thirty others were wounded. A few more Maasai had been murdered since. The Maasai politicians were at odds over the situation.

At the time, the senior MP in Narok district was sixty-three-year-old Justus ole Tipis, a thin, taciturn man with a droopy white mustache who was also national party treasurer and a chief decision maker in national politics. President Moi had recently appointed him minister of state, making him the highest-ranking Maasai in government. It was a blow to Oloitipitip, who had claimed the distinction up until his demotion. He enjoyed taking potshots at Tipis, who had some Kikuyu blood in him; the two had competed for prestige since the 1970s when Jomo Kenyatta had bypassed Tipis to make Oloitipitip the first Maasai minister.

Oloitipitip sided with the Keekonyokie and Purko on the Ntulele issue and visited Tipis's district to console the widows of the men who had been killed. The Ildamat found an ally in Tipis, who was desperate to bring new votes to the district, anticipating tough opposition in the next general elections. His rival was William ole Ntimama, a fifty-two-year-old Narok wheat farmer and businessman who headed the local party branch and the Narok county council. A full-blooded Maasai, and the son of a prominent elder, Ntimama was also managing director of Governor's Camp, a well-known tourist camp in Maasai Mara.

Both Tipis and Ntimama had started out in politics representing Maasailand in the colonial legislative council. Ntimama later worked as a schoolteacher and concentrated on business interests, but he was building up support to unseat Tipis. Tipis meanwhile was using his party clout to keep Ntimama's supporters out of civic office by blocking their nominations. In a fit of anger, Tipis clubbed one of them in the county council chambers, but since he was a key figure in the president's cabinet, the incident passed without consequence.

Ntimama supported the Keekonyokie and Purko on the Ntulele question, and it was thought that his rivalry with Tipis stood in the way of settling the problem and prolonged the bloodshed. There were two other, less influential Maasai MPs in Narok district, but they kept out of the feud.

The problems at Ntulele sparked a brief interest among the Maasai in the upcoming elections. Around Mr. Sha's bar the elders suddenly began talking politics, and savored the intrigue.

"See that man over there?" Musei said, pointing to a young man hanging out at the *duka*. "He's a spy for Tipis. They're all around now."

Some of the women were not so happy at the turn of events. They were sometimes invited to sing at Tipis's rallies, or when President Moi toured the district. They liked dressing up in their finery, but they did not want to appear loyal to a man they felt had betrayed their interests.

One day, Sekento, Semoi, Naisiawua and I drove to Ntulele trading center to find out what was new with the range dispute. When we reached Ntulele, police with rifles were patrolling the *dukas*. There were hardly any Maasai around. Naisiawua said the police had been checking Maasai *bomas* for guns and harassing some of the women. Clement ole Torome, one of old James ole Torome's sons, was a county councillor. We went to the bar he owned and found him in a back room, napping.

He climbed out of bed and led us into the empty bar. "Having police around isn't helping business," he said sleepily. I asked him if there had been any recent fighting. "I think some things have gone on which we don't even know about," he said. "People get murdered here, and the police never find out. But about a year ago some Ildamat came to a river where we water our cattle, and they had poison arrows, spears, *simis* [swords] and two guns. They wanted to fight. Our people tried to leave, but one of the Ildamat started firing his gun. He fired eleven bullets, but he didn't hit anybody. Then a Purko boy was hit in the eye with a poisoned arrow, and he died. And, later, we found an Ildamat man speared and bleeding, but he recovered. After that we had a big *baraza* [meeting] with the politicians and big shots from Nairobi. That was six months ago, but nothing has changed. The district officer said we should sit down with the Ildamat and discuss the problem peacefully. The government doesn't understand what this is about. They say, 'You're all Maasai, what's the problem? Settle together.' But we cannot. The Maasai around here are generally very polite people. They can't understand why the Ildamat did not go through proper channels for permission to stay after the drought. The Keekonyokie were here first. They let the Purko settle here because they asked in a respectful way. You cannot just move into somebody's land with force, the way the Ildamat are trying to do it. There are twenty-five Keekonyokie and Purko on the land committee now, and the government says that twelve Ildamat should be allowed to join. We had a riot the day that was announced. They had to bring in extra game wardens to control the crowd. Now it's a very tense situation. Until the views of the majority of the elders hold, there is no solution. And now we have politics involved. You know how that works. Everything concerning land ownership is corrupt. There will be more bloodshed before this problem is solved. Some of the old men—like Naisiawua here— still think it's 1914. And the moran like the tension. But it's pointless—boys who should be in school running around shooting arrows at each other."

After we left Clement, we drove to Narok and stopped for tea. Naisiawua put four spoonfuls of sugar in his tea and said there had not been such excitement since the 1950s Mau Mau rebellion against colonial rule. He had fought during those times—on the British side. He and his friends were senior moran when the uprising began, and they were hired by the local white farmers and given guns to act as security guards against Mau Mau attacks.

"We knew nothing about politics then," he said. "Our lives were carefree, just looking after cattle. We were astonished when we heard that the whites were running away from the country just because of Mau Mau! Most of the Mau Mau looked very old. Some were weak and hungry. If you pushed them, they fell down. They were mostly Kikuyu. When they tried to recruit us, we were not interested. Whenever we killed them, we always checked to see if they had money. That is when we saw how old they were. They had shaggy hair and smelled so bad we used to vomit. The government *askaris* told people they would nail their arms and legs if they helped the Mau Mau. Others were supposed to be burned or castrated. I never saw that happen.

"One time the Mau Mau took thirteen cows from one of the *bomas*. We went after them and killed eight, and the rest ran away. The district officer was a white, and he made a small ceremony and gave us seventeen cows for that. But after that, the government asked us to turn in the guns. The leader of our age-group thought it was a good idea too. He said if we quarreled among ourselves, we might use the guns to kill each other. The district officer said our age-group should be called 'Fire and Fear' because we killed so many Mau Mau. We didn't understand what it was really about. We heard after some time that the British were out, and Jomo Kenyatta was the leader. He invited some Maasai elders to Nairobi to talk and said we should forget our differences and be one nation. But we always preferred it when the British ran the government. They were kind to us and had more respect for our age-group leaders. The Africans in government don't recognize our leaders. They don't know how our culture works."

"They don't care," Semoi said.

Sekento, who was translating, looked bewildered. "What else did you do in Mau Mau?" he asked his uncle.

"One day some Mau Mau took a big ox from our *boma* and we got into a fight. They had guns, spears, swords and poison arrows. We had only spears. Our *shukas* were torn by their arrows, but none of us was injured, and we followed them. I was with a man named Leisi ole Punyua. I killed two Mau Mau, and so did Leisi. He put his spear in one and then pulled it out and stuck it into another. Before that day we used to mock Leisi because he was very small and young. You have seen him at Sha's *duka*—he's still around. The day he killed the two Kikuyu, he became great.

"Another day we went on a lion hunt, and I threw my spear and it just grazed the lion, and the lion jumped on me. The hind legs clawed my legs, and the front claws attacked my face." He showed us the scars on his temples. "Another moran threw a spear in the lion's stomach. Then Leisi went up and cut off the lion's tail before it died. Not so many men dare go up to a dying lion. Finally we had a *baraza* of moran, and we agreed we should not kill Mau Mau for nothing, only for a purpose, such as stealing our cows. But then some Mau Mau killed a Dorobo who was our friend. There were eight Mau Mau, and three had guns. They shouted that we should go back, and when we refused they were ready to shoot. I said to Leisi, 'Do you see that these men have guns?' and he said, 'Let's go forward anyway; we are seven moran, and we are going to kill them.'

"Some of our moran said we should wait and make a bigger group, but Leisi and I said we should go now, we will die together. The Mau Mau killed one of our moran. When I tried to aim at one of them, the spear went between his legs; my friend missed too. I took another spear and aimed at the neck of a Kikuyu, but that missed. So Leisi took his sword and cut one at the shoulder—cut off his shoulder *kabisa* [completely]. Then I cut off his nose. Leisi was credited with the killing because he was the first. We killed five that day. The district officer gave us eight heifers for that. He told us we could kill the Mau Mau whenever they interfered. But that day put an end to Mau Mau around here."

Chief Sayo appeared in the doorway. He said he was passing through Narok and had recognized my Range-Rover. He stayed and had a beer, but he was on his way to a meeting. When he left, Naisiawua said, "That man is useless, a beggar, a bloodsucker."

Semoi said, "He should be cursed."

We drove back to Empaash and met Nanta at the *boma*. Chief Sayo had stopped there on the way back to Ngong. He was looking for Kintolel, but the boy was out herding cattle. To spite Nanta, he took two of her goats. "You're still my wife, so these animals are mine," he told her. But she was not very angry. She still had her son. "Sayo looked funny," she said, wrinkling her nose. "His pants were too short."

23

ῥΕΤΙΤΙΟΝ

IN JULY 1982, three hundred Maasai working in Nairobi signed a petition denouncing the bickering among Maasai politicians, held a meeting, and announced plans to set up a scholarship fund and initiate other tribal development projects. The organizer was Paul ole Lumet, a thirty-nine-year-old Maasai who was public-relations manager for the state-run Housing and Finance Corporation in Nairobi.

Shortly after the meeting, I went to see Lumet at his office to ask him about it. He told me he had studied journalism on a government scholarship at Leningrad State University in the 1960s, married a Russian woman and had two children by her. He was now divorced, but his ex-wife had remained in Kenya with the children. "That's modern life, right?" he said. He was wearing a well-cut business suit and acknowledged that although he had been raised in a traditional *boma* and felt proud to be a Maasai, he felt a stronger identity as a Kenyan. "I don't practice the culture much," he said. "I speak Maasai fluently, but my children don't know the language: that's about it. I don't have that blind affection for cattle. I look at cattle as property or *nyama* [meat]. I don't know why I am like that. Maybe because I went overseas. I have several classmates who returned to the bush after they finished their education. One went back to *boma* life after he went to Makerere University in Uganda. Most of them feel proud; they want to look after cattle. They don't want the problems of employment and the harassment of city life. The culture is very entrenched. I feel disappointed that the Maasai have not developed, and I feel an obligation to help."

The first meeting of Lumet's group was held at Oloitipitip's house and attracted one hundred Maasai. William ole Ntimama attended, but Tipis and Keen did not. Lumet showed me the minutes, which began: "The meeting took place in a very friendly atmosphere and with every speaker expressing his or her opinion without fear."

Various speakers outlined the major problems facing the Maasai. The poor performance of Maasai children on national exams was blamed on the teaching system. Too few Maasai teachers were assigned to primary schools. The teachers who worked at Maasai schools were often those who'd been rejected by other districts. Some of them "lacked discipline" and "a number are either always drunk or are involved in their own businesses or politics."

Other speakers brought up the Ntulele land dispute, the "alarming rate" of land selling in Kajiado and Narok districts, the need for more Maasai in influential positions in business and government, and the unchecked damage wildlife did to livestock and people in Maasailand. Oloitipitip assured the group that his energies were fully directed toward development. He offered to speak with President Moi and the other Maasai MPs.

The minutes ended with the group's pledge of loyalty to President Moi and the ruling party and with thanks to Moi for appointing Tipis to his cabinet as minister of state.

Almost immediately the group ran afoul of the politicians. John Keen accused it of being a front to build up support for Oloitipitip. Tipis, learning that Ntimama had attended, sided with Keen.

"We were very encouraged until we talked to the politicians," Lumet said gloomily. "If they could just stop their jealousy and infighting we could sponsor students—we would do a whole range of things. Naturally, they are threatened that a real leader might come out of this group."

Professor Maloiy had signed the petition and also attended the meeting, but he was not surprised by what had happened. "I think little is going to be achieved by all of us having a suspicious, negative attitude about the politicians," he told me. "But the fact is that we have leaders who do nothing. Two of the MPs are cabinet ministers, and they have commitments to problems in their own ministries. But even if they were willing to do something for the tribe, I wouldn't expect them to be able to do it alone. They need a group, like Lumet's, to advise them. For the most part, the politicians are uneducated. Oloitipitip can hardly read and write. He has helped us get some roads and schools. But most of the politicians are concerned only with building up their own wealth. They don't want a pressure group exposing their shortcomings. It's easy for them to say a group glorifies only one leader.

"Lumet's group was not the first of its kind. A while back we had a group that put out a newsletter. But—and maybe it is inherent in Maasai culture—a new thing comes along, and interest fades away. A lot of groups are full of idle talkers, so I don't waste my time with many of them. These so-called educated Maasai—guys working in Nairobi—will decide to meet at the Serena Hotel. They have a few drinks, discuss trivial issues—women and such—and then you get a call the following day, and they say, 'Oh, we really drank a lot the other night.' Nothing gets done. It's not a very optimistic situation. If a group of Kikuyu meet, they have a drink, but you can rest assured they are discussing important issues facing their community. A Luo friend said to me once jokingly, 'Maloiy, the only reason I tolerate your insults is because you belong to a dying tribe.' And he is probably right. If nothing is done, the Maasai are a dying tribe."

"Karen Blixen called them that," I said.

"And her house, which is now being turned into a museum, was built where a very famous Maasai *manyatta* once was."

"So what's the solution?"

"I don't see an immediate solution, except we need to develop leaders. We don't need idealistic types; we need practical people who can get us roads, water facilities and boarding schools. The ordinary woman in the *boma* doesn't care what goes on in the cabinet or the United Nations. She wants clean water. But so far the Maasai have not demanded this. They have never said, 'If you don't do this, it will be your last term in office.' "

I tried to make an appointment with Oloitipitip to discuss the future of Lumet's group. I sent several letters outlining my questions and made repeated telephone calls to his secretary, who was sympathetic and who finally said, "I think the problem is that the minister cannot read your letter very well, so he does not want to see you." I had no better luck with John Keen. Twice I showed up for appointments that were not kept. I was advised to try again, in a few months.

When I telephoned William ole Ntimama, he said he would be happy to talk and asked me to come right over to his Nairobi office. I asked him why the Maasai politicians showed so little concern for their people.

"It's a big pity, isn't it?" he said. "It seems that when the Maasai leave the *boma* and get a good position in government or business they lose their tribal identity. The only thing that keeps them in touch is if they visit the family on weekends. You know, Nairobi is so sweet, maybe if I didn't work in Narok on the county council, I would get lost too. I remember when some of us started out in politics in the 1950s—before Mau Mau. Other tribes were forming political groups, and some of the young Maasai men—me, Clement Torome, Oloitipitip, John Keen, Tipis—got together with the idea of protecting the tribal identity. We were all of the same age-set—Ilnyangusi. It means, 'those who capture for themselves,' which now seems appropriate. Oloitipitip was working in the local dispensary but still a cattleman. He was the best orator then. He really shone among all of us. He was even thin in those days. That is where my political consciousness was formed. I don't know what happened, but something went wrong. I don't know if it is 'the new life,' the money chase, Western values—certainly there is less love and respect in Maasailand today. We used to be a group-acting people. Today you see examples everywhere of how the Maasai no longer help each other. A fifth of Kenya's cattle comes from the Maasai—a third, if you count the Samburu. Here is a hell of a lot of potential, and nobody to organize it.

"The Maasai are so intelligent—I would say more naturally intelligent than the other tribes. The present leaders are threatened by the young Maasai. They appoint all sorts of rejects as chiefs and assistant chiefs to stay on the safe side. We don't have any go-go people. We haven't got a young Robert Kennedy or a Tom Mboya [a Luo leader who was assassinated] type. We were really clobbered by the British, and it clipped our wings. Maybe that's at the bottom of it. We were the toughest tribe, and we got beat. I don't think the tribe has recovered from it—the loss of land, the displacement, the reserves. Its spirit was hurt, and that got transferred to the children. At the first big defeat they went under, and they are still under. Before that, we were a highly organized society—governmentally, militarily, spiritually. We were a nation, but we were crushed. And now, to the government, we are just another small tribe."

24

NASORE

WITHIN A MONTH of moving to Empaash, Agnes had finished building her hut. The other women were impressed by its modern touches. It was more spacious than the others and was divided into two sections, with a small enclosure near the entrance where lambs and kids were kept. "We will circumcise Penina in there," Agnes said, as we inspected the cubbyhole. In the main compartment of the loaf-shaped hut you could almost stand up. There were two large sleeping berths covered with smooth hide and a cooking fire enclosed by three rocks. Agnes had brought a grill from Ngong on which she set a kettle to boil. Dug into the wall was a small shelf holding tin mugs, a tea strainer, and small cans of sugar and tea leaves. There was also a kerosene wick, brought from Saikeri, but no fuel, which was in short supply lately. I had seen long lines of women with jerry cans waiting to buy kerosene in Nairobi.

Sekento and I decided to drive to Narok to see if we could find any. Semoi and Naisiawua wanted to come along. "It's nice to get a change of scene," Naisiawua said. Between Empaash and Narok there was one gas station, which also had a snack bar. They were out of kerosene, so we bought sodas and sat down at one of the picnic tables. As we did, several zebra-striped minivans of tourists returning from the lodges at Maasai Mara pulled in, and the passengers all got out to stretch their legs and use the toilets. They were mostly white Americans. Some went into the rest room and immediately walked out grimacing. "God, it's disgusting," one woman said. Those waiting in line rummaged through their handbags for wads of hotel toilet paper. Another line formed at the snack bar. There were only warm sodas and old, grease-soaked boxes of sugar cookies. It was a hot day, and some of the tourists were dressed in shorts, T-shirts and halter tops that exposed soft pink midriffs. Semoi shook his head. "Now I know I am getting old," he said. "White people running around naked—this is too much for me!"

They all stole curious glances at Semoi and Naisiawua in their blankets and beads, but none of them sat at our table. Some climbed back into the vans with their snacks. Naisiawua stuck a pinch of snuff and soda ash under his lip and said, "Look how fat these people are—their legs rub together! If a lion chased them, they would have no chance."

The spectacle of the tourists seemed to stay with Semoi after we got back on the road. He lamented what he saw as a "change" in white people. "Now, they just wander around with no real purpose," he observed. "They don't seem as tough as before."

"They used to greet us," Naisiawua said. "But either they are a bit rude or too shy these days. When I was a senior moran, there was a white district officer from Magadi who used to come into the forest with us. The moran always drink a soup made with herbs—it is like smoking *bhang* [marijuana]. It makes you ready to act. That is why so many moran always get killed. The district officer was very interested in moran life, and he spoke Maasai. One time he took the soup with us. He became wild too! He even agreed to help us steal cattle. But when the soup wore off, he forgot everything. Sometimes he asked us to bring the soup to his house for his friends."

As we drove toward Narok, Naisiawua pointed out where the white settlers had farmed during colonial times. "We had three famous *wazungu* [whites] around here," he said, "Delamere, Cole and a younger one called Nasore. Some of our fathers worked for them as herders. These whites were respectful—they spoke our language and admired our customs. Nasore used to tell jokes that his mother was a Maasai, and that it would be a sin to steal his cattle. Most of the cattle we have today came from Delamere's stock. Some were given, some we stole, and some we bought. Delamere always had a fair price for the Maasai. He wouldn't sell to any other tribe. Nasore's farm was at Naivasha. He was the richest and kindest of them. Number two was Delamere, then Cole. We always invited them to our ceremonies. They liked to talk tough like moran. After Nasore died he was buried here—with a huge bull and his dog! We thought it was strange, but he was known to love both."

Nasore I identified as Gilbert Colvile, one of the first white settlers. I had read in accounts of colonial history of a dog—a pug named Peggy—buried at the foot of his grave.

Colvile had been one of a number of English aristocrats who settled in East Africa. His father was a professional soldier trained at Sandhurst who had fought in African campaigns up to the Boer War. After his father's death in a bicycle accident in 1907, Gilbert, who also attended Sandhurst but whose military career with the Grenadier Guards was cut short by a shooting accident in which he lost several fingers, moved with his mother to East Africa. Later he became a Rift Valley rancher along with Lord Delamere, the leader of the white settlers, and Delamere's brothers-in-law, Galbraith and Berkeley Cole—all of them old Etonians. They shared a common fascination with the Maasai.

Colvile, an oddball even by local standards, was reputedly mean, miserly and stubborn. He was among the richest men in Kenya Colony and owned five large cattle ranches, including his first, Ndabibi, a forty-thousand-acre spread near Lake Naivasha. He avoided the white social scene and was said to prefer the company of his Maasai herders. In the view of most whites, he "went native," an unflattering description at the time. He was careless about his personal appearance and lived, hermitlike, in grubby shacks. He hunted with a pack of mongrels, often in company with Maasai moran. He is said to have shot 250 lions and used their uncured skins to cover his walls. He sometimes set the plains ablaze for the sheer spectacle (following a Maasai practice of burning off pasture before the rains), and once burned down a neighbor's wildlife sanctuary on the suspicion that the man was harboring lions. Late in life, he married Diana Broughton, the colony's most glamorous femme fatale, who was twenty-five years his junior. She had been married to Colvile's Eton classmate Sir "Jock" Delves Broughton, another settler, who was tried and acquitted for the 1941 Nairobi murder of Josslyn Hay, the twenty-second Earl of Erroll, with whom she had been having an affair. Several years later, in England, Broughton committed suicide. The unsolved murder became the subject of James Fox's book *White Mischief*, and Colvile is among its nobler characters.

According to Fox, Colvile had been close friends with Erroll and took pity on Diana, who, after the trial, was left with few friends. They were an unlikely pair, yet the marriage lasted twelve years, during which time Colvile gave up some of his bush habits. For Diana he bought Erroll's Lake Naivasha mansion—the Djinn Palace. She called him "Pooey." After she left him—to marry Lord Delamere's son, Tom—Colvile returned to his reclusive ways and resumed his close ties with the Maasai. But he remained friendly with Diana and Tom. The pug, Peggy, was her gift to him. Colvile died in Nairobi in 1966 at the age of seventy-eight, leaving his full estate to Diana. She died in England in 1988.

James ole Torome, the old Maasai who spoke French, told me that Nasore had sponsored part of his education.

"The whites said he was mean and stingy," I told him.

"Not at all," he said. "He was very social with the Maasai, very in touch with our people. I think he liked the Maasai better than the British."

Nasore, I had read in colonial accounts, meant "the lean one."

Torome shook his head. "No, no, no—this name comes

from the verb *a-ng'asunore*," he said. "It means, 'to start out together,' or 'oneness.' "

"We called him 'the unifier,' " Noah's grandfather told me. "He was the first one who gave beer to the Maasai." During early colonial times, the Africans were not allowed to buy alcohol, as the authorities feared aggressive consequences.

"Nasore thought differently," Sane continued. "He said the Maasai should have the right to drink beer just like any other men, and he gave it to us free. Then I think he was selling it. Before, we had only beer we made with honey from local bees, and it was used when negotiating for marriage and at ceremonies. But it was only for the elders, and they drank only about once a month. The young men never drank. The women brewed the beer, but they never touched it. If there is anyone I blame for the drinking today, it is Nasore."

The first white man Sane ever saw was Lord Delamere. "There were white men, and there were Indians who came to Maasailand," he said. "But at first we could not tell the difference." Before his family left Kinangop, he remembered Delamere scouting the area, living in a tent and watching the *bomas* with field glasses.

I asked him how he knew it was the legendary Lord Delamere.

"Everyone knew Delamere," he said. "At first we thought he was a spy. Then he came to our *boma* and discussed cattle with my father and the elders. We didn't know what he was up to. Sometimes he brought other men, and they would ask questions about the land and write down all these things, especially what we said about how the cows did here. We didn't know the whites were going to settle here. But later we became friendly with some of them."

He met Colvile after his family moved into the Maasai reserve. "He showed up with a Swahili trader who translated for him," he remembered. "He brought beads and tried to be friendly with us. He was trying to decide whether to farm or raise cattle. He spoke with my father about it. When he stayed here, he hired Maasai herders. The elders opposed it very much when he gave beer to the young men. At first the beer was rare, and then it was every place. Now the men will sell cows to buy it. The Maasai did not know the effects of the beer. Without beer, we would have continued as we were. But the beer problem now is too difficult for the elders to solve."

Musei had worked at Galbraith Cole's thirty-thousand-acre ranch at Elmenteita for several years. In 1911, Cole fatally shot one of three Maasai he caught skinning one of his sheep. He was tried for manslaughter, was acquitted and subsequently deported. Two years later, when World War I broke out in East Africa, he sneaked back into Kenya and was allowed to stay. Musei said he did not remember the incident; his employment came later. "Three of us went to work for him," he said. "One was Sha's father. Cole taught Sha how to read and write Swahili, that is why he knows about development more than some of us. If you were a herdsman for Cole, the first year you got ten shillings a month. But it kept going up until you made forty shillings. Mostly you were paid in animals. You would have a card to keep track of how many cows you would be given when you left. One cow was then a hundred and forty shillings, so we got two or three for every year. But some of us got more. We also got *posho* [cornmeal], ghee, shoes and umbrellas."

"Umbrellas—for the rain?"

"For the sun." Musei chuckled. "Delamere and Cole told us we should use them when we were looking after the animals. We built a *boma* near the *wazungu* and kept our own animals, which our children looked after. We only talked to Cole and Delamere about animals. Delamere was very ugly to look at. Cole had a smaller brother. When the war came, his brother told us to wear white *shukas* so he would know who we were because Germans were coming to fight. I left Lord Cole when my father got very old and called me home. I got twenty-seven cows, which made up for all the cows we had lost to disease right before the *wazungu* came."

Until 1918, the Maasai were exempt from the native draft, though some worked as scouts for Lord Delamere.

Two months before World War I ended, the government decided to draft three hundred Purko moran, but they resisted the plan. *Askaris* were sent to Narok to arrest them, but the moran had fled to the forest. Without orders, the *askaris* opened fire in a village where some Maasai were staying, killing two women and ten cattle. Two other women, an old man and a moran were wounded. The Maasai went on a rampage, burning down more than fifty shops in Narok and the Mara district and murdering several Indian shop owners.

Noah's family had made arrangements with an old woman named Naseyo ene Punyua to circumcise his sister Penina. She came to the *boma* one day to discuss her fees. She had been in the circumcision business for years and told me she had once worked for Lord Delamere's wife. She couldn't say which Lady Delamere she had worked for. Delamere had married twice before his death in 1931. There was both wisdom and mockery in her eyes as she talked about the old days. Life, to her, was a repetitive cycle, and she had seen it all. She claimed to be the first Maasai woman to work for whites.

"It was an unusual thing," she said. "I was married very young, and my husband died soon after. I had only one baby, but he died. I didn't like to stay idle, so I went to look for work at Delamere's farm. I don't know why, but when I was a girl I wanted my own property. I just hated to be poor. My father was against it, but I did it anyway. My mother had a very bad life. Nobody can agree to suffer the way our mothers did. I was the only Maasai woman working at that farm. The first day the Maasai who managed the laborers said, 'You are a woman, what kind of job could you do?' And I said, 'Any job.' I was a bit young and good-looking then, so he helped me. They asked me to look after the dairy and not let anyone steal milk. I also gave injections to the cows that were sick. From the dairy I was shifted to the house, where I cleaned Delamere's office. The house was very nice, and when it rained, it never leaked. I was very interested in all this. When I worked in that house it was the first time I could stay clean and not be covered with smoke. I had a small wooden house, and I slept in a bed. I was paid a hundred and forty shillings every month, and I got free milk, cream, tea and sugar. I saved all my money. All the men liked to come to my house for tea because it was clean.

"The wife of Delamere was very nice to me. She bought me a dress and shoes from Nairobi. When I left, she told me to keep myself clean, to wear clothes of the correct size and length, to show respect, never to drink from a cup used by someone else without washing it, and to keep my house clean. She said when I had a visitor to let him sleep in the spare bed, not in my bed." The old woman shrieked with laughter recalling this.

"I had seventeen cows when I left Delamere," she continued. "I built a grass-thatched house, and I cultivated seven acres of land. This was extremely unusual for a Maasai, but people still liked me. Now I circumcise girls, which is easier work at my age. I was circumcised very young because my parents feared I would get pregnant. It was very painful. How would you like such a thing done to you! It would be much better to do it at a hospital where they inject you so you don't feel it. But the hospitals will only circumcise boys. So now it is my work, and I am expert. I started with my brother's daughters. I did it perfectly. Even Kikuyu ask me to do it, but it's a different thing for them. I don't have to cut so much away. The Kukuyu like it that way, but with them the practice is dying out. Today I would not be circumcised myself. We do it because it is a custom. I would like to see it stopped completely. But I make good money doing it."

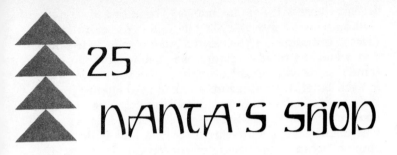

25
NANTA'S SHOP

NANTA HAD THOUGHT of a way to make money. The idea was to let tourists visit the *boma* and charge an admission fee. There were plenty of tourists passing by on their way to Maasai Mara, and it would be easy to flag them down. Mr. Sha could sell them sodas and beer.

"What do you think?" she asked.

"Are you serious?" I asked. "You really want strangers looking around your home?"

"And taking pictures?" Sekento added.

Nanta looked crushed and said we might be right. But she was desperate to make some money.

"Why don't you get together with the women around here and build a shop to sell beaded ornaments to tourists?" I suggested. Some Kikuyu had set up a kiosk at the Narok junction and started selling spears, shields and necklaces that they bought at cheap prices from the Maasai.

Mr. Sha said she could build the shop next to his bar. His wives could advise her. Sekento said his brother Richard, who was a commercial-art student, could paint a sign. We settled on a name: Maasai Women's Craft Shop. That would appeal to tourists. Mr. Sha calculated the building costs. He knew a carpenter who could do the job.

"But where will I get the money?" Nanta asked.

"You have to raise it," Mr. Sha said. "You can never succeed in business if you rely on other people." He said that when the satellite station was being built, he became friends with some Italians who had worked on the project. Later, they sent him a box of used clothes from Italy and asked if they could do anything else. "I remembered that the Italians were very religious, so we sent them a letter and asked if they would build us a church, because that would mean 'oneness,'" he said. "We thought they would like that idea, but we never heard from them again."

He suggested that some development-minded people in the area might invest in the project.

"I could ask my boyfriend at Euaso!" Nanta said.

When two of Nanta's uncles stopped by Empaash, she asked them to contribute to her building fund. They offered to give her two goats but told her she would have to collect them at Magadi, which was some hours' drive. Sekento and I agreed to take her there. We would drive her to Ngong, where she could spend the night in the hotel, and we would leave the next morning for Magadi.

Normally, Nanta did not bother much with her personal appearance. She was confident of her natural allure. But her uncles lived with her grandmother who had raised her as a girl. Nanta had not seen her in ten years, and she wanted to make a good impression. She borrowed a calico dress from one of Mr. Sha's wives, which she slipped on over her *shuka*, and she wore her son's black vinyl oxfords. Her daughter wore a dress several sizes too large. Nanta chattered the whole way to Ngong, expanding on her ideas for the shop. We left her at the Ngong Hills Hotel.

The next morning, when we picked her up, she looked exhausted. In the middle of the night two prostitutes had banged on her door and said the room was theirs. Then some drunken men came and told her to leave. She had looked for Tom Torome, the owner, but she couldn't find him, so she sat up all night in the lobby with her baby.

•   •

The plains around Magadi were like a desert. We pulled up to the *boma* in a swirl of dust. The grandmother burst into tears when she saw Nanta, hugged and kissed her, and took the baby into her arms. "I used to hold you just like this!" she said. Nanta asked how she was, and the old woman said, "I'm all right, still alive, but weak these days. I am unable to milk the cows, and eating is a problem. I just eat a little porridge. The problem here is drought and hunger. Sometimes I hardly sleep, especially when my sons are away."

The *boma* was a grouping of six lopsided, crusty huts. Nanta's grandmother asked us to come inside her hut, and some of the other women joined us.

"We have heard so much about you!" one of the women said to Nanta. "You are known everywhere!"

"My Nanta was very respectful when she was young," the old woman told us. "I was like her mother and even saw to her circumcision. We had a very close love. Now my whole body feels happy to see her."

Nanta enjoyed the attention and smoothed out the folds in her daughter's dress. The women looked at her wistfully. "There must be a lot of development where you stay," one of them said.

Nanta told them about her plans for the shop at Empaash and that the women at Saikeri were starting to cultivate the land. "And what about here—are you pushing on?" she asked.

"There's nothing happening here," one of the women said. "We just look after a few cattle and goats. Our children have no school. The young boys want to be moran. There is nothing else for them."

Another woman said, "I hate that. I don't want my son arrested for stealing cattle. We are backward around here. Nobody is learning to cultivate. The problem is water. The land is not very good, and nothing can grow. We could sell manure, but we have no roads for the trucks."

"We have problems with lions," another woman put in. "A man was attacked recently, but he survived. And we have leopards eating our goats. We report these things to the game wardens, but they do nothing. Mostly it is just women at this *boma*, and we are afraid these days to walk around with so many leopards in our area. When we are out, we always try to make a lot of noise to scare them off! The other day we saw a leopard"— the other women giggled, recalling it—"and we were all screaming and jumping and running back to the *boma!*"

Nanta told the women that two of her brother's cows had been killed by lions. Finally, she brought up the purpose of her visit: her uncles' promise of two goats. But her grandmother shook her head. "I would like to give you a goat, but the men have taken all the animals far away from this *boma*," she said. "We don't have anything to give you."

Nanta invited her grandmother to come live at Empaash, but the other women protested. "This old woman looks after our children!"

When we left, the women stood waving, and Nanta's grandmother shouted, "Don't forget us! Come back and visit again!"

Within a month Nanta had raised the money. Her boyfriend made the largest contribution, giving her an ox to sell. Her brother Tingisha sold some goats. Kindi, the other shopkeeper at Empaash, gave her money.

Mr. Sha brought the carpenter, a young Kikuyu, to discuss the building plans. Nanta insisted he come into her hut, which he did reluctantly. "Myself, I dislike these primitive places," he said. Nanta put a pot of water on the fire, added tea, milk, and sugar and let it boil. The hut was smoky and hot, and the carpenter wiped his watering eyes with his sleeve. We discussed the size of the shop and came up with a rough plan. Nanta said she wanted a cement floor and a metal roof. Mr. Sha offered his *matatu* to haul the building materials.

When the shop was almost completed, Nanta ran into unexpected problems with beads. Agnes said there were no beads for sale in Narok or at Euaso. We might find some in Nairobi, but they would be more expensive. There were two bead shops in Nairobi, both run by Indians. The Indians had brought glass beads to East Africa and introduced them to the Maasai. Before that, the Maasai wore ornaments made mostly from metal and leather.

We went into a little shop on River Road filled with Maasai women peering into the glass cabinets. But the selection was small. Agnes clucked her tongue. In her opinion, the beads were either too big or the wrong colors, and the prices shocked her.

The Indian shopkeeper, who said his family had been selling glass beads to the Maasai in Kenya for seventy-five years, confirmed a "bead crisis." It was not simply a matter of shortage—the government had recently banned their import. The beads, oddly enough, came from Czechoslovakia.

"It is a disaster," he said. "They are trying to drive us out of business."

"Who?"

"The government—the Africans." He saw it as an anti-Indian plot.

In the past two years the import duty and sales tax had gone up from 20 to 110 percent. Now the government was refusing to issue import licenses.

"It doesn't make sense," he said. "We have to pay in foreign currency, but the finished beadwork also brings in foreign currency since it is sold mostly to tourists. It is harassment—to drive us out of business and have Africans take over." He estimated that some forty-five hundred Kenyans—mostly Maasai—earned their living making beaded jewelry. He showed me a letter from the director of a craft cooperative in Kajiado which noted that the center could no longer supply its customers—mainly shops in Nairobi—and that eighty-five people, most of them Maasai women, had been laid off because of the bead shortage.

Nanta was discouraged by the news, but larger events were soon to put an even greater pall on her plans by driving away the tourists.

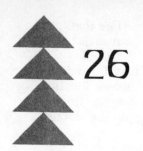

26

THE COUP

On Sunday, August 1, 1982, junior air force officers attempted to overthrow President Moi's government. It began early, before 4 A.M., with intermittent and sometimes heavy gunfire. I heard it at five o'clock—it sounded like firecrackers. Half awake, I wondered what the celebration was—maybe an Indian festival that had gone on all night—or it might have been a robbery. The police had shot some thieves on the golf course near us a few months before. But the rat-tat-tat grew louder and steadier, and it seemed to come from several directions. I switched on the radio to the state-run Voice of Kenya and heard a terse announcement in English that the government had been toppled. This was followed by some Bob Marley music. When the phone rang, I grabbed it. It was a friend calling from downtown. He said there were soldiers—army and air force men— fighting one another in the streets. He could see it from his apartment and . . . The phone went dead. The reggae music continued on the radio, then other announcements, but at that point still no clue as to whose coup this was. Students were instructed to take to the streets to show support for the "August 1st Revolution."

The rest of us were advised to "remain calm and stay indoors."

It seemed sound advice. The sound of heavy gunfire, utterly new to me, was unreal. Chuck was away. The watchman we employed had left. The phone remained dead; the electricity was off. There was nothing I could do. I made coffee on the gas stove, fed the cat and dog, and was careful to stay away from the windows. If the fighting reached my neighborhood—the vice president and the attorney general lived a few blocks away—I figured I would hide in the bathroom. I got out my motorcycle helmet for armor. It seemed funny later.

I could hear screams, gunfire and screeching tires on the other side of the valley at Pangani, the Indian shopping district. At seven-thirty the radio announcer said the Kenyan government was now in the hands of a People's Redemption Council. Police were told to change into civilian clothes; they were no longer law officers. Members of parliament were advised to hide for their own safety. Viennese waltzes were played with the distant rattle of automatic gunfire in the background. Then a loud volley, and the radio went dead.

From the kitchen window I looked out on several other houses, but there were no faces pressed to the glass. No one came out into his yard. The neighborhood was perfectly quiet, though I was certain no one was sleeping. At ten o'clock, radio transmission resumed with a brief announcement that army forces loyal to President Moi were now in charge and everything was "back to normal." Only there was still loud gunfire.

From the back deck of the house I watched looters—civilians and soldiers—crossing the forest, their arms loaded with booty. Some carried sacks on their heads. That afternoon, as the gunfire died down, three loud explosions rocked the neighborhood. Later, I learned that the wife of a German diplomat, who lived a few streets away, had been killed by a mortar shell that struck her patio. Two other shells had exploded across the street on the golf course.

By the end of the day, the major fighting was over. More than 250 people had been killed, including a Japanese tourist who had tried to film the street battles from his hotel window. President Moi came on the radio to assure the nation that he remained in control. A dusk-to-dawn curfew was declared. But the gunfire rattled sporadically throughout the evening and into the next day.

On Monday, in Nairobi, the body of an air force enlisted man was still lying outside the Ministry of Foreign Affairs as some Kenyans nervously returned to work. Some civilians were press-ganged to help collect bodies at an air force base, a few miles from our house, and rumors persisted of continuing troubles at another base in Nanyuki, a hundred miles north.

Grieving families gathered at the city mortuary to identify the dead and collect their bodies for burial. Shopkeepers grimly inspected the rubble of their shops. More than four hundred stores had been ransacked, and the downtown and suburban shopping districts looked as if a tornado had blown through. Shattered glass and debris littered sidewalks and streets. The shops owned by Indians were particularly hard hit; many Indian families had been attacked, and some badly beaten. In the Indian communities, destruction seemed as much a motive of the looters as greed. Telephones, light fixtures, even electricity meters were ripped off walls. What could not be carried away was destroyed. Books were shredded, family photographs crushed, furniture smashed, food spilled on the floors. It was African vengeance against the Indian merchant class.

Rebel threats continued to circulate. Jeeps, trucks and foot patrols of jittery police and soldiers combed the city. Africans without national identity cards were roughed up and arrested. Outbursts of gunfire sent pedestrians scrambling for shelter. A caretaker was shot dead looking out a twelfth-floor window of a downtown office building. The police swept through shantytowns, forcing residents to lie on the ground while shacks were searched for booty and rebels. Frightened looters left stolen goods piled along roads. Thousands of new shoes were laid out in pairs.

Four of the rebellion's leaders—including, curiously,

one Maasai—escaped by plane to Tanzania. The entire air force—some two thousand men—was disbanded. After a series of military trials, some of the leaders were eventually hanged.

In Ngong, the morning of the coup attempt, Sekento told me later, the Maasai were asking if the "new government" would pay higher prices for cattle. Apparently, they were prepared to go with the flow. A week earlier, I had arranged to meet Sekento in Ngong on Monday, and he told me he'd actually shown up at our meeting place after the coup, half expecting me. Instead, he was chased up the road by soldiers after some air force rebels were routed from a radio transmitter that was located near his *shamba*. During heavy fighting, the day before, one of his neighbors had been shot dead.

Chief Sayo had been in Ngong. "I was not afraid," he said. "I told people it would be better to die with this government than go along with a new one." At Saikeri, where Joseph had been, some of the Maasai had listened to the radio, but people were frightened. "There was no unity at all," he said. "People were ready to run for the hills."

At Empaash, Nanta saw soldiers passing her *boma* on the Narok road. The Maasai there assumed that Kikuyu were trying to take over the government. "We didn't like what we heard on the radio," Sekento's uncle Naisiawua said. "We thought a new government might be worse." The High Court was inundated with cases stemming from the coup attempt and looting, and the Meyoki family's land case was postponed.

It was also the end of Paul Lumet's development group. Gatherings of more than five people were banned. Professor Maloiy had driven the Narok MP, Justus ole Tipis, to the statehouse for protection the morning of the coup attempt, just hours before the minister of state's house was surrounded by rebel soldiers. "I told Tipis this was a time to really examine how the country was running, but he didn't seem to listen," Maloiy said.

A rumor circulated that President Moi, who had been at the town of Nakuru the morning of the coup, had been found by army men in a cornfield on his hands and knees begging for his life, not realizing the men had come to rescue him.

Thousands of tourists canceled vacation plans for Kenya. I sent a cable to my best friend in New York: "Just wanted to let you know I'm fine. Will be in touch soon." A week later she called. She had not heard about the trouble in Kenya and had been puzzled by my cable.

27

BARAZA

Two WEEKS after the failed coup, I took Noah to Empaash to check on his family and find out how preparations for the circumcision ceremony were going. As we drove there, Noah's eyes searched the sides of the road, looking for air force rebels who might still be hiding out in the bush, as the newspapers were reporting. But the drive was uneventful. There was virtually no traffic on the main roads; a night curfew was still in effect. I was curious to hear what more the Maasai had to say about the coup, but when we got to Empaash everybody except Semoi was gathered in the *boma* for some sort of meeting.

Mr. Sha told us that Semoi had gotten drunk the night before and attacked Agnes and Kipeno. The men in the *boma* had tried to separate them, and Tingisha had gone to the police.

"We are tired of these problems," Tingisha said. Agnes showed me her shoulder and arm, where Semoi had bitten and burned her. Kipeno's legs were bruised. "We gave him a chance to talk about it, but he refused," Mr. Sha explained. At first Noah looked ashamed, then he became angry, seeing the women's injuries. "This man—my father—should be jailed for a year!" he cried.

Kipeno said, "When the police came they didn't give

Agnes and me much time to talk about what happened. They just took him away. So now we are frightened. If our fathers and brothers say we must stay here and give this man another chance, we have no power. But I can't live like this."

We heard a truck pull up. The police had arrived with Semoi, who had spent the night in jail. Seeing the police Land-Rover, several elders came over from the bar. The two police officers proposed putting Semoi on trial—in the *boma*—to settle the matter for good. The elders agreed. The policemen told everyone to sit on the rocks.

"This will be our courtroom," one of them said and looked at Semoi. "Why is it that only your family has these quarrels and other men are not so harsh to their wives?"

Semoi remained stony-faced. No one else spoke. Finally, Semoi said the police had beaten him.

Nobody paid attention. "The only ones with bruises are your wives!" an elder shouted.

Agnes and Kipeno were asked to tell what had happened. An elder stood up and protested. "There is no reason for these women to speak; we have all witnessed what happened." But the policemen insisted. Agnes's voice was so soft they had to ask her to speak up. She said Semoi had come home drunk and told Kipeno to bring him some milk, but there was none. She and Kipeno were both inside the hut. Semoi started hitting Kipeno with his cattle stick. She ran outside screaming. Semoi grabbed a stick of wood from the fire and burned Agnes. When she tried to get away, he bit her shoulder, and she ran outside. Semoi followed and continued to try to hit the women and Penina with his stick. His blanket fell away, and he ran after them naked. The other men in the *boma* came to their assistance and held Semoi while Nanta's brother went to get the police.

One of the policemen spoke to Semoi. "This is a very serious charge. You have been a respected Maasai leader in your time, and now you are misbehaving. You have abused your wives and your daughter. You have taken off your clothes in front of children and acted in a shameful manner. You may misbehave in front of your wives, but not in front of children." Semoi stood up and said he wanted to bless the meeting. "Sit down!" the policeman shouted. "This is not a day for you to be blessing anyone. Today things are serious, and you should stand still and be firm and explain yourself. Everybody here is very angry at you."

Semoi said he wanted to divide the *boma* in half, his half and everybody else's. He said that would solve the problem.

"You have no power to do such a thing," Mr. Sha said.

"He is right," the policeman responded. "From now on this is Mr. Sha's *boma*. He is a responsible man who can be in charge."

An elder stood up and said he would like to speak on the subject of traditional Maasai law and the dividing of a *boma*. "The most important thing is that people in a *boma* must work together and help each other, not quarrel," he said. He looked squarely at Semoi, and pointed his club at him. "Are you the one who is making us meet here today? You—the age-group leader—have made everybody come and sit down here today when we have other things to do. And women are crying because of your troubling them. Did you not beat your family? Did you not beat all of them?"

Semoi said nothing.

"Tell us the mistake your family has made to make you beat them!" the elder cried.

Semoi said there were reasons, but they were personal.

"Yesterday this case was only before the *boma*," the elder told him. "But today members of the government are here. What more do you require to tell us the truth?"

Semoi remained mute. The policeman said if he didn't explain himself they would take him back to jail, or put him in Mathari Mental Hospital. "Women are human beings, you know," the policeman said. "Even if the women are your wives, you cannot abuse them like this. If you are unable to speak about this, we can say you are simply a madman who wants to kill people in his *boma*. I can assure you the doctors at Mathari will beat you until you are quite well!"

"I did not harm those women; it was a mere beating," Semoi said contritely.

Another elder called out. "Semoi is a great man, even

if you see him do such a thing." Other men shouted him down.

The police talked privately for a few minutes with Mr. Sha, Tingisha and the elders. They made two proposals: Semoi could pay a fine to the *boma*, or he could be taken to Mathari Mental Hospital. "What do you say?" they asked Semoi. He said he would pay the fine, and he got up and walked off by himself, out across the plains, not looking at his family.

"I hate him," Noah said. "They should lock him up."

"He is still your father," Agnes said. "Don't blame him for his illness."

28

EXAMS

In October, there were lions around Saikeri. A herdboy had been attacked while grazing sheep and had lost an arm. John, the Maasai with the Land-Rover, had taken him to the hospital, but he was in critical condition.

Joseph and three other schoolboys had run way from school on a lion hunt. It was not the first time, and the headmaster was threatening to expel them.

"The parents agreed with us that it was wrong for them to leave school," the headmaster said. "They said we should beat the boys in front of everyone. But I tell you, in their hearts those parents are proud to see boys hunting lions."

Joseph gave me his side of the story a few days after he had returned. A group of young moran had showed up at school late at night. They had a sword, a spear and a *shuka* for him, and told him he would be "finished" as a Maasai if he refused to come with them. Two boys from a lower class had already agreed to go. Noah was asked to come along, but he had flatly refused.

"There were ten of us who went," Joseph said. "I knew this was a bad mistake, but I saw no choice. We had no food or water, and we slept in the bush. We were shivering from the cold!" The next day they looked for lions but found none. The second day they reached Mount Suswa and found a male lion, but he escaped.

"That night we were very hungry," Joseph said. "We cut some bark off the trees and scraped the insides for something to eat. We kept saying we were very tough to carry on when we were so hungry."

Noah giggled hearing this.

The fourth day, some of the schoolboys, including Joseph, said they wanted to go home. But before the group could decide what to do, they met up with some older men who were delighted to learn of the lion hunt. They invited them to their *boma* and slaughtered a goat, and girls sang to them. But in the morning they agreed to give up. On the way back to Saikeri they found a lion making breakfast out of an eland, but they decided it was too dangerous to approach him in the middle of his meal.

"I thought moran never ran away from a lion," I said.

"These moran were not very experienced," Joseph replied.

As they got closer to Saikeri, Joseph began to worry that his father would beat him. He went instead to see Noah's grandfather. "I told him I was in trouble, and I had made a very bad mistake, and I was afraid of what my father would do." Sane sent a message to Joseph's father telling him not to beat the boy. "My father was told his hands would be broken if he tried to beat me," Joseph explained. "He could not go against what an elder said."

But the teachers and the headmaster were very annoyed. "They made us apologize in front of everybody. Then they said, 'You should be setting an example for the younger boys, and you act like fools instead. These moran are a thing of the past.' The teachers said we were working against civilization. But I told them we were taken by force! I don't want to be a moran, but I am not a coward either."

The headmaster called in the parents, who suggested beating as a punishment. But the headmaster believed a beating would be ineffective, and several elders agreed. "We have to do something to make those boys learn respect," one of the old men said. Some older moran came to the meeting and told the boys it was not their job to hunt lions. If they tried it again, the senior moran would see to their punishment.

Joseph was remorseful but worried. "These illiterate boys are still coming to ask me to go on a hunt with them. What will I tell them?"

"Tell them you are taking your C.P.E. exam in a few weeks, and you can't go," I said.

"They don't even know what that is!" he said.

The moran returned a week later, but Joseph did not go with them and somehow managed to salvage his reputation.

In the last week of November the primary school exam was given. An official from the Ministry of Education came to Saikeri in a Land-Rover with the exam papers. Chief Sayo was there with Sekento and the headmaster to supervise. The parents held a prayer meeting for their children's success. Then the six chosen boys—all with apprehensive faces—filed into the classroom to begin.

While I was waiting for Joseph and Noah, I went over to the dispensary to talk with Matthew Kivuva, the Kamba nurse who several months before had treated the men who were attacked by the lion.

"You've heard—President Moi has banned female circumcision," he said.

"I read about it."

"At least ten girls around here have been circumcised since the ban."

When Chief Sayo came in, I asked him how, since he was a government official, he would see to it that the president's edict was carried out.

"This is only rumor. They didn't ban it," he said.

"You mean you haven't heard?" Matthew asked.

"All I know is that the government wants us to keep our culture," the Chief said. "This practice will continue. What difference should female circumcision make? I have never seen a woman who was not circumcised. No one would marry such a girl! No, what we hear is only rumor."

· ·

When the boys emerged from the exam, they looked stunned. Some said they had not had time to answer all the questions. The man from the ministry drove off with the papers. It would be two months before the results were known.

"How was it?"

"Very terrible," Noah said.

"We never learned some of these things," Joseph added.

Sekento was grim. "A very tough exam," he said.

A week later, the Meyoki family was summoned to the High Court for judgment on the blind uncle's land case. I had gone with them a few weeks earlier for the final hearing. That day, Judge Todd, an elderly white wearing a wig and robes, heard evidence from both sides. He kept asking the court translator to write out the names of the Maasai on slips of paper. "I'm not used to these names," he apologized. "I don't have an ear for it." But he did listen closely to the testimony, yawning only once. The Meyoki family's witnesses included one government subchief and a former chief from Ngong who were inconsistent in recollecting details of the land-committee meeting some eleven years earlier at which the blind uncle's land had been transferred to his Kikuyu stepson. The stepson's lawyer, a distinguished Luo attorney with graying hair and an affected manner of speaking, produced documents that seemed to show that Njamba, the uncle, had sold the land fair and square to his client. Murungi Kiraitu, the young lawyer representing the Meyoki family, watched his case fall through.

The decision was issued on seven typed pages. Judge Todd found the chiefs' testimony false. He said that Njamba had surely known what he was doing all along, that he had been paid in full for his land, though the judge had found a small error of addition in the figures on the bill of sale, which appeared of no consequence. The case was dismissed, and the Meyoki family was held responsible for court costs and lawyers' fees.

Shokore could not believe it. Njamba was equally astounded.

"But your stepson proved in court that he paid you with money and cattle for the land," I said.

"It is normal when you raise a boy that he will give you money and cattle when he becomes a man," Njamba said. "But it does not mean he can take your land!"

I had no doubt the judgment was fair, but I felt sorry for Njamba. He was reasoning in terms of tribal law and tradition, relying on custom rather than modern law.

Joseph despaired of ever being circumcised.

29

SEMOI'S CEREMONY

DRIVING OUT to Empaash in early December, Sekento and I met Mr. Sha walking home from the satellite station. He flagged us down and immediately asked Sekento how his sister was. "Has she said anything about me?" he asked hopefully.

"She sends you her greetings," Sekento lied.

Mr. Sha said that Nanta's brother Tingisha had married a second wife the week before, and he had been the best man, but he had felt a little sad since his campaign to marry Janet was running into so much trouble.

Sekento asked Mr. Sha what he thought about the president's recent ban on female circumcision. "I can't believe such a thing!" he said. "Who would marry an uncircumcised girl?"

"My sister Janet is not circumcised," Sekento said.

Mr. Sha looked momentarily shocked but recovered. "Well, that is no problem; we will circumcise her when she gets here," he said.

Tingisha's new wife was a divorced woman named Tenket who had no children, and her father was rich. Her first husband mistreated her, and she had left him with her father's approval. Tingisha had given her father ten cows as well as new *shukas*, honey beer and blankets. Because Tenket had been previously married, her father did not escort her to her new *boma*. Instead Tingisha and Mr. Sha collected her and walked for four hours from her *boma* to theirs. Mr. Sha's children had cleared the bride's path of all stones and bones, in order to bring her luck. But Tingisha had run up a large debt that day at Mr. Sha's bar, where the men had celebrated. The other news, Mr. Sha said, was that two of his brothers had just been let out of jail, and we would meet them.

We stopped first at the bar. Semoi was sitting outside with some Somalis who were selling *miraa*, a narcotic leaf. If you chewed enough, it acted like a mild amphetamine. They asked us if we would like to buy some, but we declined.

Semoi was not drinking, but he was chewing leaves. He said he felt no effect and his jaws were tired. "It tastes very bitter," he said and spit it out.

The Somalis, in short-sleeved shirts and printed cloths wrapped around their legs like long skirts, said they were hoping to popularize leaf chewing among the Maasai and expand their market. They were also selling small bags of cloves and said if you chewed cloves after chewing *miraa*, you could sleep. Then they excused themselves, explaining they had business at one of the *bomas*.

"The Somalis are a tough, brave tribe, like us," Semoi said. "But sometimes they are selfish. Hindus and Somalis have the same problem with selfishness. They are very good at business. The Somalis are a bit better than the Indians, and once they settle around the Maasai, they are quite all right."

Across the road, at the *boma*, several of the women were on top of their huts with piles of cow dung, repairing the roofs. Agnes was building a second hut, where Noah would rest after his circumcision. She had just begun to plaster the frame, and Penina was helping. Other women were pegging a goat hide to the ground for drying. Noah would be circumcised on the goat hide. Kipeno was washing her baby in a puddle that had formed on the rocks. Tingisha introduced us to his new wife. She looked like a child standing next to him. Even for a Maasai, Tingisha was unusually tall and not very graceful. He said he had a "pain in his heart" from the love he felt for her. He was especially pleased about her father's wealth. Soon he would add more cows to his herd. The new wife said she was happy about the marriage because she already knew most of the women at the *boma*. Kilaso, the first wife, was the most delighted of all since "the little wife" would share her work.

Mr. Sha and the elders had decided that Semoi would not be permitted to buy beer at the *duka* anymore. "The reason for having that *baraza* was to make Semoi feel ashamed by bringing in everybody, even the women and children," he said. "We wanted him to suffer. No one can recommend him as a leader now. He acts as if nothing happened, and he still hasn't paid the fine to the *boma*. We have all lost our respect for him. If he interferes with the preparations for the children's circumcisions, then we will do this business ourselves."

He introduced us to his brothers, who planned to move into the *boma* with their wives. They had served a year in jail for beating up a Kikuyu who had killed five of their sheep on the road with his car. The car had been speeding, the brothers said, and the Kikuyu had failed to brake in time. When the man got out of his car, he screamed at them, "Why do you leave your animals on the road?" The brothers, thinking him "a bit proud," beat him with sticks and clubs, even though the man, at that point, offered to pay for the sheep. Some army men driving past broke up the fight. The brothers were arrested, tried, and sentenced to one year and eight months plus "some lashes," but they had been released early on good behavior.

"It was very bad in jail," one of them said. "We were the only Maasai. They made us work—carrying stones, building houses. We were beaten all the time with sticks, hands, shoes."

"We ate beans and *ugali* [cornmeal porridge], which we hate," the other brother said. "We couldn't talk to anyone. I felt defeated, but there was no way out."

"But now we are wearing trousers instead of *shukas*, and we have learned to build houses," the first brother said.

"But we are too poor to buy materials to make a proper house," the other brother said. Their wives were putting up new huts.

We were sitting in Agnes's hut with her and Kipeno and Mr. Sha. Agnes went outside to make sure Semoi was not around, listening. "Things have improved," she said. "Semoi is just staying home, and he is not drinking anymore. We are waiting to see what happens next. Kipeno and I have decided if he becomes violent we will both leave. We are still afraid that his aim is to kill us."

"Every night I hope he sleeps in your hut!" Kipeno said to Agnes.

Agnes laughed. "I think the same thing about you."

Mr. Sha had called in some men from his clan to oversee the circumcision ceremony. If Semoi made trouble, they would put him in jail until it was over. But first another ceremony had to be held to make Semoi an elder. The clan brothers were watching the moon, so they could pick a good day for the ritual. Until that was completed, the circumcisions could not be performed. The circumcisers had been hired. The elders and guests had been invited. Agnes and Kipeno had cleaned and repaired the beaded leather garments that they and Semoi would wear; necklaces were washed; ocher was crushed and pounded. The women had begun brewing beer to replace the batch Semoi had drunk. The loofah-shaped fruits of the *Kigelia africana* tree (the "sausage tree" it was called in Kenya) were set out on the roofs to dry. Later they would be mixed with water and honey and put aside to ferment.

Semoi came into the hut, sat down on a tin can, lit a cigarette and asked us if we would like something to eat. He looked tired and nervous. He showed us a piece of paper about a piece of land he'd been given. "Everything is quite all right here," he said. "The family is well; the animals are well. We have this new plot of land." But he said he didn't feel well and coughed.

Noah was home from school, looking after his father's cattle. He had been teaching Kintolel to write. Kintolel handed me a crumpled paper on which he had written "Charol," as he supposed my name must be written.

And he had written "Saitoti," which was Sekento's Maasai name. Noah said he had been killing small birds and stuffing them with dried grass. The birds would be attached to a frame—like a snowshoe—to make a headdress that he would wear following his circumcision. Agnes was working on a headdress made of chains and cowrie shells for Penina.

Noah and Penina had given away their childhood belongings—everything they owned—in a symbolic casting off of childhood. But their attitudes were entirely different. Noah looked forward to his initiation into manhood and the freedom and new respect it would bring him. For Penina, circumcision would mean the end of carefree days, moran boyfriends and parties.

I asked Penina if she was afraid of her circumcision.

"Yes, I fear it, but there is no choice," she said in a little whisper.

"She knows it has been done this way since the beginning," Agnes said.

"What is the reason for circumcising girls?" I asked.

"It was always done," Kipeno said.

"If somebody wanted to cut me like that, I'd want a better reason," I said.

The women laughed. "It is just normal," Agnes said. "Why do you keep asking us the same question?"

"Nobody ever really answers it," I said. "I just want to know why you do it."

"It was this way from the beginning," Agnes repeated. But after a pause, she added, "The truth is, we have the same problem. Nobody gave us the reason either. But you can't get married until you are circumcised."

Kipeno said, "Most girls are frightened before their circumcision because they think it might mean the end of them. You have to think about all the elder groups that were circumcised and survived, but you still worry you will die. The pain of giving birth is greater than that of circumcision. But these women who do the cutting are merciless. Myself, I could never do it! My father's sister did it for me. It was a business for her. My mother never talked to me about circumcision. I didn't dare ask her because I didn't want her to think I was a coward."

"The pain was not so bad for me because I fainted," Agnes said.

I asked Penina if she looked forward to marriage.

"No," she said, "I would like to remain as I am. I won't like to be beaten by my husband, and it will happen for sure."

"And what do you think about the man who will be your husband?"

"Nothing," she said. "I don't even know him except what he looks like."

The ceremony conferring full elderhood on Semoi was held in early December on the plains, under some trees, a mile from Mr. Sha's *duka*. Called Olkiteng Lorrbaa (Ox Wounds), it was a two-day purifying ritual by which a man's past misdeeds were forgiven and he was cleansed of evil and authorized to circumcise his children. The elders were hopeful this would be a second chance for Semoi.

A black ox had been smothered for the occasion, and the men divided up the tasks of butchering, chopping wood and building a fire. No women were permitted, but as I was a foreigner—regarded as a sort of neutral being—I was allowed to attend.

Semoi and his "best man" wore beaded leather capes, and their faces were painted with white chalk. Around his neck Semoi wore *isurutia*, coiled brass ornaments (actually women's earrings) that boys tied around their heads after circumcision as a symbol of "rebirth" and fertility.

The man who was to marry Penina had made most of the arrangements. He had contributed honey to make the traditional beer, had brought the sacrificial ox and new blankets for the important elders. A short, plump man with one clouded eye, he went about this cheerfully, eager to see the conclusion of the ceremony, after which Semoi might get on with the circumcisions, and he would be able to claim his bride.

Semoi was in good form, not drinking and enjoying himself. In keeping with the spirit of the ceremony, his problems were put aside and all grudges were dropped.

"When we complete this ceremony, I will be able to

retire, and my work will be only to circumcise all my children and to be asked for advice from my age-group," Semoi said. "They will consult me at home. Maybe in a few years we will be so developed that some will come in vehicles to see me. But our work as fathers is basically completed after circumcision."

I asked if Noah's grandfather would attend the ceremony, and Semoi said he was too old to travel so far.

Musei recalled how he and the other elders had selected Semoi as *olaiguenani*. To be chosen age-set leader, he said, a boy had to be known as brave, honest and a good speaker. But few boys campaigned for the job, as it meant giving up cattle raids and lion hunts. The job of *olaiguenani* was essentially to police his peers.

"It's a job that gives you headaches," Semoi said. "But my father warned me not to refuse it."

The Keekonyokie age-set leaders were often boys selected from the Teeka or Kurarru families. They were considered "pure Maasai" and held in high esteem. They did not intermarry with other sections and were known for their trustworthy character. Semoi was a Kurarru, and he had been aware he might be chosen. He was among a group of nine selected candidates, including Mr. Sha, who had been asked to speak before the elders.

"Some boys are so nervous before the elders they can hardly dare to stand or speak a word," Musei said. "But Semoi was not nervous at all. The other good speaker was Sha, but he only added to what Semoi had said."

I asked Semoi what he had talked about. "I spoke about our upcoming circumcisions and said it was important to carry out our traditions and respect the elders," he said. "I spoke from my heart."

The day he was chosen, Semoi was taken to the *oloiboni* for blessing. He was given a leather anklet, which he still wore, and a black club, which was symbolic of his authority. It was the club he had later thrown at the elders. Semoi did not mention the incident, and neither did we.

"The day after the blessing," Semoi continued, "all the moran came with spears; they were wearing lions' manes and ostrich feathers. Then, my hair was long, like yours. The moran lifted me up and carried me around the *manyatta*. I was calm. I told the old men I was ready to do what they wanted. The boy who was picked as my assistant ran away, and they had to bring him back. It was a big thing to be chosen *olaiguenani*. Even Dorobo and Kikuyu came to the ceremony to show respect. I was told to love everybody of every tribe. But I also felt confused. You are told to act like an elder. I didn't like that at first. But you are also given gifts and a good number of animals, special food at ceremonies, and respect. So there are two sides. Most of the time I traveled between the three big moran *manyattas*—at Nairragie-Enkare, Euaso and Kaputei. My work was to stay at each *manyatta* for maybe one month and see what was happening. If a cattle raid or lion hunt was held, I was consulted. But sometimes these moran were very clever; they would sneak out without informing me. The first year I wanted to be with the moran on cattle raids, getting fame from killing lions. But later I could see how some moran were killed, some killed other people, and it was a life of risk."

Naisiawua was listening and said his oldest son was pressuring him to let him become a moran, and he didn't know what to do.

"For me, being a moran was the best part of my life, and I don't want him to miss out on that," he said. "But I don't want him to go to jail for stealing cattle. We need to limit moranship, to maybe three years, so then every boy would have a taste."

Semoi said government officials had been consulting with the elders about abolishing moranship. There was talk of holding an early graduation for the current group. The moran of his group were so angry the last day of the graduation ceremony that when their mothers began packing up the donkeys to take them home, they accidentally broke a woman's leg. "Now I think it would be better if our boys went to school so they could catch up with other tribes," he said. "The moran used to be respected, but now other tribes think they are only criminals."

The elders were leaning up against tree trunks quietly talking, taking pinches of snuff, polishing their teeth with twigs, keeping watch on the roasting meat and savoring the smell of the barbecue. The younger men built a thornbush enclosure where the men would eat the meat. When it was ready, Semoi was blessed by Musei, then he and the "best man" ate from four separate pieces while the others watched. When everybody joined the feast, there was no more talking, just chewing.

The remaining meat was sent to the *boma* for the women and children. After a while the elders solemnly filed in to join the women and moran. Agnes and Kipeno, dressed in beaded leather skirts, stood outside greeting the men. The moran formed circles and began singing and dancing, leaping high in the air. When Noah and Kintolel returned with the cattle, they joined in. The girls, including Penina and her sister, Hannah, stood together, bobbing their shoulders and singing in high, clear voices, their eyes on the moran. Mr. Sha's wives, Nanta, and Kilaso joined the singing. Nanta pretended she was going to join the dancing, and the other women laughed and pulled her back as she tried to jump up like the moran. A skewer of meat had been reserved for a ritual fight between the men and women over the meat. The contest took place outside the *boma*. The meat was put down on the ground, and the men and women stood on opposite sides holding switches made from tree branches. When the signal was given, they charged toward the meat, one group whipping back the other. It was the only time women were allowed to beat men, and they took much pleasure in the flogging. Tingisha, who towered over the other men, ran from the women in mock fear. Noah cheered his mother and Kipeno. The girls jumped up and down with excitement. The women won, as tradition dictated. It was the first time I had seen Noah's family happy together.

30

CIRCUMCISION

THE DAY AFTER Christmas, Sekento and I went to Empaash for Noah's and Penina's circumcision ceremonies, arriving at the *boma* with a contingent of newly circumcised girls and boys in dark-charcoal *shukas*. The boys wore headdresses like Noah's with stuffed birds and spiral brass earrings tied around their heads. The metal chains of the girls' headpieces draped across their high foreheads. The group had come to lend support and encouragement to Noah and Penina.

The *boma* was already filled with guests, and more were streaming in. But there was no one from Saikeri. Circumcisions were large but local affairs. Joseph's father kept him home to look after the cattle.

Penina, her head shaved and wearing a beaded leather cape, was whispering with her girlfriends behind one of the huts. Noah wore a turquoise *shuka*, like a woman's, another fertility symbol, and the elders were outlining his feet with a knife on a piece of hide, cutting special sandals for him. His head was shaved, and he looked very solemn, his thoughts perhaps on the next morning, when the circumcisions would take place. I waved, but it did not seem fitting to interrupt or talk to him. Sekento and I, who stood out in our Western clothes, kept to the edges and observed.

Agnes and Kipeno were dressed in ceremonial finery, in leather capes and layers of necklaces. Semoi stood with them, wearing a long, beaded cape and smoking a cigarette. He carried a calabash of milk with fresh grass stuffed in the top, symbolic of peace and goodwill.

Agnes complained that some of the men were getting drunk across the road at Mr. Sha's bar. They seemed to prefer bottled beer to the traditional brew. Nanta was peeling potatoes and worrying about whether there would be enough food for everyone. Seven goats had been slaughtered, and she asked her brother if he thought the men should butcher a few more.

The moran, greased with red ocher for the occasion, had formed dance circles and were singing songs of self-praise. The Maasai have only one musical instrument, a long, curved kudu horn, which makes a sound like a trumpeting elephant and is used only at Eunoto, the warrior graduation ceremony. Drums and other instruments are cumbersome in a nomadic life. But the tribe has developed a unique style of singing. Today, girls and women joined in the chorus, but the moran were clearly in control. High-voiced soloists improvised over a chanting baritone chorus, while one section provided a bass beat, a deep-throated rhythmic panting, like a lion's cough. The dancers stepped forward, individually or in pairs. With straight backs they bent their knees slightly and jumped high. The best jumpers seemed to hover in the air, adding a shimmy or whipping their hair before they landed.

Semoi asked if we would like to meet the man who would circumcise Noah. He was a Dorobo, a member of a small hunting tribe that had a long association with the Maasai. In the past, the Dorobo, who were beekeepers, provided the Maasai with honey, and with smelted metal to make their spears and swords, a task too demeaning for the Maasai themselves. They also specialized in circumcisions.

This circumciser's name was Kesi. He was a short man with bright, feverish eyes; he was wearing a black-and-maroon-striped blanket, metal bracelets, two strings of beads around his neck, and metal earrings. We found him sitting on a rock, guarding his knife, which was wrapped in cloth. "So, you have come very far—perhaps from London—to talk with me?" he inquired. "Ask me whatever you like, because I am expert at this job." Semoi told us that Kesi's father had circumcised him. Kesi said he hoped his own son, though he was a schoolboy, would carry on the family tradition. He said he had performed more than a hundred circumcisions. "All of the boys were brave; none of them ran away." Sekento asked him how he was paid. "When I started, I was paid only in animals," Kesi said. "But nowadays it is more convenient to be paid in shillings."

If a boy had remained "clean," that is, had not slept with circumcised women, his family paid one hundred shillings—about six dollars. But if he had broken the sexual taboo, the price was one cow and up to six hundred shillings. Few boys failed to confess their transgressions, for fear a curse might cause the circumciser's knife to slip. Noah was "clean," Kesi said, and he had given Semoi a small discount because he was *olaiguenani*. These days, he said, there was growing competition in the circumcision business. "Some Maasai take their sons to clinics to be circumcised," he said. "It's cheaper, but I think it is very wrong to go against our traditional culture. At the clinic a nurse will wrap a boy's penis in a dressing after the circumcision, and who can be sure the thing was done properly? But with me you can see everything; you can be sure you are not cheated."

Kesi unwrapped his knife and used the cloth to polish the blade. "I have used this knife for twenty years," he said proudly. "It is very good for the job—hard and sharp."

Semoi handled the instrument, a seven-inch knife with a curved end, running his index finger along the blade, turning it over, examining the handle. "When I was circumcised, I told Kesi's father to make the blade of his knife dull—to crush it on stones—because I was ready and brave and could stand the pain," he said.

Kesi said he was very sure that Noah would not cry out. "Once I look a boy in the eye, I can tell immediately if he is brave or a coward," he said. "This boy is clean and brave."

• •

Semoi invited Kesi, Sekento and me inside his hut. Naisiawua was already inside, telling Agnes that his youngest wife was about to give birth. It would be his second child born that year. "It can happen any time now—even today!" he said. "The old women have been rubbing her stomach with fat. I don't know very much about their work, but I believe they know what they are doing. All my children have come out perfect." Agnes was cleaning a calabash with hot coals. The procedure of shaking hot coals inside the calabash gave Maasai milk a pleasant smoky taste.

Semoi showed us a basket of bottled beer and said it was only for us; we were not to share it with others. "Some of these guests are like dogs—they will eat and drink anything they see," he said. He himself did not feel well and did not want to drink. He asked if we would like to eat, but we declined. He told us his guests had given him nineteen cows and thirty sheep and goats. There would be more tomorrow, if Noah proved himself brave.

"Now you should know what to expect," he said to me. "When everyone is asleep tonight, Noah will leave the *boma*. That is our tradition. Then he will come back in the morning to face the knife."

Arriving guests stopped outside the hut and called in greetings, but the interruptions seemed to irritate Semoi. Agnes went outside. Semoi excused himself, saying he wanted to be alone for a while. Kesi watched him leave, then said, "Normally I spend the evening before a circumcision with the boy's father, negotiating the price, then just talking. Most fathers are quite calm the night before, but Semoi is not very calm."

Naisiawua defended Semoi. "No father can be completely calm the night before, not knowing if shame or greatness will fall on his family."

"No, I must disagree," Kesi said. "Semoi is not acting very normal." He opened a bottle of beer with his teeth. "I will drink until midnight, and then I must sleep, to be fresh for the job."

That evening, Naisiawua organized a singing contest between the newly circumcised boys and the uncircumcised boys. Penina and her girlfriends had disappeared. Naisiawua led the fight songs. At first they sang of the moran, naming those who were especially courageous and their deeds. They sang about lion hunts and cattle raids, meat-feasting camps and beautiful girls they had known. One group would sing until the others came up with another song that drowned them out. Then the newly circumcised boys sang songs of encouragement to Noah and to the other boys who had not yet succeeded in convincing their fathers to have them circumcised. The songs told them to be brave, but some of the songs were jesting, even insulting, suggesting that the younger boys were born cowards and would "run away" (flinch) or "kick" the circumciser's knife. This was meant to bolster their determination, and Noah and his friends sang back feisty songs, declaring their courage. The moon was nearly full, and the boys stood in a huddle in the silvery light, faces transfixed, the songs spilling out across the empty plains.

I slept that night in Kilaso's hut. Tingisha, who would be sleeping with his new wife, was worried about my safety and told me to fasten the door from the inside with a wire. The fire crackled and smoked. Kilaso fell asleep and snored. I pulled a blanket over my head to stop my eyes from watering. I could hear elders talking in other huts, and the cattle, sheep and goats moving around in the kraal. I drifted to sleep but was wakened several hours later by high-pitched screams. They sounded human. Kilaso also woke up but said it was nothing, just hyenas. My eyes felt swollen from the smoke. I fell asleep but woke up later when I heard a voice outside. I crept to the door with my flashlight, unfastened the wire and went quietly outside. Semoi was walking alone among the cattle, chanting, raising his hand and blessing them. He did not notice me. The stars were still bright, but the sky was streaked with orange as morning light began to gather at the horizon and behind the mountains.

Other men came out of their huts and joined Semoi. The women stayed inside while the men blessed their cattle sticks with cow's urine. No women would be allowed to watch the circumcision, but Musei joked that since I had long hair—like a moran—I could not be counted as female. The boys who had sung the night before formed a reception line on the rocks, watching for Noah. Kesi began his preparations, painting his face with white chalk. Semoi stood stiffly, not speaking to anyone. As the sky grew lighter, the boys and younger men rattled their cattle sticks and performed a frenzied storklike dance, some yelling out with emotion. The elders began pacing, predicting disaster. It would be a sad day, they said, as Noah would surely let down his family and the tribe. This was tradition, Sekento explained. Everyone prepared for the worst.

With a huge orange sun rising behind him, Noah appeared, first walking, then running toward the *boma*. The young men around me began to tremble, waving their cattle sticks and screaming. Noah ran past us, threw down his *shuka* and grabbed the goat hide on which he would be circumcised. Several men pinned him to the ground. An elder squatted behind him and supported his back. Kesi splashed his face with milk, then knelt down and held out the knife for everyone to see. The men drew in closer. I tried to imagine an American family gathered around a surgeon's table, watching a loved one's operation. Noah looked as if he were in a trance, his eyes closed, his arms limp. Kesi rang a small bell and began the cutting. Sekento flinched and turned away. Noah remained perfectly still. As blood poured from the wound, there was more frenzy. One boy began to jerk violently and cried out that if Noah was a coward he would take his place. The boy began hyperventilating and fell to the ground unconscious. Other boys followed, dropping one after another, overcome with emotion. The older men stood in a tight circle watching Noah's face for any trace of reaction, but his expression was placid. The cutting, following the Maasai practice by which the foreskin was loosened but not entirely removed, took several minutes, and when Kesi stood back to let the elders examine his work, he looked satisfied. Semoi, who had stood by silently, his lips pursed, splashed milk on the wound and hugged

Mr. Sha, Naisiawua and Musei. Then the men carried Noah, who remained motionless, to one of his mother's huts.

"Noah is a free man now," Sekento said. "The father can no longer dictate to him."

Mr. Sha and Musei took me outside the *boma* where the women had started milking the cows. Some men fastened a leather strap around an ox's neck and pulled it tight until the animal's eyes bulged and a large vein popped up. Then one of the men stood back a few feet and shot an arrow into the vein. The arrow had been blocked, so it did not go very deep, but only punctured the vein. The arrow was pulled out, and a calabash was used to catch the spurt of blood. When enough blood had been collected, one of the men put a lump of wet dung on the ox's neck to stop the bleeding. The blood, mixed with sour milk, was taken to Noah to drink.

The women, meanwhile, had planted a small olive sapling outside the hut where Noah was resting to symbolize the start of his new life.

Naseyo, the female circumciser, was painting her face with white chalk in preparation for Penina's surgery, which was next. She had taken off her floral-print dress and now wore a traditional *shuka* and a knit cap. The circumcision was to take place inside Agnes's other hut, as Agnes had planned it would, in the small, dark compartment where lambs and kids were normally kept. The night before, pans of water had been left outside on the roof to chill. The cold water, which was thought to act as a mild anesthetic, would be splashed on Penina. Two little girls got up on the roof and dug out a small hole to let in some light. Agnes told me to follow her inside the hut when Penina was taken in. "You have asked us so many questions about this thing, and now you can see for yourself," she said. There was none of the public drama that had surrounded Noah's circumcision. Most of the men were squeamish about female circumcision, and some had already drifted across the road to Mr. Sha's bar.

Unceremoniously, Kipeno and Nanta grabbed Penina

and took her inside. Agnes motioned me to follow. The women handled Penina roughly, which seemed to frighten her. They removed her *shuka* and laid her on the dirt floor. The hole in the roof let in only a small stream of dusty light. There were flies everywhere. The women held Penina by her shoulders, and pulled back her knees. Naseyo bent down, splashed her with cold water, and, using a curved razor, began the cutting. Penina screamed, "You are killing me! You are killing me!" The pain must have been stupendous. "Stop! Save me!" Her clitoris was sliced away, as were the outer lips of her vagina. Blood ran down her legs. I steadied myself against the wall and looked away. Penina continued to scream while the women shrieked with laughter. Finally, the cutting was over, though Penina continued to whimper, and her face was streaked with tears. Naseyo splashed the wound with milk, and then Penina was carried to a sleeping platform. "Are you all right?" I asked her. She could not speak. Outside, people were singing and dancing. The younger boys were serenading Noah, praising his courage. A second olive sapling was planted outside the hut, and guests stood naming their gifts to Penina—cows, sheep, goats. Naseyo, the circumciser, kissed me on the cheek. "Would you like to be next?" she asked. Then she winked and opened a bottle of beer with a can opener hung around her neck. A second ox was shot with an arrow, and the blood was collected for Penina. Agnes said she would also be given sheep fat to drink, as this would make her vomit and prevent infection. Two men smothered and slaughtered the sheep in the compartment where Penina's surgery had taken place. I stepped away quickly.

"Are you okay?" Sekento asked when I met him outside. "Your face is green."

The women invited me into Nanta's hut to celebrate the children's success. Agnes said, "You don't look well." I asked them why they had laughed at Penina's pain.

"It is normal," Agnes said. "We laugh; we should not be angry. There is no shortcut; it must be done. Every girl must pass that one way. This is our culture. We laugh because there is no other choice for a Maasai."

When we left that evening—the celebration would continue for another day—Sekento was very pleased, and drunk. "You know I could throw down these clothes any time and be a real Maasai," he said.

31

ISINYA

DURING MUCH of 1983, I was in New York on a writing assignment and visiting my family, and Sekento wrote to me regularly with news from Maasailand. In February I learned that three of the six boys at Saikeri, including Noah, had received passing marks on the C.P.E. examination. Joseph had failed. Sekento was optimistic that Noah and the two other boys would receive admission letters to secondary school. "We pray for good news!" he wrote and enclosed a newspaper article with the headline: "MOI BLASTS 'BIASED' C.P.E." The article said there had been wide failures on the primary school exam in rural districts, and the president, after reading through the exam, had described the questions as confusing. He asked how children from undeveloped areas could be expected to answer questions about cars when they might never have seen them. The article noted that 65 percent of the 350,000 children who had taken the exam that year would not find places in the overcrowded secondary schools.

I was sad to hear about Joseph's failure, but he had missed many more days of school than Noah. Sekento regarded the Saikeri results as a success. "The new senior class at Saikeri has ten boys, not a single girl, but at least we are growing in number due to the good results," he wrote. "We have added two new classrooms to the school, and Mary Sayo is teaching adult literacy. Chief Sayo agreed because the job keeps her away from Ngong. Joseph's mother is selling beer from her kiosk in Saikeri. Maybe it will keep the land sellers at home."

But there were problems around Kerarapon, where Sekento lived. A neighbor was stabbed to death as he was riding his bicycle to his mother's funeral. He had been stabbed six times and was found with his bicycle, three hundred shillings in his pocket and his watch still on his wrist. Apparently robbery was not the motive. Sekento said the man had been involved in a dispute over some land.

A month later there was another letter. "Good news—surprise!" Sekento wrote. "Joseph's father has paid school fees for him to attend a private secondary school near Ngong. This private school is all business. They don't care about exam results, only money. I don't know why Shokore agreed. Joseph is still pushing his father to circumcise him. Another boy who succeeded on the exam has been admitted to Dickson's school. No letter of admission for Noah or the other boy who passed. Semoi is not drinking, and he was here yesterday, promising to do something about Noah's education. He said he might send him to a private school, like Joseph. But Noah is at home herding animals. It seems to me Semoi is not very interested. It's been dry and dusty here, but—at last—we got diesel fuel for the borehole pump, so we have water. Land selling is still going on, but a little improved. The men who have title deeds will be eligible to get cattle loans, and that encourages them not to sell. Mary Sayo is pregnant. Joseph's mother is no longer selling beer, just staying home. We are busy planting at my place."

In late March another letter arrived. "Rain has started on time, very heavy. Saikeri is green, and everyone is rejoicing. The dam is overflowing. Noah wants to go to school. There is a chance he will go to Maasai High School—the private school near me. Nanta's son Kintolel is back at Saikeri herding Chief Sayo's animals.

Nanta is very angry, but what can she do? Kipeno has given birth to a second girl. Still a lot of robberies around here." Sekento's cousins' house, which was near his, had been burglarized. "Things are so bad the burglars bring trucks to haul away the cattle!"

"It's raining day and night," Sekento wrote in April. In fact, the ink in his letter was smeared. "I'm expecting Semoi to make a decision about school for Noah, but still no word." In May he wrote, "NEWS! Noah has been admitted to the same private school as Joseph. Joseph's father convinced Semoi. Chief Sayo has moved his wives to another *boma* because of quarrels with the Meyoki family. Sayo is opening a *duka* at the junction near the rifle range. (The place we always saw giraffes.) Dickson is studying for O levels, and he is now secretary of the Saikeri group ranch."

A letter from Noah arrived. It began, "The main aim of writing this letter is to let you know that I have been back to school because I know you will be very, very happy. You are greeted by everybody here, but they are remembering you very much like you are still here. The last thing is that my sister Penina has been taken to her husband. But on that day she cried and cried. I think you know that in our tribe we take marriage by force. My grandfather is having problems walking, but he greets you and says he will give you a goat when you come back. When is that? So now my pen is crying. My eyes are closing themselves. Please don't mind about my broken writing. I am improving. Joseph says hello. School work is tough."

"Very hot and dry here now, waiting for the short rains," Sekento wrote in September. "Three lions have been poisoned near Saikeri. Joseph left school to stay with the moran and is trying to convince his father to circumcise him. His father is drinking and selling more land. He still owes money to the lawyers. Noah still at school, but home on vacation." James ole Torome, the old man who spoke French, and Njamba, Joseph's blind uncle, had both died.

In October Sekento wrote it was still hot and dry with no rain, and sent the results of the general elections.

Stanley ole Oloitipitip had been reelected by a wide margin, despite the scandal surrounding his son's wedding. John Keen was voted out. Justus ole Tipis held on to his seat in Narok North, though riot police had to be called to the area to maintain peace. Some powerful friends of Tipis had convinced his rival, William ole Ntimama, to step down from the contest at the last minute, and President Moi had rewarded him with an appointment as chairman of the National Housing Corporation. Clement ole Torome, the bar owner at Ntulele and one of Ntimama's supporters, was dropped from the Narok county council. The range war at Ntulele was still unsettled, and a few more men had been killed.

"Semoi has refused to let Noah return to school following vacation," Sekento wrote a few weeks later. "No school fees. He is doing practically nothing, just herding. Joseph says he is tired of being a moran and wants to return to school, but his father is broke. Inflation is the problem now. Food is expensive. Teachers at Saikeri have not been paid for two months. Two have run away. The borehole pump is not working. No money for diesel fuel. Since the drought began, the men at Saikeri have been dipping cattle on credit. Usually they pay, and the money goes for fuel. The women at Saikeri were given their first government loan to buy cattle, and the husbands were told they would be jailed if they interfered. Mary Sayo gave birth to a girl. She is still teaching the literacy class here. Sane is okay, but very old. I saw Nanta in Ngong. Her boyfriend at Euaso was elected a councillor. She was worried about you. She said she had heard a rumor of a war in America! She was afraid you had been killed! Are you coming back?"

When I returned to Kenya in November, Sane gave me the goat he had promised and asked me if I would take him to see Semoi. He had sent repeated messages to Empaash and got no response. His eldest wife—Semoi's mother—had run away and not been seen for two weeks. It was not the first time she'd wandered off, but she had never stayed away so long. The family was becoming impatient with her senility and unexplained dis-

appearances. Throughout her life she had been forget-
ful, Sane said, prone to fainting spells and unpredictable
fits of anger. He was afraid she had got lost, or even
died, alone in the bush. She could have been eaten by a
lion. He did not feel strong enough to go look for her by
himself.

"There's no love and respect left for old people," he
complained, when no one in the *boma* would help
search for her. "My children play with me like I am
the foolish old grandfather." In fact, his son-in-law
Musanka had gone to look for her, but he had given up.

The old man had other reasons to see Semoi. He
wanted to see for himself if it was true that Semoi had
stopped drinking. He also wanted to talk with him about
some matters of inheritance. Sane was not as frightened
of his death as he had been when I first met him. His
nightmares had stopped, and his dreams took on a more
fantastic quality. "I dreamed that the Maasai were
number one," he said. "We were in charge of the world,
and everyone else was crawling around like hyenas! The
Kikuyu were just small ants that we could step on."

I took him to Empaash, and when he saw Semoi, the
first thing he told him was that he needed a haircut.
But the visit was a success. Sane spent the night. He said
that he and Semoi had stayed awake talking. Sane was
so happy about Semoi's sobriety he almost forgot about
his wife. When he got back to Saikeri, she had returned,
but she couldn't remember where she had been. She was
sitting outside her hut, muttering, making mud pies
from cow dung.

On my next visit to Empaash, Nanta was eager to fill
me in on what was really going on with Semoi. "He is
not as cured as people think," she said. "He is acting
very strange these days."

Semoi was sitting up on the rocks, by himself, and
seemed not to notice us. He was not drinking, or abusing
his wives, but Nanta pointed to her head to indicate she
thought he was crazy.

"He says he hears voices," Kipeno told me later.

"He hardly eats," Agnes said.

The women were also worried about Noah. He had lost weight and was bored staying at home looking after the animals. Agnes thought he should go back to school so that he could eventually get a job and help the family with money. "Every year our lives get worse and more cattle die," she said. She had decided to sell some necklaces to raise money for school fees.

Joseph was also at home, still trying to convince his father to circumcise him. Shokore paid no attention. When I suggested that Joseph return to school, Shokore said he had no objections, as long as I paid for it. It annoyed me. I couldn't force him to sell cows to pay for school fees—or even to be concerned about his son's future. When I tried to discuss it he said, "I'm tired of talking about this, take my boy to America, put him in school—do whatever you want."

Sekento and I tried to figure out how to get the boys in school. Sekento ruled out private schools. The teachers were often unqualified and frequently absent. Noah told us that his English teacher at the private school he and Joseph had attended could hardly read, and some of the girls had become pregnant after sleeping with their teachers. What Joseph and Noah needed, we agreed, were job skills—a vocational school. There were several possibilities for Noah, but Joseph's case was harder. The low mark on his C.P.E. exam narrowed his options. A student who failed his exam was simply tossed out of the system.

Sekento was still puzzled by Joseph's low score, since he had made up the work he had missed during school absences. The headmaster offered him the unusual chance to repeat, but he refused. I called the Ministry of Education for information about vocational schools. Sekento had heard the government was setting up job-training centers called "village polytechnics" in some rural areas, but nobody at the ministry had heard of them.

When, after a dozen frustrating calls, I still had not found anyone who knew the location of these schools, I began to doubt their existence. Finally a pleasant woman with whom I had talked several times on the telephone called back to tell me that the village polytechnics fell under the jurisdiction of Oloitipitip's Ministry of Culture and Social Services.

I made an appointment with an education officer and told Joseph to meet me in Nairobi for the interview. He showed up in a ripped vinyl jacket that I had never seen before, shoes with no laces, and ragged, muddy trousers.

"There's no water at home," he explained. But I knew it was more than the start of a drought. Joseph seemed depressed. The idea of learning a trade was not very appealing, and he was afraid that if he went away to school he would never be circumcised.

During the interview, Joseph slouched in his chair and hardly said a word. The education officer eyed him suspiciously and suggested to me that "some boys will take advantage of a person like yourself." He said the village polytechnics were open only to students who lived in the areas where they were located, and he did not know of any such schools in Maasailand.

"So what do the Maasai do?"

"You know, we are not a rich country," he said. "Maybe you can put him in a private secondary school."

I took Noah to Maasai Technical School in Kajiado, about an hour's drive from Nairobi, to speak with the headmaster. The school was the only one in the country that served the Maasai exclusively, but it took a high C.P.E. mark to get in. Driving out there, I gave Noah a pep talk. "Don't be shy. You have to speak up, act interested."

"But I am interested!" he said, offended. Noah had on a clean shirt, slacks and a sweater. He had even brought a notebook and pen. I apologized and told him about Joseph's interview. "Joseph is just very confused these days," he said.

The headmaster looked at Noah's grades and put him on a waiting list but warned us it might be a year or more before there would be a place. Noah was jubilant when we left.

"Even if it takes a year, it is worth it," he said.

Two weeks later, the government announced that Maasai Technical School would be opened the following year to all tribes on a competitive basis. I called the headmaster. He said it was unfortunate, but he would not be able to consider Noah. "I think we will be able to call this Kikuyu Technical School in a year," he said.

Dickson told me about Isinya Maasai Rural Training Center, a vocational school founded by missionaries that was also near Kajiado. Joseph, Noah and I drove out there. The small cement buildings of the school were freshly painted and bougainvillea was planted at the gateway. An affiliated primary school operated next door, and there was a dispensary, a post office and a craft workshop.

"This is a wonderful place!" Noah said. Even Joseph showed interest.

The school manager was a Kikuyu, as were most of the staff. But the aim was Maasai development. The school was funded by churches, the government and foreign aid. I wondered why no one had directed the boys here sooner. The tuition fees were low, a fraction of what a private secondary school would cost.

"So, you have fallen down on your C.P.E. exam," the school manager said to Joseph after studying the boys' school records. "You are lucky that we are going to give you another chance to prove you are tough."

"You mean we can come here?" Joseph asked.

The manager nodded.

"For sure?" Noah said.

The manager read off the courses. There was a tannery, a bead project (involving local Maasai women), and courses on agriculture, ranch management, masonry, carpentry and auto mechanics. Joseph perked up and said he would like to study auto mechanics. Noah thought for a minute and said he would too. The headmaster gave me a list of what they would need: school uniforms, mattresses, cooking utensils, kerosene cookers and food—rice, cornmeal and cocoa were among the suggested items. We went to the school outfitter's shop in Nairobi and bought black trousers and blue sweaters, socks, shoes, athletic shoes, shorts and T-shirts. The trousers were marked and hemmed while we waited, and the boys stood in front of a full-length mirror admiring themselves. The Indian shopkeeper wrapped everything in paper and tied each package with a string. Joseph and Noah proudly and incredulously carried their packages to the car. They had never owned so many clothes before. When we went to River Road, where foam mattresses, storage trunks and cooking utensils could be bargained for, the boys told me to wait in the car while they went in to negotiate. "They will ask *mzungu* prices if they see you," Joseph said.

The school dorms were narrow cement barracks with bunk beds. One of the older boys who helped Joseph and Noah unload their trunks told them to get padlocks. "There are a few thieves around here," he warned. In a few days the boys had settled in, studying English, business accounting, auto mechanics and something called "animal health," which they especially liked. There was a girls' secondary school nearby, and dances once a month. One of the girls gave Noah a heart-shaped locket. Almost immediately there were happy letters from Noah. "The work is very, very tough, but we are working hard and pushing on," he wrote. "We are learning to cook our own food. But some boys here are criminals. The teachers found them smoking *bhang* and now the parents are informed." The teachers had told some older boys to tutor Joseph and Noah, since they had been out of school for a year, but they agreed only after Noah bought them cigarettes. There were more problems. The "criminals" stole their can of kerosene. Some of Noah's things disappeared from the clothesline. The headmaster moved them to another dorm, closer to the staff housing. On Noah's first report card the teacher wrote, "He is good at his trade. Above average. Conduct very good. Keep it up!" Joseph's said, "Improve in your trade. Below average. Conduct very good, but work hard next time."

Again, Sekento and I were baffled by Joseph.

Visiting one day, I asked where the cars or trucks they worked on were. They pointed to an old tractor. "That is the only vehicle they have," Noah said. Because of the shortage of vehicles, they had not yet learned to drive.

Nonetheless, they began to discuss engines in a knowledgeable way. Noah listened to my truck and told me I had dirt in my carburetor line. "We learned about it this week," he said. "Next week I will be able to fix it."

"Maybe we will have a puncture!" Joseph said hopefully.

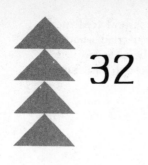

32

MEDICAL TRAINING CENTER

DICKSON PASSED his O levels with high marks in science and several months later was accepted into a two-year medical training program at Machakos Hospital, forty miles outside Nairobi. "This is perfect," he said the day I brought the acceptance letter to his father's *boma*. It had been sent to me since Dickson had no mailing address; he was to start school in six weeks. Since his exams, he had been with the moran. He was wearing a *shuka* and had let his hair grow. His best friend, Runges, a senior moran, did not look very happy when Dickson translated the news for him.

"The strangest thing happened," Dickson said. "My father called me home from the forest and told me he wants me to continue my education. He wants me to leave the moran! That's good, but now I have mixed feelings. I can't explain it. I told Runges to tell the others that I was leaving. I couldn't do it myself. I knew they would object. But I wanted to hear their views. So after he told them, we made a camp and sat around the fire and argued about it all night. They said I was abandoning them, that I had already stayed away for so many years. I felt bad, like I was doing something wrong."

"You mean you want to stay home?"

"No, I guess these are just longings for a life that heads nowhere. It's hard to give it up and become a common person like everybody else. I told my father I had cleared everything with the moran. He was happy, but he hasn't told the elders how he feels. He told me to keep it a secret between us."

At home Dickson observed the rules of moranship, one of which was not drinking milk from his family's cows. As part of his promotion to junior elderhood, his father was planning a milk-drinking ceremony that would relieve him of the restriction. But as the day for this ceremony came nearer, Dickson became increasingly nervous. "I can hardly sleep," he told me. "I have dreams of a lion marching toward me."

The morning of the ceremony, there was steady gunfire from the rifle range where the army men were in camp. Dickson's ceremony was to be combined with the circumcision of a male cousin. Just before noon, when the circumcision was to start, Joseph, who had come home from school to badger his father about his own circumcision, arrived with a sergeant major and some younger soldiers from the rifle range who were curious to see a Maasai ceremony. They were in uniform—heavy black boots with camouflage suits.

The circumciser changed from a green sweater and khaki shorts into a *shuka* and a fluffy sheepskin hat. He circled his eyes with white chalk. Some children had been watching him apply his makeup, and when he finished, he growled and playfully brandished his knife in their direction. They ran away screaming.

The soldiers watched with bewilderment as the moran began whooping, trembling and falling to the ground. When the circumcision was over, Dickson's father had to be restrained from fighting with another old man. The father refused to believe the boy had not let down the family. And then, when he was assured, he hugged all the other old men. By then, a half dozen warriors lay writhing on the ground.

"This is normal," I explained to the soldiers. "They get very emotional about circumcisions."

"They are proud. They feel something here," Joseph

said, putting his hand over his heart. "This is a big day, to see if this boy will be brave. If he had failed, this family could be ruined."

I heard a sound, almost like a braying donkey, and turned around to see Dickson howling. He was shaking uncontrollably, hopping up and down and, as if in a trance, completely unaware of us. He collapsed and lay rigid on the ground. His jaws clenched, and all the muscles in his body contracted. The women hovered over him, massaging his legs, speaking softly, but his eyes remained shut. Other boys were carried into the shade and began to revive. But when the women tried to lift Dickson he was like a deadweight. His mother glared at the soldiers, who had moved in for closer inspection, and sharply told them to step back. They meekly withdrew. Finally, a little girl was brought over and sat primly on his legs. Dickson slowly regained consciousness, stood up, angrily threw his *shuka* to the ground, and dashed naked across the plains.

"These Maasai are very queer," the sergeant major said.

That evening, Dickson's family gathered inside his mother's hut for the milk-drinking ceremony. "My son, drink the milk, and I promise you will be great afterwards," Dickson's father said to him. Four elders and two moran, one of them Runges, took part in the ritual. Dickson was trembling, and his friend tried to calm him. The senior elder drank the honey beer, spat on his chest and into the fire as a blessing, and held the gourd of sour milk up to Dickson's mouth. He pushed it away, as was the custom, first demanding gifts of livestock as a bribe. The guests and his parents named their gifts— two heifers, a ram, several goats—and Dickson reluctantly drank the milk. His mother sobbed. The elders washed his face with fresh milk. A pair of cattle sticks was given to him, symbolizing his new status, but first they were rubbed with cow dung and washed in cow's urine, honey beer and milk. This ritual insured that he would have many cattle, many children and general good luck in life. That night Dickson slept alone in his mother's bed. In the morning his mother shaved his head, and he was sent to graze the cattle. Runges and his friend returned to the forest alone.

The day Dickson was to enroll for training at Machakos Hospital he met me wearing school clothes, a felt hat over his bald head, and wide, beaded bracelets on each wrist. His mother and another woman hauled his school trunks on their backs and struggled to lift them into the truck. Dickson gazed across the valley, as if he might never see it again quite the same way.

"Why don't you help them," I suggested.

"That is women's work," he said.

At the hospital, the housemother registering students stared at Dickson's hat, offended by his impoliteness at not removing it. He told her the reason. "Well, I'm sure your hair will grow back to normal," she said, trying to make him feel better. She admired his bracelets and seemed happy to meet a Maasai. She showed us the dorm, a barracks crowded with twenty metal beds, and left us to look around on our own.

The training center was a two-story brick building, recently built. Some of the students were playing volleyball. But the hospital was old and run-down. The wards were long sheds, and some beds had been set up outdoors. Laundered sheets were spread out to dry on the grass. The psychiatric patients were also outdoors, in a fenced pen. Apparently drugged, they huddled together, some of them asleep. One woman sat alone, rocking back and forth, yelling gibberish at visitors. It was like a zoo; everyone, including us, stopped to gawk. The cafeteria was filthy. It was past lunchtime, but the tables, though cleared of plates, were mysteriously strewn with food, mostly potatoes. I could see Dickson's spirits sagging. The place gave me the creeps, and I was glad to leave.

At first, Dickson enjoyed his studies, but as the months went by he became disillusioned, telling me about male nurses striking patients who complained, and showing me a newspaper article about four dead babies found in a rubbish pit at the hospital. Earlier, a severed hand had been found in the same pit, and the garbagemen threatened to go on strike if any more dead bodies were found. The article described how a municipal council employee was "guarding the bodies from dogs and birds of prey, which were hovering above. The mutilated bodies lay in blood-bathed bandages at the corner of the pit with swarms of flies on them." There was no explanation.

A few days later Dickson quit the program, and began filling out applications to engineering school.

33

DROUGHT

DRIVING TO Saikeri in May 1984, I saw a bushbuck stagger and fall down, unable to get up. Most of the game had left the plains, but this antelope seemed to have been left behind, too weak to follow the others. It had not rained for several months, and many of the *bomas* were empty; the Maasai had started to migrate, looking for pasture and water for their weakened cattle. Joseph's father had already lost eighteen cows. He watched them die, refusing to sell them to the Kenya Meat Commission before it was too late. The women had been given seventy cattle through a government loan program, and thirty of them had also died.

Church relief workers began distributing milk powder and yellow cornmeal donated by the United States. The Maasai did not like the taste of the milk powder and tried to sell it. They were suspicious of the yellow cornmeal, being accustomed to a white variety. A rumor spread that the yellow meal was pig feed, unfit for humans. When I explained that yellow corn was preferred over white in America, no one believed me. If Americans liked it so much, why were they giving it away?

At Saikeri, school attendance plummeted. Only four of the thirty-five students in Sekento's class were attending regularly. He said the children were too hungry to concentrate on schoolwork.

I met Chief Sayo's son Kintolel in Saikeri, looking after cattle, and he gave me an ostrich egg he had found as a present. He said he had returned to his father to plead with him to have him circumcised, but had no luck. "My father is not interested in his family," he said. "All the time I have been here he is drinking and quarreling, and the elders had to stop him from beating me. I don't ask him why he tortures me this way. I know he hates me because of my mother, but it seems he is trying to ruin my life. While I am looking after his animals, all my friends have been circumcised and go to school. I would be very willing to go to school, but it is impossible. My mother has no one else to help her. I am going to ask my mother and uncle to go ahead with my circumcision without him. It is best to get it over with."

Noah was robbed a second time at school. The lock on his trunk was cut, and fifty shillings and some of his cooking pans were stolen. He was told this was a kind of "tradition." Right before graduation, the older boys always stole from the younger ones. It was not good form to make a fuss about it. He had also been in a bus accident in which several other boys had been injured.

A week later Sekento called with more bad news. "Naisiawua is dead from anthrax. His son came this afternoon to tell us. The whole family got sick. The boy said they ate a cow that had died. It must have been diseased. One of the children went for help, and Mr. Sha had his driver take them to the hospital. He tried to convince my uncle to go with them, but he refused, and nobody could force him. Everybody else got penicillin, and they're all right."

Sekento and his father were going to Empaash to visit the family. But Sekento was afraid they would be the last family members to pay respects. Naisiawua had two other brothers who lived at Euaso. But it turned out those brothers did not come at all. "You know how the old Maasai are," Sekento said later. "They say when you die, you're finished, and everybody carries on with their business."

One of Naisiawua's sons, who was about twelve years old, was staying with Sekento. He showed me a metal ring that was too big for his finger. "The day my father died he told me to get in bed with him, and he took this off and gave it to me," he said, staring at the ring and blinking back tears.

Joseph was finally circumcised. Shokore had postponed the ceremony so many times that neighbors who had loaned the family their calabashes to brew honey beer were demanding them back. The elders had berated him for the delay, shaming him into action. But Shokore was well known for procrastination. Shortly before he died, Naisiawua had told me a story about Shokore having killed a man when he was a moran, in an argument over water rights. The elders heard the case, and Shokore was told to pay forty-nine cows to the dead man's family, the standard fine for murder. This killing happened some forty years before. Shokore had still not paid the debt, but nobody had forgotten it. Naisiawua said the dead man's relatives might try to put a curse on Shokore's sons, or even his grandsons.

Because of the drought, Joseph's circumcision ceremony was a small, subdued affair. The moran danced in the *boma*, but the festivities were less frenzied than usual. People looked dirty and tired. The night before, I camped out in a tent next to the *boma*. A full moon cast an eerie, metallic light on the plains. I lay awake, listening to hyenas and the singing coming from the *boma*. But I kept thinking about Naisiawua, remembering his cheerfulness, his delight the day we brought Sekento's father to visit, his plans to build a *duka* and his desire to see his younger children educated. So why had he refused to go to the hospital?

Joseph did not flinch under the circumciser's knife. Nor did his younger brother, Tareu, who was also circumcised. Shokore looked relieved, his duty done. But there was none of the usual tumult or drunken cheer among his cronies. Some of the boys were yawning, because they had stayed up all night singing and dancing. The elders selected an ox from which to draw blood.

After several tries at darting a vein, the men gave up—it was as if the ox had no blood to spare. Another animal was selected, but I could not bear to watch. The old men sat together nursing their hangovers. The morning sun was already hot. The young boys prodded the cattle to take them out to look for water and grass, but some of the animals had to be tugged to their feet.

Soldiers at the rifle range gave Joseph antibiotics to speed up his healing, so that he could return to school. But Joseph did not return. He had bigger plans. He told me he was lining up a job with a real-estate company.

"This is a company that belongs to a man who lost in the last elections," Joseph said. "I campaigned for him, and he liked me, so he might give me a job."

It sounded farfetched to me, but I was pleased to see the return of confidence in Joseph.

A few weeks later, Joseph opened an office in Ngong. He was "branch manager" of the real-estate company, he said. "The Maasai are trying to sell land now, to make up for the drought, so I will help them, and offer advice."

"You're going to help the Maasai unload their land?" I asked.

"No, not like that," he said. "I am making sure they don't get cheated. I am helping them sell *some* land, but I am also making loan applications for them so they can develop."

Sekento and I could never figure out what it was that Joseph actually did. But he was earning more money than Sekento, and he had an office. He hired his brother William, who had dropped out of primary school, to help him. He said when Noah finished school, he would hire him as his mechanic. "By then I will probably have a vehicle." He asked if I planned to sell mine when I left Kenya. He still did not know how to drive.

Working in Ngong, Joseph lost the innocence of the boy who had dreamed of "the new life." He was learning how to make deals, the sort of hustle the town was famous for. Older men talked to him in confidence, and he adopted a swagger not unlike that of Chief Sayo. He invited me to lunch one day in Nairobi and showed up in a plaid sports jacket and yellow shirt open at the collar. He carried a briefcase. "Imported," he said, fingering his lapels.

Sekento began referring to Joseph as "the great man."

One day Mr. Sha called me from the satellite station. He shouted into the receiver, "Sha! Sha!" to let me know who was calling. He was always tense on the phone, as he did not have much experience with it. I thought he might never have watched anyone else use the phone. He told me to hold on, then asked his driver, a Maasai named Daniel, who spoke English, to talk to me. Daniel also worked as a security guard at the satellite station, and in his off-hours he operated Mr. Sha's *matatu*. Daniel said they were calling to let me know that everybody had moved out of the *boma* at Empaash because of the drought. Semoi and his wives had gone off on their own, and everybody else was now living below Mount Longonot, closer to water. The game department had given them extra grazing land to use during the drought. Later I learned they had bribed the game wardens for the favor.

All the Maasai were on the move, it seemed, and Noah met some elders from Euaso traveling through Kajiado who told him his father was sick. He asked me to take him home.

I had been busy writing some magazine articles and had not been to Empaash in almost two months. When Sekento, Noah and I got to the *dukas* we saw there was a new building, not quite finished, going up next to Mr. Sha's bar, with a sign that said "Paradise Hotel." The owner was a Kikuyu, Mr. Sha said, "but not too bad." The Paradise was a little fancier than Mr. Sha's bar and hotel. It was made of stone, and bigger. Mr. Sha had built three toilets—outhouses—behind his bar, a lure to some travelers. He did not intend to make them available to the future guests of the Paradise.

But there was hardly any business at Mr. Sha's bar. Nobody could afford to buy beer, and most of the men were busy moving cattle. The shelves in the *duka* were bare. A whirlwind of dust blew up behind the outhouses, and swept across the trading center like a small cyclone. We covered our faces from the grit.

Nanta's shop, which had never opened, had a padlock on the door. The window was boarded up. She was renting the building to Kukuyu, who were using it to store hides, which they bought from the Maasai as more of their cattle died.

Mr. Sha's driver, Daniel, suggested we take the *matatu* to Semoi's *boma*, since he knew the way. We left my Range-Rover at the satellite station and bumped across the plains. Crossing a sandy riverbed, we saw the carcass of a hyena being picked at by vultures, and farther on the skeletons of several antelopes and a dead bloated cow. It was hilly country, and going down the hills Daniel turned off the engine to coast and save gas. We climbed higher, and Daniel said he didn't know why Semoi had moved to such an isolated area. "It's a little greener up here," Noah said hopefully.

"We will have to walk part of the way because it gets too narrow up here in the rocks to drive," Daniel said. We looked back over the plains, and the satellite dishes were small specks.

Noah's family had taken up residence in an old, abandoned *boma* of six small huts, high up on Mount Longonot. There had been another family living with them, but they had moved to Lake Naivasha because water was a problem here too. Agnes and Kipeno were tired and worn, and both of them had lost weight. Semoi looked very ill. He was emaciated and could not stop coughing. When Noah saw him, he burst into tears. Kipeno and Agnes also began crying. The younger children, their faces crawling with flies, chewed on their dirty fingers, watching without comprehension. Sekento tried to console Noah, but he could not stop weeping. "This is my fault because I went away to school," he said.

Agnes composed herself, hugged Noah and told him, "Everyone is suffering; at every *boma* it is the same problem. It is not only us."

Semoi coughed incessantly.

"Why haven't you gone to a clinic?" Sekento asked.

Semoi said he had been receiving treatment from a witch doctor who had made a cut in his stomach and found, inside him, a pig's horn and several scraps of sheepskin, which he had removed. A curse of some kind had put them there, and Semoi said he felt much better afterward and had planned to continue with the treatment, but he didn't want to leave the women alone with the cattle during the drought.

Agnes and Kipeno both looked exasperated and began talking as if Semoi were not there. "The man charges three hundred shillings each visit, and I don't see any improvement," Agnes said.

"He is still hearing voices, and he complains that his head hurts," Kipeno put in. "Look how skinny he is!"

Semoi added that his skin was "darkening"; he couldn't sleep at night and found all food tasteless. I suggested we take him to the hospital, and everybody but Semoi said it was a good idea.

"I know what my problem is," Semoi said. "I am cursed because of some hatred from other people who are jealous of me." He insisted the witch doctor would know more about his problem than any doctor at a hospital. He said his sleeplessness reminded him of the time he had spent at Mathari Mental Hospital. It was the first time I had ever heard him mention it. "I didn't get better," he said. Agnes and Kipeno argued with him that he should at least try the hospital, but he walked away from us.

"We are competing here with the life of belief," Sekento said.

"If my father believes the witch doctor, there is nothing we can do," Noah agreed. He told his mother he would stay with them until the drought was over. "I can't leave you like this," he said. But Agnes said he must return to school; they would manage.

The sky was getting dark, and there was a rumble of thunder. "It's going to rain!" Daniel said. He urged us to get going, because if it was a big storm, the tracks could wash out. We tried to convince Semoi to come with us, but he told us to leave him alone.

It was a long walk, and lightning flashed across the sky. Halfway back to the truck, we heard Agnes and Kipeno shouting for us. "Wait—Semoi has agreed!" Semoi appeared behind them, the children running along barefoot behind him.

When we reached the truck, Agnes and Kipeno began collecting firewood by the armful and throwing it into the back of the covered truck. It was for Nanta and Mr. Sha's wives, they said. "We know there is little wood down where they live." As we drove off, they stood with the children, waving.

The rain came in a sudden downpour, and even Semoi smiled, but the damp seemed to aggravate his cough. Daniel flicked on the windshield wipers. He drove fast; the mud was making the track slippery. It was still raining when we reached the road. Mr. Sha was waiting at the satellite station, drenched, his baggy guard's uniform hanging in heavy, wet folds. He was relieved to see Semoi was with us and told him that everything would be fine, now that the rain had started. He promised to check on Agnes and Kipeno himself.

The next morning we went to Kenyatta Hospital. There was now a sign in the reception area: JIHAD-HARI WEZI! (Beware of Thieves!). Underneath, someone had scrawled: "Pickpockets are everywhere!" The doctor who examined Semoi was a Kikuyu woman wearing bright-red lipstick. I thought Semoi might object, but he was completely passive. I told her what I knew of Semoi's history, his sleeplessness and headaches. She checked his blood pressure, listened to his chest and ordered an X ray, which proved normal. She told us there was nothing wrong with him. "He has bronchitis, but other than that I'd say his problem is stress." She handed us a cone of paper filled with tablets. "I'm giving him Valium; it will help him sleep." She asked Noah to explain to him that he should take two before going to bed. Driving back to Empaash, Semoi actually seemed better. "I told you modern doctors know nothing," he said with satisfaction.

34

OLOITIPITIP

FOLLOWING THE 1983 general elections, Stanley ole Oloitipitip, the bumptious Kajiado South MP, was dropped from the president's cabinet. The astonished former minister, who retained his seat in parliament, responded that his latest demotion would make the Maasai "very angry," but no outcry was raised in his behalf. The Maasai were busy surviving the drought, and their interest in politics was again on a downward trend.

Oloitipitip's problems were not yet over. In the course of a long and highly publicized judicial commission inquiry in the aftermath of the aborted coup, his name was linked with Charles Njonjo, a former constitutional affairs minister under investigation for treason. A witness testified that Oloitipitip had told him, in a hotel bar, that Njonjo was a rich man with many overseas connections who need only press a button to take over the presidency. Oloitipitip admitted before the commission that Njonjo was his friend, and that he had taken tea with him long after the newspapers had begun referring to Njonjo as "the traitor" and other politicians had roundly condemned him. He blithely testified that Njonjo had promised to make him vice president. On that admission, he was promptly expelled from the ruling party and forced to forfeit his seat in parliament.

Next came a conviction for tax evasion concerning a hotel he owned. Sentenced to eleven months in jail, he blurted out in court: "What! Me sleep on the floor?" By 1984 he was suffering from heart problems, stomach ulcers and diabetes, ailments complicated by his obesity and drinking. Two Nairobi hospitals sued him for unpaid bills. Because of his deteriorating health, the jail sentence was suspended, and he was fined instead. In disgrace, he returned to his village, which was mainly populated by members of his large family, and consulted a local herbalist about his complaints.

Soon after, a by-election was called in Kajiado South to choose his successor, and the winner was Moses ole Kenah, a fifty-two-year-old former schoolteacher who had lost to him in two previous elections. Only 9,650 out of 43,000 registered voters went to the polls. The low turnout was blamed on the drought; in addition, the district commissioner had banned the practice of candidates providing transportation for voters. In the past, Oloitipitip had had trucks take his supporters to the polling stations. A newspaper sent a reporter to ask the Maasai why they had not voted. Many said they had not known of the by-election.

As his health worsened, Oloitipitip checked into Loitokitok district hospital, insisting that two of his wives be present at all times. Despite this precaution, he still feared that the staff was trying to poison him and finally left the hospital against doctors' advice to seek traditional treatment again. He died a few days later, in the care of a Maasai herbalist.

President Moi issued a brief statement of condolence to the family, but fellow politicians avoided the funeral, which hundreds of Maasai traveled long distances by foot to attend. The burial was to take place at the former minister's home, on the Kenya-Tanzania border, in a hot, dusty compound next to a traditional *boma*. But midway through the service, Oloitipitip's modern, red-tiled house suddenly caught fire. A pastor from the African Inland Church, who had been standing at the graveside some sixty feet from the house, explaining how a death can sometimes bring bounty to a people, according to God's will, paused when a woman screamed. The mourners turned to look and saw thick smoke billowing from the roof. Women, children and elders fled as moran dressed in *shukas* rushed to put out the fire. Apparently it had started in the sitting room where Oloitipitip's body had lain for public viewing the night before and where, that morning, his twenty-five sons had anointed his remains with cow fat.

When the fire was finally put out, the pastor attempted to resume the service, but people were in a state of shock, busily discussing what might have caused the fire. One man stood up on the dais and proclaimed that someone was not satisfied with the death but wanted to destroy the former MP's property as well. Several men shouted that it was sabotage, and a Land-Rover with four moran armed with clubs was dispatched to guard the family's other properties. Some of the Maasai said the fire was a divine mystery, a dark omen. But a few minutes later it was revealed that it might have been caused by a burning incense stick left stuck in the ceiling. The ceremony continued. Many mourners wept while a few women collapsed and were taken away. Speakers recounted the achievements of Oloitipitip's life, recalling how a simple cattle herder was inspired to enter politics and become his country's first Maasai cabinet minister. There were emotional calls for representatives of the provincial administration to add a few words, but none stepped forward. No important officials had attended.

A few months later, Oloitipitip's property was auctioned to pay off his debts. His large family was left in ruin.

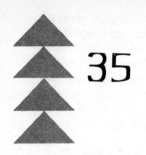

35

LAST MORAN DAYS

As THE DROUGHT tapered off, Noah's family moved to an area near Mount Suswa where the women were better able to look after the cattle on their own. Noah's grandmother was staying with the family, helping to look after the younger children.

The new *boma* was one of a half-dozen well-established Maasai settlements located along an old trade route in an area called Enkapune Oltepesi (Cave of the Acacia). There were scatterings of trees and outcroppings that made it both scenic and well protected. Noah and I drove out there one Sunday. Though there had been rain, it was still dusty, and we put blankets down on the floor of the Range-Rover to stop the red dust rising up through the vents. The game had returned to the plain; for a while a small herd of zebra galloped alongside us, and Noah counted six ostriches. There were hundreds of gazelles. When we reached the *boma*, everyone but Semoi rushed out with smiles to greet us.

Agnes said that fifteen of their cows had died, and they had only twenty-two left, but they were hopeful things would improve with the rain. She reported that Penina was happy with her husband, who did not beat her, and she had given birth to a boy. Kipeno was pregnant, apparently by a boyfriend who owned a car.

It was almost a year since Semoi had stopped drinking, but he did not look much better. He had grown increasingly apathetic and meekly did what his wives told him. He had thrown the Valium tablets into the fire and was still complaining about headaches and mysterious voices, but he had stopped coughing and gained a little weight. While we visited, he sat under an acacia tree and made no effort to join us.

Noah had two weeks off from school, and I left him at the *boma*. When he returned to Nairobi, he said his father's health was better. Several elders had come to talk with him. They had told him his problem was "bad thinking" and had offered, if he liked, to raise money for him to see the witch doctor, or to take him to a hospital. Semoi was officially still an age-set leader and was accorded respect, but no one bothered much anymore to consult him on important issues. The elders had determined that he was not well enough to help organize the moran graduation ceremony, which would probably take place within the next year.

Noah, Agnes and Kipeno had decided that Semoi's present problem was guilt over the way his drinking had hurt the family. They told him they forgave him and only wanted him to get well, and Noah said his spirits had improved during the time he was home.

The government launched another campaign to try to abolish moranhood. The issue was still too sensitive to call for an outright ban, but district officials were negotiating with various tribal sections, including the Keekonyokie, urging them to hold an early graduation for the current group of moran, and to encourage boys who were about to join to enter school instead. Dickson was critical when I went to visit him at Saikeri. "If you do away with moran and traditional culture, what replaces it?" he said angrily. "The government isn't giving us more schools or water or dispensaries. They should stop criticizing the culture and start providing the services that everybody else in this country takes for granted."

As an alternative to moranhood, the government proposed that young Maasai men consider jobs with the police or the army, for which they seemed well suited.

Joseph's brother Kureko snickered at the idea. The police had shot two of his friends during cattle raids and sent another to jail for seven months. Kureko might have gone to jail too, but his friend had refused to give names, even after the police beat him up.

Kureko considered the police—and all game wardens—enemies of the people. Soldiers were all right—he knew them from the rifle range—but their jobs had no class. Moran had style. However, Kureko agreed that moranship should be ended. "I hated it when I had to stop being a moran," he said. "I vomited for seven days when my hair was shaved. But I think if we had continued, everyone in our group would have ended up dead. So now, when I think of having sons, I want them to be educated and to go into professions." Kureko had been talking to some missionaries lately, and he thought the things they said made sense. "They speak the truth." But he was too busy with cattle trading to become a Christian himself.

In March, Mr. Sha telephoned to tell me that Kintolel had been circumcised and to invite me to a small party to celebrate. When I arrived at the *boma*, Mr. Sha and Tingisha were making goat soup in two large metal pots set over a blazing fire. Mr. Sha tossed the ends of his tie over his shoulder so they would not get in the soup while he stirred it with a sturdy twig. The men strained the fat through a sieve made of bunches of grass, using leleshwa leaves as pot holders. The small children, wearing only grimy T-shirts, were scraping the remains of the goat carcass with long, sharp knives, removing every last bit of meat, and sometimes stopping to lick the blades carefully.

Mr. Sha said that seventy-five of his cattle had died during the drought, but he still had a hundred and ninety sheep and goats, which he intended to sell to buy more cattle. Some of the goats were about to give birth and had been roped off in a maternity ward where Nanta and his wives were keeping an eye on them.

Nanta was in a triumphant mood. Chief Sayo's second wife had run away from him and taken her children; now all he had was Mary, and everybody knew what she thought of him. Apparently he did not know about Kintolel's circumcision. The surgery had been performed at a clinic with Mr. Sha, Tingisha and one of the elders as witnesses to his bravery. Nanta had not dared to hold a big ceremony and risk Sayo's interference.

Kintolel was wearing a black *shuka* and brass coils fastened around his shaved head. Several other boys, also recently circumcised and similarly dressed, had come to the celebration. Two of them were soon to join the moran, but Kintolel would be staying at home. I felt sorry for him. He couldn't go to school, and he couldn't become a moran. Tingisha said he would learn self-reliance by looking after his mother's animals.

Mr. Sha brought us cups of goat soup and said he hoped that moranship would soon be abolished. "Moran are just cattle thieves, and people waste time and money holding these big ceremonies for moran. Time gone is *gone*. Maybe small ceremonies are all right, if they are short and inexpensive." But Nanta and several of his wives disagreed. They enjoyed the ceremonies, and some of their boyfriends were moran. They did not want to give up the parties or the glamour.

I asked Kintolel if he regretted not having a circumcision ceremony, or if he minded that his father had missed this important ritual.

He glanced away when he spoke. "I always looked after my father's animals; I never did him any wrong," he said. "I tried in every way to involve him. But now it's over. He can still try to cause problems for me, but now I can face him as a man."

36

FIRE

AT SEVEN O'CLOCK on Easter morning, 1985, Mr. Sha called from the satellite station to shout that some Kikuyu had attacked his *boma* and burned down all the huts. Nobody was hurt, but most of the sheep and goats had died in the fire.

I picked up Sekento, and we drove out. The *boma* was still smoking, and Nanta was poking through the ashes looking for anything salvageable. Close to forty men and moran had gathered, armed with spears, swords, clubs, and bows and arrows. The Suswa police were there too, with rifles, waiting for the chief inspector. The police looked jittery and kept their distance from the crowd. The moran, some of them painted with red ocher, were jeering at the police to find the arsonists. "We know the names!" they cried. Trembling with rage, they jabbed their spears into the air and called for revenge. Mr. Sha and several elders tried to calm them, reminding them that the police had guns.

Nanta and Mr. Sha's wives found only a few blackened cooking pots in the debris. "We have lost everything!" Nanta wailed. The goat maternity ward was a charred rubble of bones. The smaller children, dusted with soot, were crying.

Nanta, who was at the *boma* when the fire was started, said some sixty raiders had come at dusk the night before, when Tingisha was the only man at home. One of them had a gun. Two others had held Tingisha, ordered the women out of the huts and poured kerosene around the *boma*. The women ran to the next *boma* and sent a man to Mr. Sha, who was on duty at the satellite station and saw the flames from there. The police came quickly, firing rifles into the air, and the raiders fled. Tingisha said he had recognized some of the men as Kikuyu workers from a nearby ranch.

Mr. Sha was suspicious. It seemed to him the police had come a little too quickly—as if they'd been previously tipped off. He believed the gunshots were a warning to the arsonists. Two days before, three armed policemen had beaten up a Maasai schoolboy who was looking after goats, he said. They took turns lashing him with a *kiboko* (a whip made from hippopotamus hide), then searched the nearby *bomas*—including Mr. Sha's—for weapons and collected all the spears and swords they could find. They gave no explanation but later said they were looking for cattle raiders. Mr. Sha and the boy's father took him to the hospital in Naivasha, but there were too many people waiting for treatment, so they returned to the *boma* and treated him with sheep fat. The father tried to lodge a complaint at the police station, but the police refused to take the report, claiming the inspector's signature was required, and he was away. They also refused to return the confiscated spears and swords.

Mr. Sha said the Kikuyu were trying to intimidate the Maasai, to drive them off the public land on which they had been given permission to settle during the drought. The father of the beaten boy had recently attended a local political meeting—a membership rally for the national ruling party—where he had overheard some Kikuyu talking about plans for land demarcation around Longonot, saying that the Maasai should be pushed out before the land was surveyed. He later complained to the county council.

Mr. Sha believed that the police, by disarming the *bomas*, had set them up for the raid. He said his *boma* had been targeted because he owned the *duka* and bar at Empaash. "I'm a rich man, and they want to drive me out of business and take over the trading center," he said.

Two police reporters and a photographer arrived with Mr. Sha's driver, Daniel, from the satellite station. They interviewed Nanta, Tingisha and Mr. Sha, and took pictures of the Maasai standing next to the gutted *boma*. The photographer was snapping the agitated moran when the chief inspector and three more policemen pulled up in a Land-Rover. The inspector, taking note of the pressmen, strode toward the moran. He spoke in Swahili. "My friends, I know you Maasai are tough—you could start a war, even slaughter these Kikuyu if you wanted! These Kikuyu are lucky that they picked a *boma* where there were mostly women and children!" The moran waved their spears, flattered by the characterization.

"We know who did this," one man shouted. "So why are you police only hanging around here doing nothing?"

"I ask you to stay calm. Let the police who are hired for the job handle this!" the inspector responded. "We will find the men who did this!"

The next day *The Standard* carried three large pictures with a story headlined: "GANGSTERS SET BOMA ABLAZE." The *Daily Nation* story was headlined: "RAIDERS BURN DOWN MANYATTA." In one account, Mr. Sha was reported to have ten wives and was quoted as saying that only self-restraint had prevented the moran from going after the gangsters. Neither story mentioned the underlying tribal differences, the issue of land, or Mr. Sha's allegation that police might have been involved.

Within a few days, the police had arrested four men suspected of the arson, but they were soon out on bail, each having posted bond of 50,000 shillings (about $3,000), a tremendous sum by Kenyan standards. No effort was made to arrest any of the others.

As a result of the newspaper stories, the minister who worked with Jeanne and Denny Grindall's missionary project sent twenty used coats to help out the families. The women and children found shelter in neighboring *bomas*. But the publicity brought no attention from local politicians or offers of help from the educated Maasai in Nairobi. At the time, the minister of state, Justus ole Tipis, and his rival William ole Ntimama were engaged in a bitter struggle for control of the Narok branch of the national ruling party. I called Ntimama, who said he had not seen the newspaper stories but voiced concern and promised to look into it. He didn't. Mr. Sha visited Tipis's office in Narok, but there was no follow-up.

The wildlife department, which controlled the land on which the Maasai were living, gave Mr. Sha permission to rebuild his *boma* a few miles from the old site. But the Kikuyu complained that the Maasai were using up too much water, and there was a minor scuffle near a well. "We are ready to fight now," Mr. Sha told me. "These Kikuyu can be sure we will never leave this place!"

He went to Naivasha and hired a white lawyer, T. R. Ibbertson, an elderly advocate who had lived in Kenya for thirty-five years, twelve of them in Naivasha. He was a former resident magistrate—a judge—in Naivasha, and in Eldoret, a town in western Kenya. One day I took Mr. Sha to Ibbertson's office, next door to the Kenya Grain Growers Cooperative Union on Naivasha's dusty main street.

The office was a small, shabby storefront, and Ibbertson's desktop was bare except for a large ashtray and a tattered Bible, the latter used for oaths. There was a second, smaller desk for his assistant, a young Kikuyu. Mr. Sha and I were waiting in the office, talking with the assistant, who knew nothing of the case but listened with sympathy, when Ibbertson arrived, hobbling in on his wife's arm, his ankle in a cast. He explained he would not be able to appear in court for Mr. Sha, but he would keep "watch brief." After his wife had helped lower him into his chair, he picked up the morning newspaper, which the assistant had placed on his desk, and glanced at the headline: "MAGISTRATE EATEN BY CROCODILES." He gave a hoot and held it up for his wife to see.

"I knew this chap; he once worked under me," he explained.

His wife added, "He was always a drunk, probably fell in the river."

Ibbertson did not seem very concerned about Mr. Sha's case. We discussed it for only a few minutes. But I knew there had been two previous meetings, and I thought perhaps the matter had been studied in more detail then.

The case did not reach the court for several months. The day of the hearing, Mr. Sha, Tingisha and a teenage boy named Punyua, who had been at the *boma* during the attack, were ready to testify. I met them outside the courthouse, waiting with several elders under a large acacia tree. A sharply dressed Maasai lawyer from Nakuru, who had come to the court on other business, was pressed into service as a translator. "I hope this won't take long," he told the police prosecutor and pulled back his shirt cuff to check his watch. He took no interest in Mr. Sha and his group but went inside and joked with the other lawyers. Four barefoot young men in prison uniforms with shaved heads and chained wrists were led from a police van into the courtroom.

The courthouse was typical of rural Kenya—a small, square cement building with a corrugated metal roof. It probably dated from colonial times. The British built all the prisons and most of the older courthouses in Kenya. The courtroom held nine rows of wooden benches, and there were offices off the back. At the front was a lawyers' table and a raised platform for the magistrate. The Kenyan crest—a shield with crossed spears flanked by lions—hung on the wall. The motto underneath was *Harambee* (Pull Together).

The courtroom was packed with spectators, most of them shabbily dressed and confused by the proceedings. When the gavel was struck, some people jumped to their feet; others looked around baffled. A woman nursing her baby in the first row finally shuffled to her feet when a policeman ordered her to rise. A small child squatted in the aisle and peed, but no one paid any attention. The three back rows were filled with prosperous-looking

Kikuyu farmers. Mr. Sha whispered they were friends and relatives of the men accused of the arson.

The magistrate's name was Onesmus Githinji. He was a Kikuyu and made a showy production of his entrance.

Several cases were heard before that of the Maasai: a woman tearfully described how she had been hit with a *panga*; another woman had been robbed of three hundred shillings; an old man wearing rags was accused of growing *bhang*.

The court officials and translators smirked throughout the testimony.

"Madam, you were escorting your drunken husband home, is that correct?" the prosecutor asked. There were loud giggles from the courtroom until the gavel was rapped. When the old man's case came up, wilted marijuana plants were displayed as evidence, and he sighed loudly. The four boys in prison uniforms were questioned about a robbery and murder. The woman who had been nursing her baby was accused of stealing food. She said her children were hungry, and she had no choice but to steal. The magistrate chided her for having seven children. "Haven't you ever heard of family planning?" he asked. She said her husband was dead, and began sobbing.

Finally, Mr. Sha was called to the dock and was sworn in. He explained with dignity that he was a security guard at Longonot satellite station, and that ten huts in his *boma* had been burned down. He estimated the value of the huts at about 50,000 shillings and gave a list of items lost in the fire, including 7,600 shillings in cash, and two hundred goats and sheep. He said he had not been at the *boma* when the fire started and didn't know the four accused men, but they were known and seen by other people in the *boma*, including the children.

Tingisha was called next. It was the first time I had ever seen him in Western clothing, and he looked uncomfortable. The sleeves of his jacket ended inches above his wrists. He was nervous and couldn't decide which way he was to face. A court policeman told him to stand straight and not lean on the railing. He identified himself as co-owner of the *boma* and said he recognized three of the accused men. "I have seen them around," he said.

The day of the fire, he was looking after sheep and goats outside the *boma*. "When I saw the fire, I ran toward the *boma*, but some of these people surrounded me with *pangas*. I asked them not to kill me. They took me to the *boma*."

Tingisha was asked to look around the court and see if he recognized anyone else who might have been involved. He took a long time, searching every face, lingering on the three rows of stony-faced Kikuyu. The courtroom grew restless; people fidgeted and began whispering. Tingisha said he didn't recognize anyone.

"Continue, Mr. Tingisha, tell us what happened," the magistrate said.

"One of the criminals had kerosene and another was setting fire to the huts with matches," Tingisha said.

"Were these temporary houses?" the magistrate interrupted.

"They are typical Maasai huts," Tingisha said.

The magistrate laughed. "A Maasai hut looks like an elephant lying down, is that it?" he asked. Everyone laughed. Mr. Sha and Tingisha looked appalled. Tingisha said his wives and the other women had built the huts, but they had slept in the rain after the fire. "We have suffered," he said.

The magistrate looked through his notes and said, "Ah, Mr. Tingisha, you have four wives, is that correct?"

Tingisha said he had two wives.

The magistrate asked him if he was planning to marry more wives. Tingisha said he had not yet found another wife. "But I am becoming important," he said, "and I plan to have more wives." The lawyers snickered.

"Were you ever rich?" the magistrate asked.

"I lost all my cattle in the drought," he replied.

"That is why we tell you Maasai to sell your cattle in droughts," the magistrate scolded. "How can you support so many wives and all those children? How can you send them to school?"

Tingisha said, as if by rote, "Soon we will plow the earth and plant." The magistrate nodded approvingly.

"Do you know why your *boma* was burned?"

Tingisha said he did not.

"How can you not have some idea?" the magistrate said. "There must be some reason."

Tingisha insisted there were no quarrels with the Kikuyu before the raid. "One of the criminals had a gun," he said.

"How can you be sure?" the magistrate asked. "Would you know what a gun looks like? Maybe what you saw was only a pipe that looked like a gun." The Naivasha police inspector stood up and said the gun had been recovered and identified and that it belonged to one of the accused men who worked for the wildlife department.

The boy Punyua took the stand, wearing a *shuka*, and looking very serious and not at all scared. He spoke in a mixture of English, Maasai and Swahili, which seemed to amuse everyone. He was asked to identify which of the four accused had carried the gun. He looked at the four men in the opposite dock and said he could not be sure since they looked very similar. He was then asked to look around the court and see if he recognized anyone else involved in the raid. He left the dock and walked down the aisle, row by row, scanning hostile faces. He pointed to a young man. The Kikuyu laughed. The young man said he had been in Nakuru the day of the fire and could prove it.

Court was adjourned, and the magistrate said he would make a ruling the following week. Confused, I followed the prosecutor outside and asked why he had not called more witnesses. "What about the women— they saw everything," I said.

"These witnesses are enough," he told me. Mr. Sha said the police had not taken statements from any of the women.

Mr. Sha and I drove over to Ibbertson's office and told him what had happened. He shook his head. "This magistrate is the most hated man in Naivasha," he said. "He treats everybody as if they were guilty." He showed me a letter in which he had made a formal complaint against the magistrate for referring to his age and skin color in court. "Of course, nothing has come of this or any other complaint. This is what it has come to, in Kenya."

There was, he said, nothing we could do.

The day of the ruling, the courtroom was filled with the odor of rotting meat. Flies buzzed over a bucket of meat—the evidence in a robbery case. We sat through a dozen cases. A boy explained that he had not seen his probation officer in six months because he had no money for bus fares; another boy, wearing a New York Road Runners T-shirt, was accused of disorderly conduct in a *matatu*; a sobbing Austrian businessman testified about a car accident in which his best friend had been killed; a man was questioned about some stolen sheep; two women accused of illegally brewing liquor were fined.

A prostitute took the stand. "You are a very dirty, stinking woman," the magistrate told her. "The report says you smelled so bad you drew the police's attention. You don't wash? Why are you so filthy?" Her face quivered, and tears slid down her cheeks.

Another prostitute was called. She had a baby slung on her back and looked frightened. "I am told you have syphilis," the magistrate said. "You have probably infected your daughter—do you use the same towel? When AIDS comes to Kenya it will sweep the likes of you like a broom."

It had been a busy morning, and the ruling was put off until 3 P.M. I walked around Naivasha with the Maasai, killing time. Ibbertson's office was closed. None of us was optimistic.

At three, the magistrate read from handwritten notes summarizing the evidence, then looked up. "The prosecution called three witnesses, Mr. Sha, the owner, who was not present at the time of the fire, and two others who gave eyewitness accounts. The court is uncertain that the four accused were actually among the arsonists. We have an eyewitness account by Mr. Tingisha, which I will accept. The boy's testimony I will discount. He was confused and could not identify the man who was alleged to have had a gun. But the accepted eyewitness account is not corroborated, and under Kenya law we must have corroboration. I find the four accused not guilty."

The four men stepped down, smiling, to meet their supporters, who rushed forward to shake hands.

The Maasai were stunned. Tingisha and the boy headed back for the *boma* on foot. Some police officers, waiting to load the jail van, were joking outside the courtroom. The Maasai lawyer dashed for his car. A young Kikuyu woman came up to me. She said she had been in court the previous week and had seen me with the Maasai. "I heard everything," she said. "I'm sorry. I feel so ashamed for my country to treat people like that." She opened her purse and took out two hundred shillings. "Could you give this to your friends to help them out?"

Mr. Sha and I walked up the hill behind the courthouse, over to the police station to look for the senior sergeant. We wanted to find out if there was anything we could do to reopen the case. But the sergeant was out. Nobody could say when he might be back. There seemed no point in going to Ibbertson. Mr. Sha sat down on the steps, outside the station, and looked so sad that I thought he was going to cry.

37

EUNOTO

IN MID-1985, the Keekonyokie elders agreed to hold Eunoto—the moran graduation ceremony—earlier than planned. The decision represented a concession to the government's pressure as well as a change in the elders' own thinking. The last Keekonyokie Eunoto had been held six years before, and the elders said this one might be the last. "This is historical," Joseph said, calling me with the news. With that in mind, he asked his boss for time off and headed for the bush to join the moran so that he could take part in the ritual. Noah remained in school.

A date had not yet been set, but the announcement brought a festive air to Maasailand. At every *boma* the women were repairing huts and finishing up beadwork for new necklaces and ornaments to be worn for the occasion. For the moran there was pleasure mixed with sadness during their last weeks of service. Some remained in the forest, guarding their mystique and also hoping for a last opportunity to kill a lion or steal a few more Kikuyu cattle. Other moran came home to be celebrated, and their presence, like that of heroes returned from war, added a special excitement to the ordinary routine of daily life. The women's eyes took on the sparkle of prom season. The children tagged along after the splendidly attired moran, begging to be told stories or allowed to hold a spear.

The ceremonial *manyatta* was near Mount Suswa, several miles from Noah's *boma*. Somewhat reluctantly, Noah agreed to visit the site with me, to see how the preparations were going. In a few months, Noah would be graduated himself, from his auto mechanics course. He said he would be too busy at school to attend the Eunoto ceremony. "It might be the last one," I said. "How can you miss it? Can't you come just for one day?" He would not be swayed.

Noah was not officially eligible to take part, since he had not been a moran, and he had no interest in joining up for the last few weeks as Joseph had. "I have exams to study for," he said stubbornly.

"When you finish your course, will the school help you find a job?" I asked.

"I don't know," he said and seemed not to want to talk about that either. We had stopped on the way to visit his family. Semoi, who seemed very tired, had asked Noah when he was coming home—for good.

"Look at that, Noah—maize!" We splashed through a rocky creek and came up a hill where three Maasai women were weeding a small field of corn. I had never seen a Maasai *boma* planted with corn. The women waved and we stopped to talk. Their husband, a stout man in a *shuka*, proudly showed us a generator and pump and a pipe system that he had installed to bring water from the creek.

"How did you learn to do this?" I asked.

"That's my secret," he said. "People around here laugh now, but when the next drought comes they will see I have beans and corn stored to feed people; then they will change their minds!"

Euaso trading center, a few miles from the ceremonial site, was lively with business, its small tin-roofed shops built around a dusty market square where goats and sheep were sold. Prospective Maasai buyers were crowded around, inspecting, pinching, examining the animals from all angles, and striking bargains. Two *matatus*—one with lettering on the back that said

"Maasai Express"—were parked outside the bar. A driver was changing a flat tire while some moran watched idly, leaning against their spears, their legs crossed at the ankles, like herons.

"Maybe you'll have a garage here one day," I said to Noah.

"Maybe," he said.

We stopped at the bar for a soda. It must have been one of the oldest bars in Kenya. The sagging mud walls were decorated with old Maasai buffalo-hide shields and yellowed photographs, including one of Chief Sayo many years ago, when he was a slim young hunter. Two very drunk Maasai elders in blankets sat in a corner with a dozen empty beer bottles lined up on their table like bowling pins. Nanta's boyfriend the councillor came in, wearing a sports jacket that was too small to button over his protruding stomach. He bought Noah and me a soda. "I'm busy, busy, busy these days," he said, and wiped the sweat on his brow. He threw a disparaging glance at the barman taking another round to the besotted elders.

After Euaso, the road was a narrow dirt trail that gave way to smooth, flat volcanic rock. Mount Suswa rose to our right, its tall red crater worn to a sharp point. Much of the forest around the old volcano had been hacked for firewood. Brushfires had swept some sections, leaving charred stumps of acacia, crooked and bare, like bolts of lightning fixed to the ground. The surrounding plain was deep with grass. The wildflowers were scattered like bright confetti.

Crossing the plain, stopping to pull long grass from the grille on the truck, we met three moran painted with red ocher and carrying spears and shields decorated with clan markings. They said they were heading for Mount Suswa to hunt leopards in the caves. It would be their last chance. One of the moran asked in English if I would like to buy his spear and shield after the Eunoto ceremony. He would be returning to school and needed money for fees.

Many of the moran's mothers were already at the ceremonial village, putting finishing touches of dung plaster on the large huts. Noah and I counted thirty-six huts (seventy-two if double entrances were included) arranged in an oval along a north–south axis, representing the historical migratory route of the Maasai. Technically, there were supposed to be forty-eight huts—forty-nine, counting the *osinkira* (a large ritual hut), which would be constructed during the ceremony. But sometimes during the building, Noah said, there were miscalculations, or aesthetic considerations came into play, so the number of huts could vary. The Maasai considered forty-nine an auspicious number.

Overseeing the women's work was the ceremonial leader, Letangwua ole Lasiti, a majestic man who wore metal earrings, a neckband of red, black and white beads, and a plaid blanket. He shook hands with Noah. "Today I greet you as a man," he said, acknowledging Noah's changed status since his circumcision. Letangwua had been a moran with Noah's father and was the *olaiguenani* of the senior division of their age-set. He had visited Semoi recently and had brought a case of beer, which Semoi refused even to taste. Noah explained that his father had quit drinking. "He seems more settled these days," Letangwua said, but added it was too bad he would not be attending the ceremony. Noah's eyes darkened, and he looked away. I realized then that his ambivalence about the ceremony was because of his father's inability to assume his duties.

Letangwua noticed Noah's discomfort. "Look at this," he said, sticking out his tongue. It was inky black. Noah laughed. Letangwua explained that the *oloiboni* had given him a special herbal medicine that had turned his tongue black, a ritual that authorized him to supervise the ceremony. "If anybody else says he is in charge, I just show him my tongue," he said. He showed us a black *o-kiuka*, the club that signified he was an age-set leader. It was the same type of club Semoi had thrown at the elders a few years back, after his drinking began. "I have two clubs like this," Letangwua said, "but usually I keep them locked up in a briefcase so nobody can curse them or steal them."

I asked Letangwua about the Eunoto ceremony—at which the junior moran would be promoted to senior rank—and he told me it was the most significant of the long cycle of male graduation rituals, which began with circumcision. It would be followed by several smaller ceremonies, which would confer the status of junior elderhood on the group and the rights to marry and own property. But despite these concluding rituals, after Eunoto the days of full-blown warriorhood would be finished for the group.

The ceremony began in late October, on a full moon. A strong, hot wind was blowing across the plains. The air was heavy with dust. The Keekonyokie moran were to arrive in regiments—in stately single-file processions of twenty or thirty at a time—from Euaso, Saikeri, Narok, Nairragie-Enkare and the Kaputei plains. Hundreds of celebrants had gathered at the *manyatta* to await them. At first, you could not see them. There was only the distant trumpeting of kudu horns and the clang of bells strapped to the warriors' thighs. A deep chanting grew louder as they finally appeared on the plains, still far in the distance. They approached the *manyatta* with a slow, rhythmic step, their footfalls resounding with bells, and paraded into the *manyatta*, some in head-dresses made of black ostrich feathers or lions' manes. They wore red cloths tied around their hips, some ornamented with spangles; many had ritual scars, like welts, in patterns across their chests. Their ornate hairdos were caked with grease and red ocher; the same paint had been applied to their legs in swirling patterns. With each step, they thrust out their chins, the movement co-inciding with a deep bass grunt—*Hhooohn! Hhooohn! Hhooohn!*—a warlike sound, which in the old days was fair warning to all who heard it.

Letangwua, dressed in a full-length cape of dark hyrax fur, stood with commanding dignity, reviewing the troops as they circled inside the *manyatta*. The moran looked straight ahead, with expressions of grave and sullen pride that seemed remarkable, even for the Maasai. The women and girls backed away a respectful distance. Mr. Sha, who was watching with me, picked out several of his nephews who were taking part. I spotted Joseph, his hair a bright-red mop, his younger brother, Tareu, and some of Dickson's friends. It was startling to see Joseph, the real-estate tycoon, dressed as a moran, his expression no less fierce than the others.

By late afternoon, all of the moran had arrived. It was the first time the entire group had come together since the ceremony preceding their circumcisions. There were predictable skirmishes between rival groups—pushing, shoving, wrestling—and some warriors restrained their comrades from inflicting injuries on each other or themselves. No emotions were held in reserve. Some moran trembled and writhed on the ground, high on the potent herbal brews concocted in the bush.

No one was seriously hurt, but the women fled the *manyatta*. Joseph broke up fights and told his friends to "act sensibly." When the moran were worn out, they assembled outside the *manyatta* where the elders gave final instructions. The old men waved their clubs and fly whisks and sternly warned that ancient differences were to be put aside in the interests of peace and community. The moran half listened and worked on each other's hair plaits. Some held hands or draped their arms around each other's shoulders. Many were quite young, their military service cut short by the early graduation. Some were schoolboys who had joined up at the last minute. But Dickson's friends, including Runges, were men in their early twenties who had spent years in the bush. With long pigtails and flinty eyes, they seemed of another era, and their swagger and belligerence intimidated the younger moran.

Chief Sayo was on duty in his khaki uniform and felt beret, patrolling a makeshift refreshment stand and hobnobbing with local government officials and politicians who were seated on tree-shaded benches. Beer was being sold out of the back of a *matatu*, and the elders formed a line. Some of them carried bottle openers; others relied on their teeth to pry off the caps. One of the oldest, a man named Livingstone, proudly told me in English that he was the father of Letangwua. He had learned English while attending a mission school in 1931 and had served with the King's African Rifles during World War II. "I have seen much of the world," he said, and named Tunisia, Egypt, Saudi Arabia and Burma among the countries he had visited as a soldier. After the war, he worked as a driver, but eventually returned to traditional life. "It's very difficult for the Maasai to go outside," he said. "I was glad to come back. We are not like the Kukes [Kikuyu]."

That evening, as the wind died down, I set up a tent outside the *manyatta*, made a fire and watched the full moon rise. In the darkness, the valley seemed to draw in on itself, and the flanking mountains stood like a wall barring the outside world. The sky thickened with stars; I was sorry Noah had not come with me.

Most of the moran left the *manyatta* for the night to drink more of their powerful herbal soup and sleep in bush camps. The older men were singing drunkenly in their huts. A few children ran around in the dark, too excited to sleep, and several boys tried to calm a moran who cried out for others to join in a lion hunt. Around nine o'clock I noticed a reddish-brown stain spreading across the face of the moon.

A string had been tied around the perimeter of the *manyatta* as a symbolic protection against bad luck, and I climbed under it and went inside. The Maasai were watching the moon with surprise, some with fear; it seemed the eclipse was unexpected, and troubling. A full white moon is auspicious for the holding of major ceremonies, but when the moon disappears—"dies"— the Maasai become circumspect. The moon's dark phase is symbolic of death, and significant activities are curtailed at that time to avoid the possibility of bad luck.

The shadow on the moon—the color of ocher—continued to creep. I stood with Joseph, his mother and some of his school friends from Saikeri, all of us looking up at this strange sight. The Maasai were silent, then some of the women cried out, "The moon has died!" Others began singing a song which tells the legend that links the moon with death. According to the story, Naiteru-kop, the creator of the earth, instructed Leeyio, the first man, that when a child died he must dispose of the corpse with the words, "Man die and come back again; moon die and remain away." When, after some time, a child died, Leeyio became confused and said,

"Moon die and come back again; man die and stay away." He realized his mistake, but it was too late. After that men died and did not return, but the moon was always reborn.

An elder scorned the women's concern. "This is nothing new; I have seen such a thing before."

"It is blood from the war in Uganda spoiling the moon!" another man yelled.

The moran began trembling. "It is a curse," one of them said bitterly. Others shouted, "Enemies have cursed our ceremony!" Some proposed going on a cattle raid, before it was too late.

An old woman sobbed. "These moran are right—the world is ending! We will all die!"

An elder shouted her down. "It might be a good thing," he said. "It is a message from Engai that the Maasai should not be ending moranship."

A schoolboy who was with Joseph said, "It is only an eclipse, a natural thing."

Letangwua seemed to agree. "Calm down, go back to your huts!" he ordered. I returned to my campfire. At midnight the moon was completely dark, and the air was still.

Two schoolboys in warrior dress came by and asked about the eclipse. "What is this thing on the moon?" one of them asked. I used rocks to explain the positions of the sun, the earth and the moon.

I asked the boys how long they had been moran.

"Two weeks," one of them said. "After this we go back to school."

"Being a warrior is useless," the other said. They asked to sleep in my Range-Rover. Inside the *manyatta*, the women were still singing, "Moon come back." The shadow was slowly receding, letting out a fuzzy edge of light.

The next morning, before dawn, a moran stood outside my tent and announced, "Wake up! It's disco time!" I heard the blasts of kudu horns, the sound of bells, boisterous singing and foot stomping. It was still dark with only a tinge of orange spreading along the horizon. Inside the *manyatta*, hundreds of moran were charging back and forth, wearing ostrich feathers, lions' mane headdresses, and billowing red and white *kanga* capes. Dust was flying everywhere; there was terrific agitation and deafening noise. Various groups were boasting of their courage, putting down the others. Cowards were scorned. "You were good only for carrying water!" they sneered at a small boy, whose face clouded with surprise and shame. When it was light, the moran removed their capes and formed dancing circles. Leaving their shoes and sandals in a pile, they sang and took turns jumping into the air, tossing their heads like lions. The young girls stood to the side, solemnly singing, their small, shaved heads crowned with spired beads that shook like the plumage of birds. The elders took time out to rest, bundled in blankets under the trees.

The major events of the ceremony were to take place over four or five days, but by the third day Joseph said the program was running behind schedule. A delegation that had been sent to Narok to find a sacred olive tree—required before the ceremony could proceed—had not returned. "People are worried their truck might have broken down," Joseph explained. The elders mulled over the problem, scanning the plains for some sign of them. A few of the warriors flew into wild fits and passed out. The women bustled about, attending to them with the purposefulness of nurses on battlefield duty. The singing and dancing continued, but some moran, apparently worn out, sat ouside the *manyatta* making cosmetic repairs on their hairdos and painted legs.

That evening I joined a group of women, including Joseph's mother, in one of the huts reserved for the wives of respected Ilukumae clansmen. It was like a pajama party, with the women gossiping, talking about old boyfriends, recalling girlhood days and singing softly. It seemed their worry about the eclipse had passed. Later, Joseph joined us, but he looked distracted. I asked him if he was enjoying the ceremony.

"It's good," he said. "But last night I was having dreams about work. I've been away a month. I don't know what's happening at my office." The ceremony, however, fit in with his career strategy. "I'm a solid politician. Some day when I am campaigning, these

266 ▲ MAASAI DAYS

moran will remember I was with them." As if already calculating the potential votes, he told me there were 1,076 moran taking part in the ceremony. He had counted them himself.

Nanta, Agnes and Kipeno showed up the next day. Semoi's wives apparently felt no hesitation about attending without him. Nanta had left Kintolel at home to help Tingisha look after the animals.

When Sayo realized Nanta was on the premises, he came drunkenly over to me and said she must leave immediately. "She is ruining this ceremony and everybody wants her to go!" he shouted.

"Why not tell her yourself?" I asked.

"I know you two are together!" he roared. "You are wearing the same shoes!" Nanta was wearing red plastic sandals just like mine that I had given her. "I have the authority to dismiss you from this ceremony," the Chief said.

The women laughed when I told them, but Nanta said she would leave and pulled her cape up like a hood, as if to disguise herself.

A short time later, Sayo grabbed me by the back of my shirt. "Out! Out! Out! You have insulted the crown," he shouted.

Everyone turned to watch. Letangwua, hearing the commotion, rushed over and stood between me and the Chief. Nanta, it seemed, was still around. Letangwua spoke quietly but firmly. It was agreed that both Nanta and I would stay.

Sayo staggered off. Letangwua said archly, "That man is our model for development."

The ceremony had drawn the interest of other outsiders in addition to me, some with connections to the tribe. Local officials made brief appearances and posed for photographs with the moran. A young Dutch couple hiking across Kenya came upon the ceremony by chance. They were deeply tanned, dressed like flower children of the sixties. The anthropologist whose specialty was beads was there, worried that one of her competitors might also show up. Three Japanese set up a high-tech camp with a portable generator and beach chairs. One of them, who wore a kimono, was a veterinarian who had worked with the Maasai. But there was little mingling among the outsiders, which struck the Maasai as strange.

"It seems as if there is jealousy between your people," one of the moran observed, grouping us together.

A woman from New York, who had come with expatriate friends from Nairobi, reported that her passport and airline tickets were missing from her tent. "It was stupid to bring them," she said. No money had been taken. Mr. Sha's driver, Daniel, who was wearing a sports jacket and slacks, but who had briefly joined the moran's exuberant dancing, informed Letangwua. "This is a serious case," he said. "We are not a stealing people."

Letangwua ordered the moran to stop their dancing and gather around him. He explained the problem. One moran shouted, "Who is the coward who would steal from guests!" Others echoed his anger and offered to kill the culprit. Letangwua ordered the thief to return the stolen items. "If he is afraid to show his face, he can leave them outside tonight," he said. The items were not returned, but Letangwua did not believe the moran had been involved. "This is a big ceremony," he explained the next day. "You can see that Kikuyu could slip in here easily."

That night, around the campfire, the two schoolboys asked Letangwua to tell about when he was a warrior. "Was it different from now? Did you kill more lions?"

"Our group killed twenty-four lions with manes," Letangwua said. His stiff fur cape bunched around his neck as he held out his tin cup for a whiskey refill. He had worked his way through a third of the bottle that Joseph had advised me to bring for him. But as much as he drank, he remained steady. "There are fewer lions with the big hair today," he said. "Lions are like Europeans—they come with different kinds of hair. Some without." The schoolboy-warriors asked the leader which group was the bravest, theirs or his. He was diplomatic. "About the same," he said.

Letangwua told us that the Purko Maasai had agreed to stop moranhood entirely, and that their leader had signed a kind of treaty to that effect with the government. But he said the Purko leader was "lazy," and might have been bribed. The Keekonyokie had not yet resolved the matter. "Have you noticed that our guests from the government are enjoying this ceremony and want to have their pictures taken with my boys?" he asked. "All of them will drink at least four cups of our honey beer, and they will boast to their friends that they have been to this great ceremony. But the problem with moran is cattle raiding. Too many go to jail these days."

We heard the whoops of hyenas. Letangwua chuckled and said that the night before the Japanese were frightened because they thought they had heard lions. The moran told them the lions might eat them. After that, the Japanese built a fence around their camp. "They are not a very social people," one of the schoolboys said, glancing at their brightly lighted camp.

Before he retired for the night, Letangwua advised me to stay out of the *manyatta* until morning. "Tonight the moran can become wild from soup," he said. An elder sitting with us said, "I would pray for any woman who went in there tonight."

During the night, the moran had begun unplaiting one another's hair, working quietly in pairs, removing the strands of wool that had been twisted into their own hair. There were clumps of greasy red yarn scattered on the ground in the morning. At dawn, the *manyatta* was quiet as the moran sat morosely on wooden stools or goat hides outside the huts, and their mothers anointed them with milk in preparation for the hair shaving. Many of the moran whimpered and cried as the women scraped their scalps with razors. Some trembled and passed out or tried to run away, only to be dragged back. Greasy plaits fell to the ground, and children raced around grabbing them up and tossing them into the air. Joseph remained stoical as his mother worked on his head. But the shaving was traumatic for his younger brother. Tareu's eyes filled with tears, and his thin shoulders shook with anger. He resented this premature retirement. His father had been a moran for fifteen years, while his moranship had lasted only a year and a half. For this, he had given up school.

By the fourth day, the ceremony had begun to take on the aspect of a surreal three-ring circus. The moran sang and danced, their shaved heads gleaming with grease and red ocher. They looked like an alien race from a science-fiction movie. Outside the *manyatta*, the mothers of the forty-nine moran judged the most distinguished of their group were building a second village of small temporary huts. The elders were making a ritual fire with friction sticks and overseeing the sacrifice of two selected bulls. They suffocated the bulls with a piece of soft hide from a woman's skirt, slit their dewlaps, and let the moran take turns lapping at the blood.

When the women completed the small village, they started building a cupcake-shaped ritual hut called the *osinkira*, in which final, secret rites were to take place. Two moran were chosen to lead the rites and were given dark-blue beads as a mark of their position. Joseph told me that the Eunoto, literally the "planting" ceremony, was moving toward its climax. The massive olive trunk, finally brought from Narok, was "planted" as the center post of the domed *osinkira*. The circumference was marked with a rope cut from the hide of a sacrificial ox. The hide of the second bull was spread out to dry, held down by forty-nine pegs, one for each moran whose mother had helped build the ritual house. Eerily, the skulls of cattle the moran had slaughtered in the forest were placed around the base of the house.

After the meat was roasted, and the men had eaten, all the mothers were called to sit in a circle inside the *manyatta*. Three moran, including Joseph, handed out chunks of meat to them, flirting with them—calling them women rather than mothers—and making ribald jokes hinting at their sexual prowess. This was a tradition, denoting the change in their status as men. The women laughed with embarrassment and tried to swat the moran's legs.

At seven-thirty the next morning, Joseph, Daniel and I joined the pilgrimage up Mount Suswa. Hundreds of moran marched ahead of us with bells strapped to their thighs. We walked at a leisurely pace for almost three hours, across open plain, through thickets of acacia and finally up the mountain into forest. Where the terrain became steep, a column of shiny red moran's heads appeared like trail markers leading up the hill. The barefoot warriors scampered over boulders, grabbing at trees to haul themselves up. One whittled a walking stick for me. They assembled, halfway up the volcano, by a large euphorbia tree on a ledge designated a sacred site. Below us, the plains looked like an empty ocean floor.

The elders had arrived earlier and slaughtered an ox that somehow had been coaxed to climb the mountain. The moran lined up to drink blood, wiping their mouths with the backs of their hands. The hide of the sacrificial ox was cut in short strips to make finger rings for the moran. The meat was roasting. Joseph said the moran would be blessed later, and the elders would give them a new group name. A smoke signal would be sent up when the confirmation was completed.

The three of us decided to hike back early, since it would be difficult to climb down in the dark, and Joseph said the moran would travel quickly. Some young moran were also leaving, and we climbed down with them. They bragged about which of them were the toughest. Joseph said the best moran were crooks. One boy accused Joseph of not being a real moran. But he protested and said he had stolen cattle. He accused two of them of stealing gasoline from the filling station in Ngong. When we reached the *manyatta* the animosity seemed forgotten.

Later that evening, Letangwua came by my campfire and pointed out the puffs of smoke rising from Mount Suswa. Two hours later, in a light drizzle, the moran filed toward the *manyatta*, with kudu horns, bells and chanting sounding their approach. Joseph, Daniel and I went out to watch their arrival. The moran's faces were painted with ghostly white chalk and they yelled out their new name—Ilmirisho (Those Who Will Not Be Defeated). The elders responded, "Bless that name!" and snapped their leather whips and waved cattle sticks to keep order. The moran began panting and shaking as they drew near the *osinkira*, the large ritual hut. Under penalty of a curse, only those who had not broken the sexual taboos were allowed to enter, and everyone watched with curiosity to see which ones would go inside. Close to a hundred moran were able to squeeze inside and the others dispersed quietly until the only sounds from the *osinkira* were the elders' voices making blessings. After a while, the women standing outside retired to their huts.

When the rain had stopped and the moon broke through the clouds, Joseph, Daniel and I built a fire outside my tent. Two moran came to sit with us. Neither they nor Joseph seemed particularly concerned about not taking part in the ritual going on inside the *osinkira*. Earlier, I had read an anthropologist's account of the symbolism. According to him, the *osinkira* represented the mother's hut in which a husband first sleeps with his new bride. The "planted" center post of sacred olive wood had phallic connotations. The moran, who would soon become eligible to take wives, would each urinate in the hut as a representation of ejaculation. I was curious to know what Joseph and his friends had to say about this, but I was uncertain how to broach the subject.

I asked the moran if they knew what would happen that night in the ritual house, but it took a little pressing to get an answer. Finally, one of them said the moran would urinate in a special hole dug by the center post, and they would be blessed with fresh milk and cow dung.

"Why do they do that?" I asked.

"It is just our custom," they said.

They only shrugged when I related the interpretation that I had read.

A moran who had offered to sell me his ostrich-feather headdress came to find me. He said he had spent five years in the bush but wanted to start school right after the ceremony and needed the money now. I bought it as a souvenir.

"I was a good moran," he said. "I have stolen ten cows and killed six men, but I am tired of that life. For five years my brain has been sleeping."

I was too tired to ask whom he had murdered, or to care if it were true.

Joseph and his friends and Daniel returned to the *manyatta* to join in the final celebrations. In the morning, everyone would pack up and leave. Letangwua drifted by to collect the remains of the whiskey. The two schoolboys wandered near, and I stuck two cans of spaghetti in the fire for them. They found it an exotic cuisine. After they had eaten, they said they were tired, and we sat silently staring into the flames.

Suddenly, five moran sprang out of the dark, shouting and waving swords. I jumped up and edged toward the Range-Rover. The schoolboys stood their ground, demanding to know what they wanted.

They wanted the ostrich-feather headdress, which they said had been stolen from them.

"You better give it to them," one of the schoolboys said. "I think they can kill you."

I got into the truck, locked the door, and handed the headdress out the window. They grabbed it and fled into the dark.

All the time I had known the Maasai, I had never before been made to feel frightened—or given any thought to the possibility. It had surprised me when the English father of a teenage girl I had invited to another Maasai ceremony would not let her attend. His apprehension had seemed preposterous. But faced with five warpainted moran waving swords, I had a glimpse of the terror the Maasai must have presented at the height of their power. They were still terrifying to the Kikuyu farmers whose ranches they raided. The schoolboys— like me—seemed shaken. They piled up rocks to throw in case of further trouble. Daniel returned from the *manyatta*, happily drunk. When he heard what had happened, he said he must report it immediately to Letangwua.

"Don't worry, it's over," I said. "Get some sleep. Anyway, Daniel, you're drunk."

Daniel drew himself up, offended. "I am a pure Maasai," he declared, "and for us sometimes the alcohol works. If I don't go now, I may be too quiet in the morning. Now I am angry—I should go!"

When Daniel returned, he brought with him three older moran whom Letangwua had sent as guards. They sat down at the campfire, relieving the schoolboys. Daniel stretched out on the backseat of the truck. I crawled into my sleeping bag. The moon shining through the tent flap made eerie shadows. I couldn't sleep. I heard cattle bellowing and hyenas cackling. The wind was blowing, and tree branches scraped the tent. There were shrieks and laughter from the *manyatta*, the sounds of passing footsteps and of men stopping at a nearby tree to urinate. The moran guards talked softly, then I heard them snoring. Much later, when I had dozed off, I was awakened by a strange sound I could not identify. I peered through the flap. One of the guards was having a vivid dream—or a nightmare. He tossed and growled like a lion.

The sun was hardly above the horizon the next morning when Letangwua and a delegation of elders came to my tent and handed me an ostrich-feather headdress. From the beadwork, I saw it was the same one the moran had taken the night before. Daniel climbed bleary-eyed out of the truck and brushed the wrinkles from his jacket. My guards sat warming themselves around the fire, their knees pulled up to their chins. I was still confused. Letangwua said I had bought the headdress from its rightful owner, and the five moran who claimed it was theirs would be punished. He apologized, took off his beaded neckband, which I had admired, and gave it to me as a present.

38

GRADUATION

A FEW WEEKS after the Eunoto ceremony, Joseph met me for lunch in Nairobi. "The Maasai don't even know what lunch is," he said, toying with a plate of French fries. His sandwich—a "tuna melt," my suggestion— was untouched, except for one trial bite. Joseph said it was sickening. The idea of eating fish or chicken— "Kikuyu food"—was, despite his growing sophistication, still more than he could bear. This was a celebratory lunch. Joseph had been elected youth-wing chairman for the Saikeri branch of Kenya's ruling party. Officially embarked on a career in politics, he said he hoped to run for councillor in a few years. He had also switched jobs. He was now working in Nairobi as a veterinary-drug salesman. He was glad to be out of the land-selling business; he suspected that his former employer was a crook.

"I'm writing a book," he announced and asked if I could type up his manuscript. He took a notebook out of his briefcase. I glanced at the first few pages, a collection of sixty-three Maasai proverbs. "Corrupt gifts darken the mind" was one. From the wording and punctuation, I had doubts he had written them.

"Where did you get these?" I asked him.

"I copied them from books," he said proudly.

"You can't make a book by copying other people's books," I explained.

"But *my* book will be longer and better," he protested. "I'm adding some stories that Noah's grandfather told me."

Dickson was studying irrigation engineering. He had been accepted into a four-year program at Jomo Kenyatta College of Agriculture and Technology near Thika town. The government provided his tuition and a small monthly allowance. In return, he was expected to work for the government for three years after his graduation. Built with Japanese aid, the college had seven hundred students and was one of the most modern and best-equipped colleges in Kenya. It looked like a state university in the American Midwest, but many of the teachers were Japanese.

The dormitory rooms had modern furniture and balconies. Dickson was among the few Maasai students; his roommate was another. They had put up a sign on their door that read "Strangers in a Strange Land." But Dickson had no trouble fitting in. He had joined the karate club and was aiming for a black belt, and he had a picture of Laura Branigan, the pop singer whose version of "Gloria" was then popular, taped over his bed, and was learning to break-dance. Movies were shown at the school, and he liked spy thrillers in which the CIA, the KGB or Mossad were featured. He asked if I had any Marvin Gaye or Kenny Rogers tapes. He liked them both, and his roommate had a cassette player. His desk was spread with charts and books, geometry exercises, drawing tools. Other students asked to "rent" his notes. Above his desk, he had put up a snapshot of himself as a moran, under which he had written: "The Desert Wanderer: Further Studies in the Bush." Whenever I visited, Dickson climbed down the fire escape to meet me. It was faster, he said.

One day when I was going to see Dickson, Agnes appeared in Nairobi, and I brought her along. When we went up to see Dickson's dorm room, Agnes said she had never climbed stairs before. Dickson gave us a tour. The students stared at Agnes, who was barefoot and wearing a *kanga* cape and necklaces, but she did not seem to notice. She was puzzled to see students playing badminton in the gym and put her hands over her ears to shut out the disco music playing over loudspeakers.

I was surprised Agnes had come to Nairobi without Semoi's permission. She had come by bus, paying her fare with money she had earned selling milk at the market in Euaso. The bead crisis had passed, and she had made some new necklaces to sell. We took them to the gift shop at the Kenya National Museum. The manager was so impressed she decided to make tags for each necklace, with Agnes's name and a few lines about her tribal background. Agnes said the women at Empaash, including Nanta and Mr. Sha's wives, had formed a women's cooperative. There were plans to open Nanta's shop, and some sixty women had agreed to contribute crafts. They were planning a fund-raiser, and local officials had been invited.

The family was prospering. Kipeno's father had given them some cows to make up for the drought. Semoi was "quiet." But I worried about him, and about the effect of his illness on Noah. I remembered long talks with Semoi, when Sekento's uncle Naisiawua was still alive. But Semoi was no longer interested in talking about the past, or the present. He seemed to be in another world entirely. He had had no reaction when I told him that Noah was finishing his auto mechanics course.

The day of Noah's graduation ceremony in March 1986, Sekento and I picked up Joseph in Nairobi, at his office. Joseph was dressed in a trim beige safari suit, his hair carefully patted down. "The great man," Sekento murmured when we saw him waiting at the curb. Sekento was a little downcast. None of the boys in the latest senior class at Saikeri had passed the primary school exam. Out of a possible score of seventy-two, the highest scorer had earned only twenty-seven points. Saikeri had scored the lowest of any school in Kajiado district. The long drought of the previous year was partly to blame. The school had fallen into disrepair, and the roof was leaking. The MP who had replaced John Keen had done nothing for Saikeri. There was no money to pay Mary Sayo, so her adult literacy class was discontinued. "But at least there is rain," Sekento said. He and his sons had just finished planting the *shamba*.

At Noah's school in Isinya, the rains had not started. It was a hot, sunny day, not a cloud in the sky. The auto mechanics, the tanners, the livestock managers and the carpenters were to receive certificates. About sixty students would be graduated, and the dusty schoolyard was filled with displays of their work. There were few traditional Maasai among the hundred or so parents and relatives admiring the exhibits. Noah's family did not attend since the women were busy looking after the cattle. Noah was pleased to see Joseph. When the school manager saw him, he seemed surprised. "Ah, you have become a big man, I see," he said, noting Joseph's sharp appearance.

The graduation was to start at one o'clock. A half hour before, all the students, their families, the teachers, children from the primary school and a group of Maasai women from the center's bead project lined up along the dirt driveway, awaiting the arrival of the guest of honor, Stanley Metto, an assistant minister for culture and social services. The Maasai women sang traditional songs, bobbed and waved fly whisks, while the schoolchildren clapped.

The mood was festive, but as time passed and there was no sign of the assistant minister, the younger children became fidgety in the heat, and some local officials and policemen paced back and forth. After an hour, the singers gave up, all eyes focused on the main road. I took some pictures of Noah and his friends and the school, and finally Joseph, Sekento and I sat in the Range-Rover, just to get out of the sun. Most of the people lined up along the entrance had sat down and were wearily fanning themselves with the graduation programs. Some of the parents were worried that the ceremony wouldn't end in time for them to make bus connections home. There was no place for them to stay overnight.

Reluctantly, the school manager agreed to start the program without the guest of honor. But at three o'clock, before the certificates were handed out, two government

Land-Rovers pulled in. An official explained that the assistant minister was unable to attend but offered no reason or apology for his absence. Instead, he had sent a representative, Ezekiel Chemoiywo, a commissioner of social services.

For the next hour, the guests and students endured a series of long-winded speeches. Every minor official was given time at the podium. The previous year, a teacher whispered to me, Stanley ole Oloitipitip had given a rousing speech.

The commissioner told the gathering that 42 million shillings—just under $3 million—had been allocated by the government to support the nation's village technical schools. (These were the government-run vocational schools the Ministry of Education had claimed to know nothing about when I was looking for schools for Joseph and Noah.) He urged the Isinya graduates not to "flock" into towns looking for work but instead to form cooperatives in rural areas, in line with district development strategies. A number of parents got up and left to catch their buses. Just before dark, Noah was handed his certificate and a toolbox.

He was at a loss to find a job. The school had no program to help the graduates. Noah inquired at a few gas stations in Nairobi and was told he lacked experience. I mentioned the problem to the manager of the local Esso station, an Indian named Mr. Jiva. He said he might have a job for Noah and asked me to bring him for an interview.

Noah showed up with his report card and mechanic's certificate. Mr. Jiva said he needed a man in his injection-pump workshop. The station serviced diesel trucks. Noah knew a great deal about diesel pumps, it turned out, which made him perfect for the job. Mr. Jiva agreed to give him a tryout and shook his hand. He added, "Honesty is the foundation for good business." He said he'd had problems in the past with employees stealing spare parts and money, but he had never hired a Maasai, and he believed the Maasai were "honorable people." Noah—ecstatic at his luck—was told to report to work in two weeks, which would give him time to visit his family.

I was soon to leave Kenya. Chuck had received a journalism fellowship to study at Harvard for a year, and after that he would be posted to Poland. Before we left, Mr. Sha called from the satellite station on Nanta's behalf, inviting me to the women's fund-raiser at Empaash. I had not seen her for more than a month, but I remembered Agnes telling me about the cooperative the women at Empaash had formed.

The fund-raiser was held in the lot next to Mr. Sha's bar, where chairs had been set up under a canopy to accommodate the invited officials. Only two county councillors—one of them Nanta's tubby boyfriend—showed up, but there was a man from the Voice of Kenya who recorded the women's songs for later play on the weekly Maasai-language radio show. Mr. Sha, Daniel and Kintolel attended, along with a few dozen other Maasai. Mr. Sha's *matatu* was again up on blocks, the front end dented from hitting an antelope on the road. Mr. Sha had recently married his fifth wife, a local girl, having finally given up on Sekento's sister. Janet remained single but disappointed the Sekento family by getting pregnant.

Mr. Sha and Tingisha had given up hope that the men responsible for the fire at his *boma* would be brought to justice. There had been no recent problems with Kikuyu neighbors, however; the only bad news was that hyenas had eaten off the udders of two of Nanta's cows.

The Paradise Hotel remained unfinished. Mr. Sha had heard that the owner was bankrupt and was trying to sell it. But Mr. Sha did not regret the extra expense of having built the outhouse toilets to thwart the competition. The Maasai looked up to him for it, and those who lived nearby made it a habit to use them daily. "Sometimes," Mr. Sha said, "there is even a line."

Kintolel had grown tall, and his filled-out features resembled his father's. But he had retained his mother's winning smile and still held my hand, as he had since he was a boy. He had given up the *shuka*, and wore a blue guard's uniform, cast off by Mr. Sha, with a pink, open-collared shirt. His shoes were laced, and he carried a short cattle stick and a club, a fancy metal-tipped type, similar to the kind his father preferred.

Nanta was co-director of the women's group and clearly its most popular member. She danced and waved her fly whisk and sang directly into the microphone of the Voice of Kenya tape recorder, making everyone laugh at her audacity. The group's chairwoman was the hefty gap-toothed wife of a local government chief. Like the other women, she wore a red-and-white-printed *kanga* cape, a turquoise *shuka*, a beaded headpiece, and layers of jangling necklaces. Her plump arms were encased in colorful plastic bracelets, and a large white vinyl pocketbook dangled from the crook of her elbow, a special mark of her high status.

When it appeared that all the guests had arrived—the elders assuming the seats of the missing officials—Mr. Sha, who was wearing his green tie with the Kenyan crest, made a short speech. He noted the absence of "some important politicians" but urged all those who had taken the trouble to come to make generous contributions to the women's cause. He walked back and forth, hammering the end of his club into his open hand to emphasize his points. He said he was a great supporter of women, since they were more development-minded than men. He said they should be respected, for it was women who had raised money to put a new roof on the school. In his closing remarks, he said, "We need active men, women and children! Too many of our people have been sleeping—wake up!" There was wild applause, and the women began chanting *"Harambee! Harambee! Harambee!"* (Pull together!) as men stepped forward to make contributions.

Noah reported to work, but I did not hear from him until two days later when he quit. He called me from Nairobi to tell me, but he wouldn't say why. I picked him up at the downtown post office, and we drove around because I couldn't find a place to park.

I asked him what had happened, but I did not feel much sympathy.

"Nobody would tell me what to do," he said sulkily.

"What about Mr. Jiva?"

"He wasn't around."

I tried to picture Noah at the station. The other mechanics and gas attendants were older Kikuyu men. Perhaps they had given him a hard time or made some tribal slur. Noah was nineteen, but he looked much younger. I was suddenly sure that in some way, which he would not tell me, his dignity had been affronted.

I suggested we stop by to see a Lebanese mechanic I knew to see if he needed an assistant. Noah did not seem very enthusiastic, and the man had no job to offer but took his name.

We went to see Sekento, who was equally disappointed, but Noah was no more forthcoming when Sekento asked him what had happened on the job. "I won't go back," he said.

"Did you tell them you were quitting?" I asked.

"No, I just left."

Sekento told him he'd have to go back and formally resign, that he couldn't just walk away. The three of us drove to the station, and Sekento and I waited in the car while Noah went in to tell Mr. Jiva, who was sitting behind his desk in the front office. We watched through the window. The exchange was brief. Mr. Jiva stood up and shook Noah's hand, but his expression was mystified.

"Okay, I did it," Noah told us, getting back into the car.

"So, what now, Noah? Are you going to look for another job?" I asked.

"No, I'm going home." The tone of his voice was so hopeless and the decision so unexpected that neither Sekento nor I said anything but only glanced at each other with surprise. Sekento picked up his newspaper and stared stonily at the front page. A number of reproachful speeches ran through my mind, but I kept my anger to myself as I drove downtown. When I dropped Noah off at the bus station, he gave a weak smile and said he was sorry for "all the trouble." He asked us to visit him at Empaash. Sekento and I watched him walk to the crowded bus stand, his hands stuck in his back pockets. He didn't look back.

"What can you do?" Sekento said as we drove to Ngong in weary silence.

As days went by and I began packing up to leave Kenya, my anger toward Noah lessened. It *was* his life. He was not the first Maasai to give up a job and return to the *boma*. It was one of the intriguing aspects of the Maasai that had drawn my original interest. I had gone out to the Rift Valley to meet "real Maasai," but over the years, I had been caught up with Joseph and Noah and their dreams of a "new life." I had come to believe that "development" was the only solution for a people whose time of grace seemed to be expiring, and whose land was running out. But I knew they weren't a "dying tribe," as some supposed. They would get along. The change would come gradually, but they would survive. In the end, I was not really sure that Noah would be better off in a Nairobi grease pit, working with wrenches, staring up at the underbelly of a diesel truck. I suspected it would be his children—and others of the next generation—who might someday make the leap and enter professions where influence made a difference.

I made a last trip to Saikeri, with Sekento, to visit Noah's grandfather. We left the Range-Rover at the bottom of the big hill, as I had done the first time I'd come there by chance with Ndika, the hitchhiker. I'd recently heard that Ndika, who had moved away after he was cursed, was reformed and married. The road was still blocked by fallen boulders, and some men were sitting in a shallow cave alongside it roasting meat. "If everybody got together they could fix this road in a day," I said to Sekento. He shrugged. His request for a school transfer had again been turned down. His wife, Rahab, had recently given birth to a second daughter. He was worried about rising school fees for his other children and had applied for a loan, which he was not sure he would get, to build a larger house.

It was a long hike to Sane's *boma*. A soft rain was falling. It reminded me of my first days in Kenya, in June, riding a motorcycle. The bike was now sold; my other belongings were crated for shipping. We passed a *boma* where a circumcision had taken place. The boys were dancing. We met some Tanzanians who had decided to settle here and told them to be on the lookout for Chief Sayo.

Mount Suswa stood in the misty distance. It had been raining off and on for a week. I had never seen the Rift Valley so green, which was the best way to remember it. As we walked, Sekento picked wildflowers—purple daisies, flame lilies, hibiscus, miniature irises—and made a bouquet for me.

Sane's hut was thick with smoke. He sat by the fire, wearing two blankets, his wife next to him. Two cattle sticks, which he needed for walking, were propped up beside him, and a small tan puppy slept at his feet. He had seemed despondent the last time I visited, and I was surprised to find him robust and talkative. He said he was fine, "but a little bit of a fool now." He had some aches and pains, he said, but lived day to day. His wife needed medicine for her eyes. Noah's sister Penina was visiting and brought her baby son inside, asking her grandmother to look after him. The baby bawled, and the puppy tried to lick the tiny bare feet. Sane said he was pleased that affairs with Semoi had been settled. I remarked on his good health, and he responded with a story about an old man who never came out of his hut as he prepared to die. But one day he went out to look at the cattle, and he became younger each day after, "like a snake shedding skin." Soon the old man's sons were old men, and they died, but he lived on. Sane said the same thing was happening to him. He didn't fear death now—he was at peace and ready. A few months before he had "died" for a few days. All the women began crying; like the moon, he came back. Death was pleasant, he had discovered. The experience so astounded him, he had called a missionary to discuss it. He and his wife had recently been baptized, and the missionary had given them Biblical names.

"You can call us Abraham and Sarah now," he said.

I spent sad days saying good-bye to the Maasai. I planned to return on visits, but I still wondered if I would see them again. Dickson, Joseph, Noah and Sekento promised to write. I visited Noah at his family's *boma*. He was wearing a *shuka* and was relieved when I told him I understood his decision. He said that he and Joseph might open a *duka* at Euaso, and I should not think his education was totally wasted. Agnes and Kipeno thought building a shop was a good idea. "Maybe you can help fix Mr. Sha's truck," I suggested, but auto repair did not seem to interest him anymore. Preparations were under way for the circumcision of his youngest sister, Hannah. Semoi was no better—or worse—than before. He shook my hand and spat a blessing on my travels. When I left, Agnes ran up to the truck and asked when my plane would be leaving. "We will stand here at exactly that time and look up for your airplane," she said. "If you look down, you will see us waving."

Several months later, I was in Massachusetts. Snow was falling, and squirrels had left tracks on the roof next door. A frozen branch scraped the window, and I thought of Noah. I had been listening to a tape of "Shauri Yako," a popular Swahili song he and I used to sing in the car. It had become our traveling anthem during trips to Empaash. I wrote him a letter, describing the scene outside the window. I had to describe what snow is, what squirrels look like. There had been a Kenyan recently selling sisal baskets—"Kenya bags"—near Trinity Church in Boston. I stopped and spoke to him in Swahili. He was happy, but already I had forgotten many words. Sometimes I have imagined I might run into the Maasai unexpectedly. I turn corners and half believe they may appear, no stranger a sight than the kids hanging out around the Harvard T-station with their Mohawks and purple hair.

"Sometimes I wish I had wings, so I could fly to where you are lost," Noah writes in his letter. On the envelope for his return address he has written "From Kenya." I wonder how far he walked to mail it. He has not received my letters and blames the "criminals" in the post office. He is certain I have written to him. I picture him sitting under the big acacia tree outside the *boma*, hunched over his grimy notebook, composing the letter. The rains have not started, he writes, but the cattle are still fat. He has started a school. There was none in the area. He has twenty-two students, all little ones, whom he is teaching to read and write. The parents pay him twenty shillings a month for each child, and he is pleased with his students' progress. He has given up the *shuka* and wears trousers, as befits a teacher. His income supports the family. Joseph has fallen in love with a girl named Regina, who works in a bank. He and Noah are still thinking about opening a *duka*. Overall, he writes, everything is fine. "People and cows are in a good mood."

CHARACTERS

NDIKA, hitchhiker from Saikeri

Joseph ole Meyoki's family:

SHOKORE, Joseph's father
NTERUE, Joseph's mother
NJISHA, a wife of Shokore
WILLIAM, Joseph's brother
KUREKO, Joseph's brother, a warrior
TAREU, Joseph's younger brother
NJAMBA, Joseph's blind uncle

KIRAITU MURUNGI, lawyer for Joseph's family

Noah Kipetuan ole Semoi's family:

MUSANKA, Noah's uncle
SANE, Noah's grandfather
SEMOI, Noah's father and leader of his age-set
AGNES, Noah's mother
PENINA and HANNAH, Noah's sisters
KIPENO, Semoi's youngest wife
RESIAN, Kipeno's daughter
RIMAS, Semoi's ex-wife

WILLIAM OLE SEKENTO, teacher at Saikeri Primary School
RAHAB, a teacher and Sekento's wife
EDGAR, ALEX, DANIEL, JEREMIAH, GIDEON, GRACE, Sekento's children
EDWARD, Sekento's father
JOYCE, Sekento's mother
JANET, Sekento's sister
NAISIAWUA, Sekento's uncle at Empaash
DICKSON LEPONYO OLE NTIKOISA, student at Oloolaiser Secondary School
STEPHEN, Dickson's older brother
RUNGES, Dickson's warrior friend

JEANNE and DENNY GRINDALL, American Presbyterian missionaries
WILSON, chairman of the Saikeri land committee
TOM OLE TOROME, owner of the Ngong Hills Bar
CLEMENT OLE TOROME, Narok county councillor
JAMES OLE TOROME, one of the first school-educated Maasai
PROFESSOR GEOFFREY M. OLE MALOIY, chairman of the physiology department at the University of Nairobi
MATTHEW KIVUVA and TITUS KIMILU, full-time nurses at the Saikeri clinic
JOAKIM OLE MEREU, field enumerator
CHIEF SAYO, government subchief of Ngong and Saikeri
MARY, the chief's youngest wife
LOUISE, Mary's daughter
LENKENWUA, a wife of Chief Sayo
NANTA, Chief Sayo's ex-wife
KINTOLEL, Nanta's son
TINGISHA, Nanta's brother
KILASO, Maryene Sayo's sister and Tingisha's wife
TENKET, Tingisha's second wife

MR. SHA, bar owner at Empaash, watchman at Longonot satellite station
DANIEL, MR., Sha's driver
DANIEL KISAI, guard at Longonot satellite station
KINDI, shopkeeper at Empaash
T. R. IBBERTSON, Mr. Sha's lawyer
PUNYUA, boy who testified at the arson trial
ONESMUS GITHINJI, Naivasha magistrate
LEKASHU, old man with cataracts
FRANCIS, eye clinic orderly at Thogoto

KOIMARISH, Maasai clairvoyant ("the man who talks to God")

THOMAS, Samburu *lais* (fortune-teller)

MUSEI, senior elder at Empaash, a friend to Semoi

LESEI OLE PUNYA, warrior friend to Sekento

NASEYO ENE PUNYUA, female circumciser, former maid to Lady
Delamere

KESI, male circumciser

LETANGWUA OLE LASITIS, Eunoto ceremony leader

MR. JIVA, Nairobi gas station owner

NASORE (GILBERT COLVILE), colonial rancher

LORD DELAMERE, first leader of Kenya's white settlers

GALBRAITH and BERKELEY COLE, colonial settlers

SIR "JOCK" DELVES BROUGHTON, colonial settler, tried and acquitted for
murder of Josslyn Hay

JOSSLYN HAY, the twenty-second Earl of Errol, colonial settler

DIANA BROUGHTON, wife of Jock Broughton, later married Gilbert
Colvile, then married Lord Delamere's son, Tom

The Politicians:

DANIEL ARAP MOI, Kenya's president

STANLEY OLE OLOITIPITIP, flamboyant Maasai cabinet minister

JOHN KEEN, Maasai member of Kenya's parliament

JUSTUS OLE TIPIS, Maasai member of Kenya's parliament

WILLIAM OLE NTIMAMA, Maasai businessman and politician

CHARLES NJONJO, former constitutional affairs minister investigated for
treason

PAUL OLE LUMET, organizer of Maasai development group

TOM MBOYA, Luo leader who was assassinated

ABOUT THE AUTHOR

CHERYL BENTSEN was born in Cranston, Rhode Island, and has a B.A. in journalism from New York University. From 1973 to 1976 she was a reporter for the *Los Angeles Times* and their first woman sports reporter. In 1976 and 1977 she worked for the *New York Post*. Her articles have appeared in *Newsday, The Daily News Sunday Magazine, New York* magazine, *Look,* and *Ms.,* among other publications. At present she and her husband, Charles Powers, are living in Warsaw, Poland.